Digital Platforms and Global Law

To Edi and Jack

To were-rabbit,
Baroness in the Trees

Digital Platforms and Global Law

Fabio Bassan

Professor of International Law, Department of Business Economics, Roma Tre University, Italy

 Edward Elgar
PUBLISHING

Cheltenham, UK • Northampton, MA, USA

Cover image: Scaccchi [Chesss] 2014, by Anna Scalfi Eghenter, ph. Ela Bialkowska/
OKNOstudio, private collection

Published by
Edward Elgar Publishing Limited
The Lypiatts
15 Lansdown Road
Cheltenham
Glos GL50 2JA
UK

Edward Elgar Publishing, Inc.
William Pratt House
9 Dewey Court
Northampton
Massachusetts 01060
USA

A catalogue record for this book
is available from the British Library

Library of Congress Control Number: 2021947651

This book is available electronically in the **Elgar**online
Law subject collection
http://dx.doi.org/10.4337/9781800889439

ISBN 978 1 80088 942 2 (cased)
ISBN 978 1 80088 943 9 (eBook)

Printed and bound by CPI Group (UK) Ltd, Croydon, CR0 4YY

Contents

Introduction to Digital Platforms and Global Law: Work Plan

Digital platforms are hardware or software structures that provide techno-logical services and tools, programs and applications for the distribution, management and creation of free or paid digital content and services, including through the integration of multiple media (integrated digital platforms).

Various authors have investigated the topic of digital platforms, from the standpoint of substantive law. In particular, it is discussed whether the instruments of competition law and regulation are adequate to regulate an evolving phenomenon that transcends the classic framework of the transna-tional company. However, the research found in the literature is apparently not systematic, as it focuses on specific aspects (the relationships with competition law,[1] with the protection of personal data,[2] with copyright and intellectual

---

[1] A. Ezrachi, M. Stucke (2016), *Virtual Competition. The Promise and Perils of the Algorithm-Driven Economy*, Harvard University Press (in particular 56–81); id. (2017), Artificial intelligence & collusion: when computers inhibit competition, *University of Illinois Law Review*, 2017, 1175 *et seq.*; E. Calvano, G. Calzolari, V. Denicolò, S. Pastorello (2019), Algorithmic pricing: what implications for competition policy?, *Review of Industrial Organization*, 55(1), 155–171; A. Deng (2018), What do we know about algorithmic tacit collusion?, *Antitrust*, 33(1), 88 *et seq.*; M. Maggiolino (2018), *I Big Data e il Diritto Antitrust*, Diritto dell'economia; S. Mannoni, G. Stazi (2018), *Is Competition A Click Away?* Editoriale Scientifica; OECD (2017), *Algorithms and Collusion. Competition Policy in the Digital Age*, 39–40; OECD, Big Data: bring-ing competition policy to the digital era, Background note by the Secretariat, DAF/COMP(2016)14, 29–30.

[2] O. Lynskey (2017), Aligning data protection rights with competition law rem-edies? The GDPR right to data portability, *European Law Review*, 42, 793 *et seq.*; I. Graef, M. Husovec, N. Purtova (2018), Data portability and data control: lessons for an emerging concept in EU law, *German Law Journal*, 19(6), 1359 *et seq.*; I. Graef (2016), *EU Competition Law, Data Protection and Online Platforms: Data as Essential Facility*, Wolters Kluwer; J. Polonetsky, O. Tene (2013), Privacy and Big Data: making ends meet, *Stanford Law Review Online*, 66, 25 *et seq.*; J. Lerman (2013), Big Data and its exclusions, *Stanford Law Review Online*, 66, 55 *et seq.*; M. Corrales, M. Fenwick, N. Forgó (eds) (2017), *New Technology, Big Data and the Law*, Springer; A. Waldman (2018), *Privacy as Trust: Information Privacy for an Information Age*, Cambridge University Press.

property,[3] with the foundations of democracy,[4] and with global governance.[5]

The lack of effectiveness of the tools adopted so far in practice reveals, from an analysis that goes beyond substantive law, a more complex reality. In order to understand it, I believe we need to gain more insight into the supranational legal space in which digital platforms operate. The research must start from reality; therefore, I shall investigate international (state) and transnational (companies) practice – recent practice that has, however, quickly (almost 'instantaneously') become common practice – and try to qualify it legally, departing from the mainstream – if not unanimous – assumption in literature, that the solution to the changing phenomenon lies in state regulations and has a regulatory nature.[6]

---

[3]   W. Schuster (2018), Artificial intelligence and patent ownership, *Washington University Law Review*, 75(4), 1945 *et seq.*; V. Falce (2018), Copyrights on data and competition policy in the digital single market strategy, *Italian Antitrust Review*, 1, 38.

[4]   E. Benvenisti (2018), Upholding democracy amid the challenges of new technology: What role for the law of global governance?, *European Journal of International Law*, 29(1), 9 *et seq.*; L. Casini (2018), Googling democracy? New technologies and the law of global governance: afterword to Eyal Benvenisti's foreword, *European Journal of International Law*, 29(4), 1071 *et seq.* On this topic see also C. O'Neil (2017), *Weapons of Math Destruction. How Big Data Increases Inequality and Threatens Democracy*, Penguin; J. Bartlett (2018), *The People vs. Tech. How the Internet Is Killing Democracy (and How We Save It)*, Ebury Press, 159; N. Srnicek (2017), *Platform Capitalism*, Wiley; D. Gerber (1994), Constitutionalizing the economy: German neo-liberalism, competition law and the 'new' Europe, *American Journal of Comparative Law*, 42(1), 42; A. Hatje (2010), The economic constitution within the internal market, in A. von Bogdandy, J. Bast (eds), *Principles of European Constitutional Law*, 2nd edn, Hart, 590–591, where it is further remarked that the concept of economic constitution is the 'engine' of the EU integration process (593); A. Gerbrandy (2019), Rethinking competition law within the European economic constitution, *Journal of Common Market Studies*, 57(1), 128.

[5]   N. Tusikov (2018), *Chokepoints: Global Private Regulation on the Internet*, University of California Press; M. Rioux, K. Fontaine-Skronski (eds) (2015), *Global Governance Facing Structural Changes. New Institutional Trajectories for Digital and Transnational Capitalism*, Palgrave Macmillan; H. Krause Hansen; T. Porter (2017), What do Big Data do in global governance, *Global Governance*, 23(1), 31–42; M. Campbell-Verduyn (ed.) (2018), *Bitcoin and Beyond: Cryptocurrencies, Blockchains, and Global Governance*, Routledge.

[6]   I have tried to point out in other works that more complex explanations are also more compatible with a coherent interpretation of the reality in the making. Namely, I questioned the assumptions from which scholars generally start, i.e. that the regulation of these markets is the goal of governments and institutions; that digital platforms operate in relevant contestable markets; that the current regulatory matrix is suitable and adequate, with appropriate measures, to foster market developments: see: F. Bassan (2019), *Potere dell'algoritmo e resistenza dei mercati. La sovranità perduta sui servizi*, Rubbettino. That (part of) the solution can be a non-state one and there is room for international organizations, E. Benvenisti explains in Upholding democracy amid the

The study of the consequences of the digital revolution requires us to be more radical: we need to focus on what constitutes the subjectivity of these new dominant protagonists of the international economy. It is a classic topic, approached with classic research tools; the subject of the research, however, is totally new and the results can be surprising.

This research develops as follows.

The first chapter starts from the urgent need to bring the ecosystem of digital platforms back to a state of unity. I start with the terminology, by providing a definition of digital platforms that allows us to narrow the perimeter of the research (section 1).

The definition serves the purpose of illustrating the current ecosystem of digital platforms. I use the same tools and follow the same perspectives from which states and regulators are currently facing the digital evolution. It is not my intention to delve into all of these issues, each of which would require several monographic studies. My intent is rather to bring approaches, tools and practices back to the system, and to investigate in two directions.

The first consists in understanding whether the actions (and reactions) of states and regulators towards digital platforms show contradictions, or have a lowest common denominator, or are at least consistent with each other and, in the latter case, whether such consistency is in turn consistent with the real evolution of digital platforms.

The second direction consists in understanding whether a line of continuity or at least of consistency can be identified also in the errors, if any, made in approaching the digital evolution that, while not revolutionary in itself, is the basis of a revolution, both in individual relations and in the relations between states, international organizations and multinational companies.

Therefore, I review the regulatory profiles (section 2), focusing my analysis on the European Union approach, which represents the most advanced frontier of market intervention for the defence (or the development, depending on the approach) of continental European welfare, which Brexit has now freed from compromises with British welfare.

The digital revolution is part of a European regulatory evolution that was already fast and that the pandemic has further accelerated; the typical 'perfect storm', where the effectiveness of the interventions is difficult to predict and can only be assessed a posteriori. Nevertheless, the European Union (EU) cannot afford the regulatory inertia that this situation would impose. Therefore, by means of regulations, the EU tries to take a stand on the global scene, recovering its disadvantage at industrial level.

---

challenges of new technology: What role for the law of global governance?, in (2018) *European Journal of International Law*, 9–82.

In the reform of competition rules (section 3) the difference between the European and the US approach towards digital platforms grows bigger. The ineffectiveness of the traditional tools of antitrust law (in the US) and competition law (in the EU) has led the United States to take action towards possible break-up measures, and the European Union towards 'regulated competition', with which it attempts to promote competition through the typical instruments of regulation *ex ante*. Hybrid competition, actually.

The digital evolution is based on the control of data and the ability to manage it (section 4). Data protection thus becomes a parameter of regulatory effectiveness. Again, the two prevailing models (US and European) diverge. The reason lies in the different cultural approach, of course, but also in the different balance of interests between market freedom and individual rights (no longer consumer rights only). The European regulation imposes a ladder, the rungs of which are based on the principle of proportionality. Already at the core of many cultures, the European Union principles have become global standards (via the Brussels effect) and have also imposed themselves on digital platforms. These, by transforming risks into opportunities, have made them their own, not merely by integrating them into their business but also by using them to develop and protect it.

The opposite approach guides the two sides of the Atlantic as regards the effects of the evolution of digital platforms on democratic principles, with freedom of expression in the foreground (section 5). Here too, the reason lies in constitutional foundations and traditions, but also contingent events: the Trump 'saga' has led public opinion, not only in the United States, to question checks and balances and the prevalence of interests. In the 'tug-of-war' of interests, once the ideology or what remains of it is removed, the debate focuses on how well democratic structures will hold in the face of technological progress. It is an old debate: the dominant narrative has been affirming that globalization is incompatible with democracy since the last decade of the past century. The context, however, is new, because the challenge is no longer the globalization of markets (now classified as 'regional globalization') but that of digital platforms. However, the question remains the same: the compatibility of the phenomena (globalization, digitalization) with the structure and institutions of democracy (which differ according to legal and cultural traditions). But again, the question is still wrong, because it presupposes a Ptolemaic vision of international relations, with the state (indeed, the democratic state) at the centre, which is incompatible with the reality of the evolution of both trade and technology.

The temptation to manage new phenomena using tools that do not have the typical limits of legal tools (e.g., territoriality and enforcement) becomes strong. Hence the 'ethical drift', consisting of principles considered useful in 'Middle-earth', to territories not reached by the rules (section 6). Yet, ethics can only trace a path, on which the road (the rules) must then be built. There is much confusion and misunderstanding here, where law and technology are not parallel worlds but join together and hybridize each other.

The distributed ledger technologies, which allow many different applications (cryptocurrencies, smart contracts, etc. ...) complicate the scenario even further (section 7). They are themselves ecosystems, in addition to those of digital platforms and those of artificial intelligence, and raise questions as to which law would be applicable at the intersection of systems, when digital platforms use artificial intelligence, or blockchain, or both (in the latter case, the intersection is between three systems).

I shall first look into the differences in the approaches, tools and perspectives, to ask whether all these interventions (or non-interventions) in the market, and the ensuing debates, are consistent with the definition of digital platform that we have suggested and with the reality of its evolution (section 8). The unity of the platform as an ecosystem, on which engineers and economists now agree, produces effects that states and regulators seem not to have really taken note of.

The unity of the ecosystem, on a legal level, translates into order. Private legal systems are numerous and have been investigated for at least a century. If we accept – as I believe is appropriate – this shifting of the platform from an ecosystem (which qualifies its action on the market) to an order (which identifies its institutions and powers) we can lay the foundations of a unitary approach, which is still missing and, seemingly, most needed.

The second chapter starts from these assumptions and investigates whether digital platforms can qualify as private legal systems, starting from the qualification of digital platforms as transnational companies and their placement within transnational law (section 1).

Compared to transnational companies, however, digital platforms have additional elements that lead to their classification as legal systems (section 2). They exercise regulatory powers when they adopt the behavioural policies of the community of users of which they are composed; executive powers, when they take action to enforce the rules adopted; and jurisdictional powers, when they establish independent dispute resolution systems – de facto, arbitration systems. More refined systems (that of Facebook, for instance) provide for real courts, as well as guarantees and protections similar to those of a state (section 3).

If we add to these elements an autonomous payment system and, potentially, in the near future, an autonomous currency (whether a cryptocurrency, or a stablecoin pegged to one given currency or to a basket of currencies, is of little importance for our purposes), the private ordering of platforms becomes complete and increasingly autonomous, almost independent: in other words, sovereign (sections 4 and 5).

This is the starting point for a new presentation of digital platforms, for they are multinational companies, but have evolved to the point of constituting real legal systems.

This new presentation follows a dual path. The first path (Chapter 3) consists of the relationship between these private systems and the other existing public and private orders. In the first place, state systems are relevant (section 1). The classifications developed in Chapter 1 seem useful here, and particularly the distinction between the platforms' internal and external environments. The legal approach allows us to provide assumptions and justifications for such a distinction. Private international law provides all the tools (starting from *renvoi* between legal systems) to define and qualify the relationships between digital platforms and states, and shows the ineffectiveness of the regulatory tools presently used, which do not grasp the evolution of the platforms at institutional level.

From another point of view, public international law makes it possible to define the relationship between the private transnational systems of digital platforms and international law. The path is different if one follows either the monist or the dualist approach, but the outcome is the same (section 2). It is no coincidence, therefore, that the most refined tool examined, i.e. Facebook's Oversight Board, supplements its internal norms not by referring to state laws but to the principles of public international law, beginning with those on the protection of human rights.

The relationship between the platforms' private transnational systems and the *lex mercatoria* (section 3) – when the latter should be recognized as an order, which is still the subject of heated and articulated controversies – exists when the *lex mercatoria* evolves (via arbitration awards or generally accepted principles and practices (GAPP)) by applying the internal policies of digital platforms. It is a predictable development, if the principles and paths of the European regulatory circle apply (Chapter 1, section 2).

It is therefore not only possible but, I believe, entirely probable that another question arising is the relationship between one transnational digital order and another (i.e., between two digital platforms). The more the *lex mercatoria* develops in terms of digital systems, the more these will be able to integrate and share rules and principles, not just protocols and standards (Chapter 3, section 4).

The second path (Chapter 4) concerns the possible qualification of digital transnational private legal systems as subjects of law. Their being transnational is beyond doubt. But are they also subjects of international law? Again, the path is different if one follows the monist theories based on decentralization (section 1) or the dualist theories based on the pluralism of legal systems (section 2). The outcome here appears different at first sight, since the subjectivity of digital transnational legal systems seems admissible in international law according to the monist approach, but is denied by dualist theories.

This divergence, however, becomes merely apparent if we follow the dualist approach of Arangio-Ruiz, which defines the subjects of international law as de facto 'powers' (section 3), as they both exist and are independent. For Arangio-Ruiz, natural and legal persons are not subjects of international law. Conversely, international organizations (among others) are subjects of international law. They have internal law (which governs relations within the organization) and external law (which governs relations between the international organization and other subjects of international law). Arangio-Ruiz defines the internal law of international organizations as international interindividual law.

Well, the analogy with digital platforms is evident. They too are powers, like international organizations, and constitute a legal system whose law, which applies to the community of users, is 'international interindividual'. Digital platforms can then also qualify as subjects of international law, insofar as they participate in the interstate law of international relations.

This conclusion, on closer inspection, coincides with a branch of evolution of the theory of global law, defined as the law of non-state governance communities.

These findings lead to the concluding chapter, Chapter 5. It can be affirmed, based on the evidence of Chapter 2 and the conclusions drawn in Chapter 4, that there is a global law of digital platforms.

Compared to this, the regulatory matrix used so far by states to tackle the rise of digital platforms is inadequate, for the reasons illustrated in Chapter 1, and because it does not take into account the legal evolution of digital platforms highlighted in Chapters 2 and 4 (Chapter 5, section 1).

Therefore, the need for a new paradigm arises: a new matrix equipped with new tools. The playing field must shift from the current matrix of market regulation – which governs the relationships between companies and between states and companies – to that of negotiation, which presupposes a relationship between peers. This evolution does not conflict with what is already considered, in the European Union, to be the main evolution of regulation: self-regulation (the 'law of digital platforms'), which then becomes co-regulation via negotiation with independent authorities and national governments.

If the paradigm change that I propose is consistent with the current developments of the institutions and of the markets, then the tools of uniform law that are emerging – the negotiation between private and public norms and the codification of private law – become central. We may see such codification as the first phase of regulation (self-regulation) or, shifting our analysis to the level of legal systems, the internal law of platforms: what Arangio-Ruiz calls international interindividual law (section 3).

The centrality of these tools is not new: during the 1980s, the codification of uniform law was already one of the assumptions and premises of globalization, which developed strongly in the 1990s. They will be useful again, in the different form that I am suggesting here, to regulate digital globalization too, which is no less rapid than the general globalization of the 1990s, but bears implications that go far beyond the markets.

The new paradigm is described in the last section of the chapter (section 4).

1. Digital platforms: protagonists of the self-age

1. WHAT WE TALK ABOUT WHEN WE TALK ABOUT DIGITAL PLATFORMS

The first issue to face is giving a definition. It is not difficult to understanding what a digital platform is. It is harder, however, to give a suitable definition of it, for at least two reasons.

The first is that the market provides services, to which the platform becomes instrumental: there is no conceptual idea of a platform in itself, which can then find sectoral applications. Going back from practice to a technical formula is therefore not easy, since the constituent element risks being so general that it becomes useless for classification purposes.

The second reason is that the definition is always functional to an objective: the engineers qualify the digital platform based on the technical characteristics, the economists focus on the market, the jurists consider the balancing of protected interests operated by the legislator and from private autonomy, and therefore highlight regulatory and contractual aspects.

1.1 Definitions from the Technological Perspective

The engineers' main aim is to open the technological black box of digital platforms and understand their technical and innovation content. Studies adopting this view focus on the technical developments and functions. Hence, a platform can be defined as an extensible codebase of a software-based system complemented by third-party modules;[1] a building block that provides an essential function to a technological system and serves as a foundation upon

---

[1] A. Tiwana, B. Konsynsky, A. Bush (2010), Platform evolution: coevolution of platform architecture, governance, and environmental dynamics, *Information Systems Research*, 21(4), 675–687; K.J. Boudreau (2012), Let a thousand flowers bloom? An early look at large numbers of software app developers and patterns of innovation, *Organization Science*, 23(5), 1409–1427.

which complementary products, technologies, or services can be developed;[2] a set of components used in common across a product family whose functionality can be extended by applications;[3] a set of subsystems and interfaces that form a common structure for/from which derivative applications can be developed and distributed.[4] Key aspects, depending on the definition, may be: ease of use and immediate appeal for users; trustworthiness and security (clear terms and conditions are necessary as well as privacy protection and guarantees in terms of intellectual property and data ownership); connectivity through the use of APIs that allow third parties to extend the ecosystem of the platform and its capabilities; facilitation of exchanges between users (producers and consumers); providing value to the community and as a function of the size of the community (the bigger the community, the more value the platform can provide to all parties involved); ability to scale up without causing performance degradation.[5]

Digital platforms are simultaneously governed by centralized and distributed control (i.e. the paradox of control),[6] so that the core unit of analysis should not be the core of the platform, but its boundary resources:[7] distributed actors who collectively determine boundary resources.[8] These reconstructions, albeit technical, have a significant impact on the legal qualification of digital platforms in terms of multinational or transnational companies, if we consider

---

[2] P. Spagnoletti, A. Resca, G. Lee (2015), A design theory for digital platforms supporting online communities: a multiple case study, *Journal of Information Technology*, 30(4), 364–380 at 364.

[3] M. Ceccagnoli, C. Forman, P. Huang, D. J. Wu (2012), Cocreation of value in a platform ecosystem: the case of enterprise software, *MIS Quarterly*, 36(1), 263–290.

[4] X. Xu, V. Venkatesh, K.Y.Tam, S.-J. Hong (2010), Model of migration and use of platforms: role of hierarchy, current generation, and complementarities in consumer settings, *Management Science*, 56(8), 1304–1323, at 1305.

[5] M. de Reuver, C. Sørensen, R.C. Basole (2018), The digital platform: a research agenda, *Journal of Information Technology*, 33, 124–135. According to A. Ghazawneh and O. Henfridsson (2015), A paradigmatic analysis of digital application marketplaces, *Journal of Information Technology*, 30(3), 198–208, digital platforms are 'software-based external platforms consisting of the extensible codebase of a software-based system that provides core functionality shared by the modules that interoperate with it and the interfaces through which they interoperate'.

[6] D.Tilson, K. Lyytinen, C. Sørensen (2010), Digital belowstructures: the missing research agenda, *Information Systems Research*, 21(5), 748–759.

[7] O. Henfridsson, B. Bygstad (2013), The generative mechanisms of digital belowstructure evolution, *MIS Quarterly*, 37(3), 907–931.

[8] B.D. Eaton, S. Elaluf-Calderwood, C. Sørensen, Y. Yoo (2015), Distributed tuning of boundary resources: the case of Apple's iOS service system, *MIS Quarterly: Special Issue on Service Innovation in a Digital Age*, 39(1), 217–243.

control not only in terms of governance but also of technology (Chapters 2, 3 and 4).

1.2 The Market-Based Definition According to Economists

Economists define the digital platform as a two-sided market, a place for exchanges of information, goods, or services between producers and consumers as well as the community that interacts with the platform,[9] or a business based on enabling value-creating interaction between external producers and consumers.[10] The community itself is an essential piece of the digital platform.[11] Hence, classifications are based on the services provided: social media platforms like Facebook, Twitter, Instagram, and LinkedIn; knowledge platforms like Wikipedia, StackOverflow, Quora, and Yahoo! Answers; media sharing platforms like YouTube, Spotify, and Vimeo; service-oriented platforms like Uber, Airbnb, and GrubHub.

---

[9] J.-C. Rochet, J. Tirole (2003), Platform competition in two-sided markets, *Journal of the European Economic Association*, 1(4), 990–1029. Platforms deliver 'a digital service that facilitates interactions between two or more distinct but interdependent sets of users who interact through the service via the Internet' (OECD (2019), *An Introduction to Online Platforms and their Role in the Digital Transformation*, OECD Publishing). A platform is

> an undertaking operating in two (or multi)-sided markets which uses the Internet to enable interactions between two or more distinct but interdependent groups of users so as to generate value for at least on of the groups ... Platforms are generally known as 'two-sided' or 'multi-sided' markets where users are brought together by a platform operator in order to facilitate an interaction (exchange of information, a commercial transaction ...). European Commission Staff Working Document, Online Platforms accompanying the document Communication on online platforms and digital market, 15 May 2016, SWD 2016 172, p. 2.1.

This definition appears to be very similar to the one provided by T.K. Koh, and M. Fichman (2014), Multi-homing users' preferences for two-sided exchange networks, *MIS Quarterly*, 38(4), 977–996, at 977. We can find the same definition in European Commission (September 2015), Public consultation on the regulatory environment for platforms, online intermediaries, data and cloud computing and the collaborative economy, available at https://ec.europa.eu/digital-single-market/en/news/results-public -consultationregulatory-environment-platforms-online-intermediaries-data-and- cloud.

[10] G. Parker, M. van Alstyne, S. Choudary (2017), Platform Revolution: *How Networked Markets Are Transforming the Economy and How to Make Them Work for You*, W.W. Norton.

[11] One challenge for digital platforms is the chicken-and-egg problem: the platform needs both the producer and the consumer sides to ensure a valid value proposition, but neither side is willing to join as long as the other side is not populated: see B. Caillaud, B. Jullien (2003), Chicken & egg: competition among intermediation service providers, *RAND Journal of Economics*, 34(2), 309–328.

The reason for this definition lies in the need for economists to apply already existing (conventional) categories and practices: those typical of multi-sided markets,[12] from which direct and indirect network externalities originate.[13]

As the economic research on two (multi)-sided markets is mostly focused on financial and pricing dynamics of competition, this is the main topic that economists are investigating, also with reference to digital platforms. One of the main difficulties inherent in the definition is to include both platforms that are based on an economic exchange (e.g. Uber, Airbnb) and those based on a non-economic exchange (typically, the data of community participants, for social networks). Hence, the need to give an economic value to the data, to include the latter in the definition and (among other things) subject them to the

---

[12] A. Gawer, M.A. Cusumano (2002), *Platform Leadership: How Intel, Microsoft, and Cisco Drive Industry Innovation*, Harvard Business School Press. M. Pagani (2013), Digital business strategy and value creation: framing the dynamic cycle of control points, *MIS Quarterly*, 37(2), 617–632 at 625, points out that a
> multisided platform … exists wherever a company brings together two or more distinct groups of customers (sides) that need each other in some way, and where the company builds a below structure (platform) that creates value by reducing distribution, transaction, and search costs incurred when these groups interact with one another.

Within this perspective, a platform can be categorized in terms of its production process scope: (1) internal platforms, enabling recombination of sub-units within the firm; (2) supply-chain platforms coordinating external suppliers around an assembler; and (3) industry platforms where a platform leader pools external capabilities from complementors. In the latter two types, platforms not only provide a stable core but also mediate between different groups of users. A platform mediating different groups of users, such as buyers and sellers, is a typical multi-sided platform. See also: J.C. Rochet, J.Tirole (2003), Platform competition in two-sided markets, *Journal of the European Economic Association*, 1(4), 990; J.C. Rochet, J. Tirole (2006), Two-sided markets: a progress report, *RAND Journal of Economics*, 37(3), 645–667; M. Armstrong (2006), Competition in two-sided markets, *RAND Journal of Economics*, 37(3), 668–691; D.S. Evans, R. Schmalensee (2008), Markets with two-sided platforms. *Issues in Competition Law and Policy (ABA Section of Antitrust Law)*, 1; D.S. Evans, R. Schmalensee (2016), *Matchmakers: The New Economics of Multisided Platforms*, Harvard Business Review Press; L. Filistrucchi, D. Geradin, E. van Damme, P. Affeldt (2013), Market definition in two-sided markets: theory and practice, *Journal of Competition Law and Economics*, 10(2), 293–339; A. Hagiu, J. Wright (2015), Multi-sided platforms, *International Journal of Industrial Organization*, 43, 162–174.

[13] Network externalities imply that a technology grows more useful as its installed base of users increases. They are direct when the value of the platform depends on the number of users in the same user group, and indirect when it depends on the number of users in a different user group. See M.A. Schilling (2002), Technology success and failure in winner-take-all markets: the impact of learning orientation, timing, and network externalities, *Academy of Management Journal*, 45(2), 387–398.

typical antitrust dynamics – and rules – which would otherwise be ineffective.[14] It is a case in which the theory influences the practice or, according to another approach, constitutes one of those self-fulfilling prophecies. Constitutional protections are the losing party (below, section 5).

If these are the aims and the needs, we can understand how the classifications of digital platforms inferred from this economic definition depend on their business model, their form of interaction, their governance, their ownership structure.[15]

---

[14] N. Jentzsch, A. Harasser, S. Preibusch (2012), Monetising Privacy – An Economic Model of the Pricing of Personal Information, ENISA Report (www.enisa .europa.eu/activities/identity, accessed February 2021); A. Acquisti, C.R. Taylor, L. Wagman (2016), The economics of privacy, *Journal of Economic Literature*, 54(2), 442–492; OECD (2013), Exploring the economics of personal data: a survey of methodologies for measuring monetary value, OECD Digital Economy Papers, No. 220; A. Acquisti, L.K. John, G. Loewenstein (2013), What is privacy worth?, *Journal of Legal Studies*, 42(2), 249–274; S. Preibusch, K. Krol, A.R. Beresford (2013), The privacy economics of voluntary over-disclosure, in R. Böhme (ed.), *Web Forms, Economics of Information Security and Privacy*, Springer, 83–209; J.W. Jerome (2013), Buying and selling privacy: Big Data's different burdens and benefits, *Stanford Law Review Online*, 66(47), 48–53; J. Farrell (2012), Can privacy be just another good?, *J. on Telecomm. & High Tech. L.*, 10(2), 251–265; L. Brandimarte, A. Acquisti (2012), The economics of privacy, in M. Peitz and J. Waldfogel (eds), *The Oxford Handbook of the Digital Economy*, Oxford University Press, 547–572; K.L. Hui, I.P.L. Peng (2006), The economics of privacy, in T. Hendershott (ed.), *Economics and Information Systems*, Elsevier, 471–497; R.A. Posner (1981), The economics of privacy, *The American Economic Review*, 71(2), 405–409; G. Stigler (1961), The economics of information, *Journal of Political Economy*, 69(3), 213–225.

[15] A. Asadullah, I. Faik, A. Kankanhalli (2018), Digital platforms: a review and future directions, Paper presented at the Twenty-Second Pacific Asia Conference on Information Systems, Japan. Namely, the business model can be classified as: integrator platform model (Apple iOS, Google Android), product platform model (Linux, Cloud computing initiatives) and multi-sided platform model (Facebook, Alibaba). As for the interaction mode, one can make a distinction between collaborative (Wikipedia) and competitive (videogames on consoles) platforms. As for governance, Open platforms (Linux, Wikipedia) are different to Closed ones (Apple iOS, Google Android). Finally, as for ownership structure, there are property-based platforms (Sony, Microsoft) and open-source platforms (Linux, R). See also: OECD (2019), *An Introduction to Online Platforms and their Role in the Digital Transformation*, OECD Publishing, 22–25; D.S. Evans, R. Schmalensee (2010), Failure to launch: critical mass in platform businesses, *Review of Network Economics*, 9(4), 21–23; D.S. Evans, R. Schmalensee (2016), *Matchmakers: The New Economics of Multisided Platforms of Entry*; N. van Eijk, R. Fahy, H. van Til, P. Nooren, H. Stokking, H. Gelevert (2015), Digital Platforms: An Analytical Framework for Identifying and Evaluating Policy Options, The Hague, p. 46.

1.3   Legal Definitions

The definition of digital platforms by jurists is both contractual and regulatory, as it must satisfy the needs of both private and public regulation (below, section 2).[16] It is also peculiar, and revealing of the inherent difficulties and pitfalls, that no definitions of digital platforms can be found in binding regulations. The EU expressly chose not to adopt a one-size-fits-all approach and to rely on a sector-specific, problem-driven approach.[17] It is therefore clear that, since the definitions are functional, and the function with respect to digital platforms is regulatory, jurists have not provided definitions other than those functional to antitrust, competition or regulatory analyses. Recent examples are the European Commission's proposals for the Digital Services Act, the Digital Market Act and the Digital Governance Act, focused on the regulation of platforms, of which, however, the rules do not provide a definition other than that of gatekeepers, for platforms enjoying very special positions on the market.[18]

---

[16]   The study Liability of online platforms (Panel for the Future of Science and Technology, European Parliamentary Research Service, STOA, February 2021) defines online platforms as entities which: (i) offer 'over the top' digital services to users; (ii) are or can be operated as two- or multi-sided market business models; and (iii) allow the overall facilitation of interaction between the different sides of the market, even when there is no direct interaction among them.

[17]   See European Parliament (2017), Resolution on online platforms and the digital single market (2016/2276(INI)), paras 6–7.

[18]   The Proposal for a Regulation of the European Parliament and of the Council on contestable and fair markets in the digital sector (Digital Markets Act) COM(2020) 842 final, designates (Article 3) as gatekeepers:

> 1. A provider of core platform services shall be designated as gatekeeper if: (a) it has a significant impact on the internal market; (b) it operates a core platform service which serves as an important gateway for business users to reach end users; and (c) it enjoys an entrenched and durable position in its operations or it is foreseeable that it will enjoy such a position in the near future. 2. A provider of core platform services shall be presumed to satisfy: (a) the requirement in paragraph 1 point (a) where the undertaking to which it belongs achieves an annual EEA turnover equal to or above EUR 6.5 billion in the last three financial years, or where the average market capitalization or the equivalent fair market value of the undertaking to which it belongs amounted to at least EUR 65 billion in the last financial year, and it provides a core platform service in at least three member states; (b) the requirement in paragraph 1 point (b) where it provides a core platform service that has more than 45 million monthly active end users established or located in the Union and more than 10 000 yearly active business users established in the Union in the last financial year; for the purpose of the first subparagraph, monthly active end users shall refer to the average number of monthly active end users throughout the largest part of the last financial year; (c)

1.4 A Functional Definition

At present, I believe that the most adequate definition, being general (it includes all existing platforms and also future ones) but not generic, is the following. Digital platforms are hardware or software structures that provide technological services and tools, programs and applications for the distribution, management and creation of free or paid digital content and services, including through the integration of multiple media (integrated digital platform). A digital platform can be open source or commercial and can be structured for public access or for a limited target, subject to registration.[19] It may include information, interactive services, file sharing, downloading and uploading, and streaming services, as well as communication and sharing of multimedia content.

Digital platforms constitute real communities, closed or open, depending on whether they require registration or not. Operating system platforms like Android (Google) and iOS (Apple), social networks (Facebook, LinkedIn), payment platforms (PayPal, Apple Pay, Square), consumer communication apps (Twitter, Instagram, Skype, WhatsApp, Telegram, WeChat, Line, TikTok, etc.), Fintech apps (Kickstarters), health care apps (PatientsLikeMe), as well as permissioned blockchains, are closed communities. Search engines such as Google, or sales platforms, are open ones, ranging from simple marketplaces with or without intermediation (eBay, Airbnb, Home Away) to intermediate forms such as transport applications (from Uber to car/motorbike/bicycle sharing), to platforms that sell directly, distribute and deliver, such as Amazon, to permissionless blockchains.

Whether the platform is closed (a social network, a mobility app), open (a search engine) or partially open (a marketplace) is relevant as regards the

---

the requirement in paragraph 1 point (c) where the thresholds in point (b) were met in each of the last three financial years.

[19] As highlighted by M. de Reuver, C. Sørensen, R.C. Basole (2018), The digital platform: a research agenda, *Journal of Information Technology*, 33, at 127, for digital platforms, openness does not merely relate to organizational arrangements like entrance and exit rules but also to openness of technologies such as APIs and software development kits (SDKs). Different levels of openness are found in practice for mobile platforms like iOS and Android (A. Benlian, D. Hilkert, T. Hess (2015), How open is this platform? The meaning and measurement of platform openness from the complementors' perspective, *Journal of Information Technology*, 30(3), 209–228), digital marketplaces (A. Ghazawneh and O. Henfridsson (2015), A paradigmatic analysis of digital application marketplaces, *Journal of Information Technology*, 30(3), 198–208) and payment platforms (J. Ondrus, A. Gannamaneni, K. Lyytinen, The impact of openness on the market potential of multi-sided platforms: a case study of mobile payment platforms, *Journal of Information Technology*, 30(3), 260–275).

economic definition, which qualifies the platform as a 'waterproof' or 'porous' ecosystem. But it is even more so as regards the legal definition, for the more the platform is closed, the more the ecosystem may be legally qualified as a private legal order (see Chapters 2 and 3).

The common features of digital platforms are, on the one hand, the ability to process a large amount of data and, on the other, the use of algorithms for data extraction, and also for the purposes of customer or user profiling. The profiling mechanisms are now so refined (through 'recommendation algorithms') that they are de facto individual, and determine a knowledge of the preferences and habits of each user so profound as to allow the supply of tailored goods and services under economic conditions ad hoc for each ('reserve price').[20]

If we abstract from the daily life of the markets and investigate the path that digital platforms are taking, it is clear that in the coming years the Internet of Things (IoT) will make digital much of the world that is still partially analogic (or physical). It will imply an interoperativity (via API and standards) that will let platforms operate and integrate each other.[21] Hence, digital platforms are becoming interconnected digital structures: real ecosystems.[22] The development of the blockchain strengthens this trend.

The evolution and progressive 'aggregation' of these ecosystems accelerates, albeit in an original way, the overcoming of gaps through the transition from public ordering (via *ex post* verification through independent agents) to

---

[20]   The reserve price is the price that the digital sales platforms offer to each potential buyer, determining it on the basis of his/her previous purchasing experiences and on a series of additional data that allows it to accurately qualify the spending capacity and the propensity to purchase. The price of each asset is therefore not fixed, but is tailored to each prospective buyer.

[21]   For instance, the agreement between Google and Apple that in the spring of 2020 allowed their respective operating systems (Android and iOS) to interface in order to create a unique base platform worldwide for tracking and notification of exposure to Covid-19.

[22]   A. Hein, M. Schreieck, T. Riasanow, D. Soto Setzke, M. Wiesche, M. Böhm, H. Krcmar (2020), Digital platform ecosystems, *Electronic Markets*, 30, 87–98; R. Kapoor (2018), Ecosystems: broadening the locus of value creation, *Journal of Organization Design*, 7(1), 12; R. Adner (2017), Ecosystem as structure: an actionable construct for strategy, *Journal of Management*, 43(1), 39–58; M.G. Jacobides, C. Cennamo, A. Gawer (2018), Towards a theory of ecosystems, *Strategic Management Journal*, 39(8), 2255–2276. According to this work, there should be a paradigm shift in literature by integrating the intra-organizational technical perspectives on digital platforms and the inter-organizational economic, business, and social perspectives on ecosystems, which are based on complementarity and generativity. The notion of ecosystem to define digital platforms will be useful when we locate the investigation at the level of legal ordering.

private ordering (via private employees), theorized by Williamson with the 'fundamental transformation' in the development of firm theory.[23]

Moreover, even on a legal level, the 'technological' notion of ecosystem should lead to that of ordering, which despite having similar characteristics arises differently in closed, waterproof platforms, and in open, porous ones. Taking note of these evolutions makes it possible to make up for the current gaps in the legal definition. We shall look more closely into this aspect in Chapters 2, 3 and 4.

2. DIGITAL PLATFORMS FACING THE REGULATORY ENVIRONMENT: THE TWENTY EUROPEAN MILESTONES

Digital platforms operate in the market and create the rules that govern it. Let's start with the latter. For the sole purposes of interpretation, to define the framework and outline the scenario, we start from some assumptions (twenty). Let's call them European milestones, since they are the foundations on which the European Union intends to carve out a role in the global digital economy, via regulation. Since European standards constitute the highest standards and at the same time a measure of legal protection, they become de facto paradigmatic, and are therefore a good starting point for the investigation.

2.1 One: The Era of the Necessary European Policy of Sustainable and Inclusive Growth

We are in a new phase of the European Union: the era of the 'necessary European policy of sustainable and inclusive growth'.[24] Growth must be sustainable and inclusive: Germany, the economic engine of the Union, is aware that the regionalization of globalization makes the European market even more strategic, so that competition between member states' legal systems is no longer an interest to be pursued but a danger to avoid.[25] This also produces

---

[23] See O. Williamson (1991), *The Nature of the Firm: Origins, Evolution, and Development*, Oxford University Press; O. Williamson (2002), The theory of the firm as governance structure: from choice to contract, *Journal of Economic Perspectives*, 171–195. We shall see in section 2 that the two positions, respectively of Calabresi and Williamson, are compatible with each other and consistent with the regulatory evolution, in which public and private regulation constitute communicating vessels and their relationship depends on contingencies.

[24] F. Bassan (2020), La nuova Unione Europea: una politica di crescita sostenibile e solidale necessaria, *Astrid Rassegna*, 320.

[25] In the European Union, the combined provision of powers attributed to European institutions for some policies (some exclusively, such as monetary policy, others

direct effects on regulation and on the tools used to implement it: increasingly European regulations (not directives) and a single, general body of legislation.[26]

Sustainability and solidarity are now linked: the former no longer refers only, typically, to the environment or corporate governance, and also integrates the principle that value must be kept as close as possible to the link in the chain that produced it.[27] Hence, the focus is on the extraction of value achieved by digital platforms via algorithms and the need for a regulation consistent with this evolution.[28] Hence also, the link with solidarity, since the production chain is no stronger than its weakest link.[29]

2.2   Two: The Rules Embedded in Technology

In the current evolutionary framework, the hardware (terminals, networks) is Chinese, the cloud predominantly American, and all that remains for the European Union is to define the rules.

However, two clarifications are important to interpret the real data. The first: technological evolution drives intelligence, which was once centralized in the cloud, towards distributed ledger technology (DLT) or decentralized systems (today the cloud edge, or proximity data centre, tomorrow directly into objects), or combinations of these. Among the consequences of this evolution is that there is reasonably greater competition between companies to occupy spaces that are still empty. The instruments of competition, if concentrated on

---

concurrently) and not for others (for example, fiscal policy, which remains with the member states, or economic policy, which belongs to the states and which the Union can only coordinate) has consolidated over time into a complex system in which cooperation and competition between state systems coexist, and prevail over each other according to economic and political contingencies.

[26]   Regulations are directly applicable in the member states, while directives must be transposed into their respective law systems. Therefore, the use of regulations makes EU law stricter. This is combined with the recent codification, via regulation, of entire sectors. The codes replace (via regulations) a set of rules (regulations and directives) stratified over time, and by so doing they standardize and simplify. Specific rules for different applications (which can also be numerous) originate from this clear and simplified regulatory basis.

[27]   M. Mazzucato (2018), *The Value of Everything – Making and Taking in the Global Economy*, Penguin. According to the author, platform-based models are not necessarily data-extractive, but they are and will continue to be data-intensive.

[28]   Financialization and digitalization have led to the emergence of new ways of doing business, in which value creation and value extraction are increasingly separated. See M. Mazzucato (2018), Mission-oriented innovation policies: challenges and opportunities, *Industrial and Corporate Change*, 803–815.

[29]   U. Malvagna and M. Rabitti (2020), Filiere produttive e Covid-19: tra rinegoziazione e co-regolazione, *Nuovo Diritto Civile*, 4, 369–410.

the repression (USA) or prevention (EU) of monopoly structures, could there-fore only be partially useful to regulate the transition phase.

Second: the rules, in the digital world, are embedded in technology (below section 7). Failing to understand this leads to serious mistakes, like the one Germany recently made, for example, when it adopted a law on the notification of exposure to Covid-19 which provided for a centralized database, and had to modify it after two weeks because it was incompatible with the decentralized model that Google and Apple had spread in the meantime on all mobile ter-minals.[30] Therefore, defining the rules means guiding technology, directing it towards the protection of rights that the European Union believes are the basis of its shared continental welfare.[31]

The digital welfare of continental Europe now proceeds in two directions: access and protection. It includes data protection as per the General Data Protection Regulation (GDPR), but also solidarity (which is necessary as it applies to states, but also to companies: hence contractual tools to allow equal-ity and overcome the asymmetries of abuse of dependence) and sustainability (environmental, corporate and value-chain).[32] Digital platforms cannot be asked to be responsible for this too: it is up to the states to take action.

The most important among the tools in the toolbox is interoperability, more effective even than break-ups,[33] and guaranteeing both competition between platforms and also the setting up of new ones. After all, the European project GaiaX, a federation of national clouds to foster minimum protocols and stand-

---

[30]　Google and Apple have thus agreed on a fundamental choice that has divided governments and has forced some of them to reverse the choices (database centrali-zation) already made (Austria, Germany, United Kingdom, Sweden even with GPS). France remained the only one to have maintained a centralized system despite its limited compatibility with the Apple and Google platform.

[31]　Think not only of freedom of expression but also, in the Internet of Things, of health protection, transportation, provision of essential services, etc. Only if taken into account right from the outset, in the development of protocols and technological stand-ards, can these rights be guaranteed. European welfare must therefore be reviewed and integrated into technology.

[32]　Above, note 27. Bringing value creation and value extraction back to the same plan is one of the functions of sustainability, as it is understood today by the European Commission.

[33]　We shall see in section 3 that the US antitrust approach, which justifies inter-vention in the market only in the event of an intent to monopolize and admits it in the most disruptive form (the break-up, in fact) is less efficient than the 'regulated compe-tition', an approach that the European Commission has been supporting since 2020 with a series of proposals for regulations, which base the opening of markets on the interop-erability of platforms and technologies.

ards consistent with European welfare, goes exactly in this direction.[34] This is a fundamental prerequisite for the transition – which is already taking place – from the (centralized) platform economy to the (distributed) blockchain economy, to the (decentralized) artificial intelligence economy, in which the data multiplies exponentially because data is no longer generated only by users but also by things (IoT).

2.3   Three: Rules and Extra Costs: Who Is Going to Pay?

The issue for the Union is how to make efficient a system in which the rules make technologies more expensive instead of cheaper. Without some form of public intervention, the market is based on an inexorable Darwinian process in which, all other features being equal, the least expensive product survives.[35] Assigning these extra costs is a choice of industrial policy, which we can re-categorize today in the necessary European sustainable and inclusive growth policy. The answer to the question 'who is going to pay?' was the origin of the awarding of many Nobel Prizes for economics and is, however, often the most pragmatic starting point.

One can assume that states pay the extra costs, to promote their own welfare.[36] Sharing mechanisms can be created alternatively, as has already been done in the past, for example with the universal service.[37] According to a third

---

[34]   The European GaiaX project is still at an initial stage and may evolve in two directions, or in a third one consisting of an integration between the two. The first is the least ambitious: a federation of national clouds aimed at sharing protocols and standards ('GSM model'). The second sees an intervention by governments and an industrial policy, which is expressed in an 'Airbus model' collaboration, and therefore with European companies that actively participate in the development of technologies which integrate the rights that the Union wants to guarantee.

[35]   This was the case, for example, with GSM, a European technology that at the beginning of the 1990s competed with others (CDMA, in the United States) and then prevailed all over the world thanks to its efficiency and reduced costs.

[36]   Much of the debate on the use of National Recovery and Resilience Plans is based on the costs attributable to the member states of the European Union for achieving the goals of sustainable digital development.

[37]   The solutions chosen by the European Union in the 1990s for overcoming state monopolies in public services were numerous and different from each other. In telecommunications, the justifications for public monopolies were based on cross-subsidies (for example, between local and long-distance calls), unsustainable in a competitive environment, in which newcomers would have attacked the richer (long-distance) market. The solution was to allow competition on all services, identifying a 'cluster' of essential services that each member state decided to guarantee, quantifying the net cost of providing these services, and attributing it to all operators on the market in proportion to the market share achieved (starting from a minimum deduction of 4%).

scenario, the market pays for these costs, provided that they correspond to a welfare shared by EU and some non-EU countries and that therefore the companies themselves believe they apply everywhere, making themselves part – if not promoters – of that higher level of protections on a global scale. This is what happened, for example, with the GDPR, initially opposed by digital platforms but then used (by Facebook, for example) as a justification for not sharing data, or (by Apple and Google) as the basis of the shared platform for Covid-19 notification applications, demonstrating that companies can easily turn risks into opportunities.

The Brussels effect is not automatic, and the degree of effectiveness of the rules is measured by the market.[38]

2.4   Four: The European Regulatory Matrix Is Blowing Up

The regulated markets in Europe constitute a 'matrix', composed of vertical silos (banking, insurance, financial markets, energy, transport, etc.) each subject to specific regulation, and horizontal silos, applicable to all sectors (competition, personal data protection, consumer protection). In the matrix, each box corresponds to an interconnection point between vertical (sectorial) and horizontal (general) rules, regulations and standards.[39]

The 'matrix' approach provides answers to many legal questions, not least that of the hierarchy of sources, which is clear in continental national legal systems but less evident in the relationships between legal systems. In the event of a conflict between vertical and horizontal silos indeed, reference has often been made to the hermeneutic criterion of specialty (the special rule prevails over the general one), which has generated a series of regulatory misunderstandings. The matrix simplifies the work of the interpreter, replacing the notion of prevalence of the rules with that of coordination (of the rules) and cooperation (of the competent authorities).[40]

---

[38]   See: A. Bradford (2020), *The Brussels Effect: How the European Union Rules the World*, Oxford University Press.

[39]   I developed the regulatory matrix theory in detail in: F. Bassan (2019), *Potere dell'algoritmo e resistenza dei mercati in Italia. La sovranità perduta sui servizi*, Rubbettino.

[40]   According to the reconstruction and interpretation that I provided in 'The power of the algorithm' (*Potere dell'algoritmo*, above, note 39), the matrix provides for coop-eration between independent national authorities, which should be adequate to resolve conflicts of competences and fill gaps. Nevertheless, there have been difficulties in the application, because independent authorities – and the courts – have applied the general criteria of interpretation: to overcome the conflicts they have therefore classified as 'special regulations' those of vertical silos and 'general regulations' those of horizontal silos. Hence, special rules have prevailed, in all the cases where the vertical silos could

Matrix regulation, which has worked satisfactorily up to now, is, however, imploding under the pressure of digital evolution. Vertical silos are no longer parallel: they converge or spread apart according to contingent urgencies and needs. A few examples: banks sell insurance, financial and mixed products, and the regulatory issue is raised here again in terms of prevalence or cross-regulation.[41] The convergence between telecommunications and television is prehistoric and the frontier has shifted to the audiovisual content of digital platforms, which grew in their *ante litteram* sandbox (in Europe, the 2000 Directive on electronic commerce, in the USA, the Telecommunications Act and the Communication Decency Act both of 1996, which over the years have guaranteed them exemption from liability)[42] and are now too big to care.[43] And what about the convergence in transport, where the degree of substitution has long since exceeded the threshold of the markets?

As for horizontal silos (competition, protection of personal data and consumer protection), they are overcoming the historical constraints that have now become unbearable.[44] This is the territoriality for data protection (*Schrems I* and *II*),[45] the economic and turnover thresholds for competition law ('mod-

---

be considered 'complete'. In cases of 'incompleteness' the general rule prevailed again. With the proposed 2020 regulations on DMA and DSA, the European Commission is now trying to bring the subject back to the original terms, providing for cooperation between national authorities. The eventual conflict must be resolved on the level of cooperation, not of prevalence (below, section 2.19, Nineteen: Regulation, Today).

[41]   V. Colaert, D. Busch (2019), Regulating finance in a post-sectoral world: setting the scene, in V. Colaert, D. Busch, T. Incalza (eds), *European Financial Regulation: Levelling the Cross-Sectoral Playing Field*, Hart Publishing.

[42]   In the European Union, the e-Commerce Directive imposed a 'notice and take down' procedure, according to which internet service providers (ISPs) were not responsible for the content disseminated on the websites they hosted, but were required to remove it or disconnect them as a result of a request from the authorities. Similar provisions were in the US Communication Decency Act. When digital platforms took over from the ISPs, the rules were not changed consistently, and the guarantees – justified if applied to small operators, i.e. internet connectivity providers – were also applied to the platforms, which therefore operated for twenty years in the absence of rules, or at least of those rules that governed the activity of companies that competed on the same markets but originated from regulated sectors.

[43]   Speaking to the European Parliament's Internal Market Committee, Internal Market Commissioner Thierry Breton said that digital platforms may have become 'too big to care' (6 October 2020). He stated this in the context that they 'tend to neglect the consequences of their actions in our daily environments, whether it be in work [or] in our social lives, but also when it comes to our democracy'.

[44]   Below, sections 3 and 4.

[45]   In *Schrems I* (CJEU, 6 October 2015, Case C-362/14, *Max Schrems v. Data Protection Commissioner* – 'Safe Harbour'), the CJEU ruled that national data protection authorities have the right to investigate individual complaints related to EC deci-

ernization'),[46] and the definition of the consumer as the beneficiary of the protection.[47]

2.5   Five: The Transition Regulation

The fifth assumption concerns the regulatory reaction: the classic regulation by subjects has rapidly become regulation by activity and then by products.[48] Recently, the failure of a regulation that follows the evolution of the markets

---

sions and legal instruments based on these decisions, but also made very clear that only the CJEU is authorized to declare such a decision or instrument invalid. The CJEU also declared the Safe Harbour agreement invalid. The main reason for this ruling appeared to be the fact that the CJEU found that in adopting Article 3 of the Safe Harbour agreement, the EC exceeded its powers by making a shortcut to the adequacy procedure that should be followed according to Directive 95/46/EC. Following the invalidity of the Safe Harbour agreement, the EU–US Data Protection Shield (Privacy Shield) mechanism was implemented in order to replace the Safe Harbour agreement and to function as an instrument for EU/US data transfer.

In *Schrems II* (CJEU, 16 July 2020, Case C-311/18 *Data Protection Commissioner v. Facebook Ireland and Maximillian Schrems*), while the Court of Justice invalidated Decision 2016/1250 on the adequacy of the protection provided by the Privacy Shield, Commission Decision 2010/87 on standard contractual clauses for the transfer of personal data to processors established in third countries was deemed valid.

[46] In 2019, French, German and Polish governments jointly proposed options for modernizing EU competition policy. It follows the German 2030 industrial strategy proposals of 5 February 2019 and the Franco-German Manifesto for a European industrial policy fit for the 21st Century, of 19 February 2019. The European Commission Proposal for a Digital Market Act of December 2020, originates from here.

[47] Communication from the Commission to the European Parliament and the Council, New Consumer Agenda Strengthening consumer resilience for sustainable recovery, COM(2020) 696 final.

[48] F. Annunziata (2020), MiFID II as a template. Towards a general charter for the protection of investors and consumers of financial products and services, EU financial law private and public enforcement of EU investor protection regulation, in R. D'Ambrosio, S. Montemaggi (eds), *Quaderni di Ricerca Giuridica della Consulenza Legale, Bank of Italy*, 90, 21–59; R. D'Ambrosio (2020), The liability regimes within the SSM and the SRM, law and practice of the Banking Union and of its governing institutions, in R. D'Ambrosio (ed.), *Quaderni di Ricerca Giuridica della Consulenza Legale, Bank of Italy*, 88, 503–529; V. Colaert (2020), Product governance: paternalism outsourced to financial institutions?, *European Business Law Review*, 31(6), 977–1000; A. Marcacci (2017), European regulatory private law going global? The case of product governance, *European Business Organization Law Review*, 18(2), 305–332; D. Busch (2016), Product governance and product intervention under MiFID II/MiFIR, in D. Busch, G. Ferrarini (eds), *Regulation of the EU Financial Markets: MiFID II and MiFIR*, Oxford University Press 123–146; R. Mellenbergh (2014), MiFID II: New governance rules in relation to investment firms, *European Company Law*, 11(3), 172–177.

was commonly recognized. A new era has begun, which recent events (the pandemic, too) have accelerated.

We are presently halfway, fording the river when it is in flood – not exactly the best situation for developing strategies. The old rules are no longer effective, the new ones are not yet in force. The European Commission that took office on 1 December 2019 has taken exceptional decisions to face an exceptional crisis (the pandemic), but has also structured a medium- to long-term intervention to address the market.[49]

2.6   Six: The Regulatory Circle

The Commission's strategy has now been simplified by the withdrawal from the European Union of the United Kingdom, which had brought into the EU with it an aversion to the codification of continental Europe. Legal traditions thus return to their origins, each in their own way.[50] The EU Commission can therefore now move towards a new regulatory paradigm, no longer spurious, based on a general codification typical of civil law, applicable to all sectors, and therefore based on general principles, with specific applications (not 'sectoral', but based on single products or services) that arise from the market, according to the 'regulatory circle', which I illustrated in my previous writings.[51]

In a nutshell: the best practices on the market are adopted by the national regulatory and supervisory authorities as benchmarks and brought to the forum of the European authorities, which develop technical standards or, when necessary, proposals to the EU Commission, which then adopts executive acts, or launches legislative acts that the EU Council and EU Parliament then approve, making them binding. The advantage of the 'regulatory circle' is that the best practices are binding (self-binding the companies that adopt them) immediately, or as soon as the national and European authorities propose them as standards or guidelines.

---

[49]   DSA, DMA, DDA, Recovery Plan for Europe, ESM, are all tools that, together with the interventions of the European Central Bank (Pandemic emergency purchase programme (PEPP) and longer-term refinancing operations (LTROs)), intend to promote the sustainable technological development of the European Union.

[50]   In the European Union, member states and European institutions have attempted to make civil law systems compatible with common law ones. The civil law system is based on the framework of Roman law, with core principles codified into a referable system, which serves as the primary source of law. Common law (judge-made law, or case law) is the body of law created by judges and similar quasi-judicial tribunals by virtue of being stated in written opinions. With the United Kingdom's exit from the Union, European legislation is now based on a single legal model, i.e. continental civil law. The harmonization process therefore tends to be more effective and faster.

[51]   F. Bassan, *Potere dell'algoritmo*, above, note 39, at 23–45.

The application rules of the codes are therefore no longer defined by 'silos' but by product. Hence there are a few rules of public regulation, which have been codified, and numerous specific applications that change in real time due to market practice. In this pragmatic way, and also dictated by the pandemic emergency, the regulatory dilemma that has seen opposing principles of prevalence and cross-regulation for a decade has been resolved.[52]

2.7   Seven: Enhanced Cooperation Regulation

This evolution produces direct effects in terms of technological innovation and digital platforms, since in the modernization of the regulatory framework, the national authorities of several member states can coordinate and negotiate jointly,[53] as well as effectively sanction any non-compliance (with what, however, is an agreement reached on the basis of a commitment made by the platform). This applies to competition, and should also apply to the regulatory authorities, coordinated with each other both vertically (with the supervisory or regulatory authorities of the same sector in the other member states and with the European one or, failing that, with the European Commission) and horizontally (with authorities from other sectors in the country of origin).

2.8   Eight: Ethical Regulation

What has been said is also relevant on a peculiar front of technological innovation, not ignored by scholars, but still without solution: the relationship between ethical principles and legal rules, separated by the curtain created over two centuries of general theory of law and now torn down by artificial intelligence. When we remain on the level of rules, the responsibility of the algorithm seems ineffable, since the algorithm can be, depending on the case, more

---

[52]   A common solution to regulating mixed (hybrid) products or activities is represented by the principle of prevalence (or predominance). The issue has typically arisen in the market for unit-linked and index-linked insurance policies (plans offered by insurance companies that integrate both life insurance – covering the risk of death – and investments, which offer the opportunity for the investor to generate capital). On this topic, see N. Dacev (2017), The necessity of legal arrangement of unit-linked life insurance products, *UTMS Journal of Economics*, 8(3).

[53]   E. Mastenbroek, D.S. Martinsen (2018), Filling the gap in the European administrative space: the role of administrative networks in EU implementation and enforcement, *Journal of European Public Policy*, 25(3), 422–435; W.P.J. Wils, Ten years of Regulation 1/2003 – a retrospective, *Journal of European Competition Law & Practice*, 4(4), 293–301; D.J. Gerber (2007), Two forms of modernization in European competition law, *Fordham International Law Journal*, 31(5), 1235–1265.

or less autonomous from both its creator and its users, and often the choice is one of opportunity; therefore credible representations must be created.[54]

The regulatory circle is part of the solution, not of the problem: it permits human intervention (thus, the algorithm will not do it by itself) to select the best practices, which are transformed into benchmarks and therefore into rules and, in this perspective, it also implements the rules of Asimov (rules 3 and 1).[55]

The European Union is now beginning to regulate these issues, differentiating regimes according to the degree of risk that the use of the algorithm produces and the activities in which the risk can be generated.[56] The principle according to which human intervention is in any case necessary, in one of the phases of production or use of the algorithm, to prevent its autonomy from turning into independence, constitutes the fundamental prerequisite of the legislation under discussion.

2.9   Nine: The Communicating Vessels of Regulation via Subsidiarity

Public and private regulation are two communicating vessels. Public regulation intervenes when private regulation fails: subsidiarity applies, since private self-regulation may be sufficient, and public regulation only intervenes to fill any existing gaps.[57] However, one must not confuse the failure of regulation with that of the market.[58] It is more than a reconstructive hypothesis because it

---

[54]   Below, section 6.

[55]   The Three Laws of Robotics (known as Asimov's Laws) were introduced in Asimov's 1942 short story 'Runaround'. The Three Laws are: (1) A robot may not injure a human being or, through inaction, allow a human being to come to harm. (2) A robot must obey the orders given it by human beings except where such orders would conflict with the First Law. (3) A robot must protect its own existence as long as such protection does not conflict with the First or Second Law. Asimov also added a fourth, or zeroth law, to precede the others: (0) A robot may not harm humanity, or, by inaction, allow humanity to come to harm.

[56]   Below, section 6.

[57]   I. Bartle, P. Vass (2007), Self-regulation within the regulatory state: towards a new regulatory paradigm?, *Public Administration*, 85(4), 885–905.

[58]   J. Tirole (2017), *Economics for the Common Good* (translation by S. Rendall), Princeton University Press, 160 ff. argues that economic regulation addresses six prototypes of market failures: (1) negative externalities or spillovers; (2) informational asymmetry; (3) buyers can become victims of their own actions; (4) implementing the exchange may exceed the individual's capacities; (5) market power; (6) inequality.
    In turn, at times regulation itself can fail. See R. Baldwin, M. Cave, M. Lodge (2012), *Understanding Regulation: Theory, Strategy, and Practice*, Oxford University Press, 2nd edn, 68–77; M. Lodge (2002), The wrong type of regulation? Regulatory failure

always works and therefore becomes a general rule. If put in this perspective, we understand the strategy of the new European Commission, which entrusts the concrete application of the rules and principles to the market and the regulatory circle.[59] And one also understands the EU Court of Justice, which (*Schrems II*) does not limit itself to cancelling the flawed public regulation but suggests developing the private one in the meantime (the standard contractual clauses), to be possibly framed within the other.[60] Here, the task of regulators, guarantors and supervisors becomes decisive, in the role they must exercise in the 'circle'.

2.10   Ten: Regulation and Codification of Uniform Law

From this point of view, the activity of subjects unfairly ignored in the last historical phase, which has effectively produced the codification of uniform law, becomes decisive again. UNIDROIT and UNCITRAL are the venues in which international contracts have found standards commonly applied today and are again (the most) appropriate in the current phase in which European rules have territorial constraints,[61] and public intervention must be residual, limited to providing the guarantees that the rules between private individuals fail to ensure (see Chapter 5).

2.11   Eleven: Co-Regulation, Clearing House

This evolution is fully part of the mainstream thinking on which the European regulation of the last two decades has been based, according to which co-regulation, necessary if self-regulation is ineffective, is a clearing house for communicating vessels, where private and public regulation meet, and public

---

and the railways in Britain and Germany, *Journal of Public Policy*, 22, 271–297; P.N. Grabosky (1995), Counterproductive regulation, *International Journal of the Sociology of Law*, 23(4), 347–369; C. Sunstein (1990), Paradoxes of the regulatory state, *University of Chicago Law Review*, 57, 407–441; R. Merton (1936), The unintended effects of purposive social action, *American Sociological Review*, 1, 894–904.

[59]   F. Bassan, *Potere dell'algoritmo*, above, note 39.

[60]   On 16 July 2020, the Court of Justice of the EU (CJEU) issued its judgment in *Data Protection Commissioner v. Facebook Ireland Limited, Maximillian Schrems* (Case C-311/18, '*Schrems II*').

[61]   See: D.J. Gerber (2010), *Global Competition: Law, Markets and Globalization*, Oxford University Press; A.S. Papadopoulos (2010), *The International Dimension of EU Competition Law and Policy*, Cambridge University Press; H. Hovenkamp (2003), Antitrust as extraterritorial regulatory policy, *Antitrust Bulletin*, 629–655; M. Bazex et al. (1987), *L'application extra-territoriale du droit économique*, Éditions Montchrestien, Cahiers du CEDIN, No. 3, 11.

intervention is allowed on a subsidiary basis and in compliance with the principle of proportionality. Co-regulation is to be understood here, obviously, as cooperation between regulatory authorities and the market in the formation of the rules that the latter is unable to establish via self-regulation.[62]

2.12   Twelve: Co-Regulation and Enhanced Regulatory Cooperation

It follows from the above that co-regulation finds specific application no longer in vertical silos (indeed, they no longer exist) but in intersectoral applications and often beyond the borders of a member state. Hence the need for that cooperation between authorities in both vertical and horizontal directions referred to in milestone six, which allows for a differentiated regulatory evolution based on the legal needs and sensitivities prevailing in the various legal systems.

2.13   Thirteen: Regulation and Digital Platforms

Digital platforms are the new players in the market (autonomous ecosystems) and cannot be the recipients of classic regulation, which is ineffective: it is a radar against which they fly too high, or too low (depending on the cases and interpretations). Because they were born unregulated.[63] Because they have so far operated in the absence of regulation.[64]

Therefore, today – and this is one of the objectives of this research – the issue arises of their placement in the legal space in which they actually operate, and which is national, transnational and probably, as we shall see, international.

---

[62]   Co-regulation has been defined as a form of industry association self-regulation with some oversight and ratification by government (P. Grabosky, J. Braithwaite (1986), *Of Manners Gentle: Enforcement Strategies of Australian Business Regulatory Agencies*, Oxford University Press); to be distinguished from 'enforced self-regulation', involving a subcontracting of regulatory functions to regulated firms (I. Ayres, J. Braithwaite (1992), Responsive Regulation, Oxford University Press, 103). For a broader overview on self-regulation, see: R. Baldwin, M. Cave, M. Lodge (2012), *Understanding Regulation: Theory, Strategy, and Practice*, Oxford University Press, 2nd edn, 146 ff.; J. Black (1996), Constitutionalising self-regulation, *Modern Law Review*, 59, 24–55; A. Ogus (1995), Rethinking self-regulation, *Oxford Journal of Legal Studies*, 15(1), 97–108. More recently: I. Rubinstein (2018), The future of self-regulation is co-regulation, in E. Selinger, J. Polonetsky, O. Tene (eds), *The Cambridge Handbook of Consumer Privacy*, Cambridge University, 503–523; C.T. Marsden (2011), *Internet Co-Regulation: European Law, Regulatory Governance and Legitimacy in Cyberspace*, Cambridge University Press.

[63]   See: H. Feld (2019), *The Case for the Digital Platform Act: Market Structure and Regulation of Digital Platforms*, Roosevelt Institute.

[64]   Below, section 5.

2.14   Fourteen: Digital Platforms and AI – The Relationship between Ecosystems

Algorithms and artificial intelligence are independent and self-regulated eco-systems which, when inserted into the ecosystem of digital platforms, become their operational tools and impose their implementation rules. The issue of an intervention (co-regulation) is therefore raised to regulate artificial intelligence in a way that is independent from the regulation of the platform, but consistent with it. The two sets must have autonomous but coherent rules, since both must be applicable in the subset constituted by their intersection (below, section 7).

2.15   Fifteen: Responsible Ecosystems

The regulation referred to in the previous point is legitimate and necessary, when it comes to digital platforms, to guarantee and protect the rights on a contractual level, but also to identify and distribute the responsibilities on a non-contractual level (when the damage is produced by an illicit act – below, section 6); public regulation, subsidiary, via the regulatory circle. Old rights are no longer enforceable, new ones must be guaranteed. However, it is a matter of understanding (and accepting) that the rules cannot be imposed from top down, but are developed through cooperation via the regulatory circle. With digital platforms, the best that states can achieve is to negotiate, influencing best prac-tices and establishing which of them should become benchmarks and standards on the basis of the welfare that the Union wants to guarantee (see Chapter 3).

2.16   Sixteen: Middle Enterprises

This regulatory approach is opposed by the 'middle enterprises' (nothing to do with medium sized enterprises). I refer to companies that have no bargaining power with transnational digital platforms, and cannot count on a regulatory basis that, on the one hand, protects them, and on the other, guarantees the legitimacy of their work, if compliant. Legislative, regulatory, judicial solu-tions – rules by principles, 'mercatory' applications – leave middle enterprises exposed to both negotiation (they have no power) and compliance risks (they have no certainties).[65]

Here, too, the old rules are sheet music without instruments. The solution exists and has been indicated and practised by the European institutions in

---

[65]   See, among others: T. Butler, L. O'Brien (2019), Understanding RegTech for digital regulatory compliance, in T. Lynn, J.G. Mooney, P. Rosati, M. Cummings (eds), *Disrupting Finance*, Palgrave, 85–102.

recent years as a priority: it is called co-regulation (see above, milestones six and eleven) and provides for the participation in the formation of the *lex mercatoria* by the regulatory authorities to compensate for market asymmetries. It allows companies to guarantee certainty, as regards compliance and strength, in negotiating with digital platforms.

Co-regulation also includes the reconstruction of a level playing field on a contractual level, a regulatory competition tool that the European Commission's proposal for a Digital Market Act has introduced as an *ex ante* measure.[66]

Regulation must push these companies towards environments (distributed today, decentralized in the near future) where competition is not yet driven by gatekeepers. Pushing the 'middle enterprises' towards market segments still open to competition and which are the prerequisites for the progressive digital evolution, is a typical act of industrial policy. Or rather, what I have indicated here to be the 'necessary sustainable and inclusive growth policy'.

2.17   Seventeen: Lockdown Economy

On these assumptions, the pandemic has had a significant impact. The persistent lockdown (2020–2021)[67] changes the picture. On the one hand, the power of digital platforms has grown, to the point of exceeding the psychological threshold of abuse (the US Federal Trade Commission's intervention against Facebook and that of the US Department of Justice against Google are historic events and will have consequences).[68]

The fact that the German government had to change a law adopted a few days earlier (on the notification of exposure to Covid-19) because it provided for a centralized database, incompatible with the decentralized system imposed a few days later by Google (Android) and Apple, with the additional aim of better protecting personal data, did not get the publicity it deserved.[69] An agreement between duopolistic operators on the global market has the power to impose itself on governments as it is instantly applied to all active smartphones and not notified to any regulatory or supervisory authority.

From this first point of view, therefore, even if experienced, in fact, as a revolution (game changer), the pandemic has rather produced an acceleration of the evolution already under way (game accelerator).

---

[66]   Below, milestone 19, and section 3.
[67]   I'm referring to the effects of the Covid-19 pandemic.
[68]   Below, section 3.
[69]   Below, sections 3 and 4.

2.18   Eighteen: The Superstition of Algorithm Transparency

On the other hand, the pandemic has accelerated the transparency of the processes of artificial intelligence. This is an important point, for the transparency of the processes was precisely what was missing to allow digital transnational platforms to submit products and services to the regulatory and supervisory authorities and finally enter the regulated markets.

The notorious transparency of the algorithm, which cannot go to the origin of the source code due to industrial property rights,[70] settles on the process level: disclosure about the steps, the instructions provided to the algorithm, must be sufficient for the supervisory authorities.[71] What they produce, by virtue of machine learning, can become reasonably predictable if the initial instructions are known. However, this is certainly not a final solution. The

---

[70]   M.E. Kaminski, G. Malgieri (2020), Algorithmic impact assessments under the GDPR: producing multi-layered explanations, *International Data Privacy Law*, 1–20; M. Brkan, G. Bonnet (2020), Legal and technical feasibility of the GDPR's quest for explanation of algorithmic decisions: of black boxes, white boxes and fata morganas, *European Journal of Risk Regulation*, 11, 18–50; G. Malgieri (2019), Automated decision-making in the EU member states: the right to explanation and other 'suitable safeguards' in the national legislations, *Computer Law & Security Review*, 35(5), 2–26; M.E. Kaminski (2019), The right to explanation, explained, *Berkeley Technology Law Journal*, 34(1), 189–218; B. Casey, A. Farhangi, R. Vogl (2019), Rethinking explainable machines: the GDPR's 'right to explanation' debate and the rise of algorithmic audits in enterprise, *Berkeley Technology Law Journal*, 34, 143–188; S. Wachter, B. Mittelstadt, C. Russell (2018), Counterfactual explanations without opening the black box: automated decisions and the GDPR, *Harvard Journal of Law & Technology*, 31(2), 842–887; S. Wachter, B. Mittelstadt, L. Floridi (2017), Why a right to explanation of automated decision-making does not exist in the General Data Protection Regulation, *International Data Privacy Law*, 7(2), 76–99; I. Mendoza, L.A. Bygrave (2017), The right not to be subject to automated decisions based on profiling, in T.E. Synodinou, P. Jougleux, C. Markou and T. Prastitou (eds), *EU Internet Law: Regulation and Enforcement*, Springer, 77–101; J. Powles, A.D. Selbst (2017), Meaningful information and the right to explanation, *International Data Privacy Law*, 7(4), 233–242; L. Edwards, M. Veale (2017), Slave to the algorithm? Why a 'right to an explanation' is probably not the remedy you are looking for, *Duke Law & Technology Review*, 16(1), 18–84; G. Malgieri, G. Comandé (2017), Why a right to legibility of automated decision-making exists in the General Data Protection Regulation, *International Data Privacy Law*, 7(4), 243–265; M. Perel, N. Elkin-Koren (2017), Black box tinkering: beyond disclosure in algorithmic enforcement, *Florida Law Review*, 181 ff.; M. Perel, N. Elkin-Koren (2016), Accountability in algorithmic enforcement, *Stanford Technology Law Review*, 473 ff.; B. Goodman, S. Flaxman (2016), European Union regulations on algorithmic decision-making and a 'right to explanation', ICML Workshop on Human Interpretability in Machine Learning, New York.

[71]   Below, sections 4, 5 and 6.

battle is about to begin, the regulation must be ready and modernization of the rules is not enough.

2.19   Nineteen: Regulation, Today

Therefore, the European Commission is accelerating the Digital Services Act (DSA), the Data Governance Act (DGA) and the Digital Market Act (DMA), also addressed to platforms,[72] to which the Platform-to-Business Regulation (2019/11501) already applies. It provides indeed for general rules and contractual application.[73]

The DSA stands as a core of fundamental rules for the digital economy, equivalent to the GDPR and with the same goal of 'globalizing' rights.

At the same time, the Commission launches the modernization of competition rules, to make them effective in the new framework and with the new digital market structures.[74]

We shall see the contents and impacts of these new tools, which are still being defined, in the next section. Again, the European Strategy for Data[75] is not corollary; rather, it closes the perimeter; similarly with the 'Digital Finance Strategy'[76] the 'Retail Payment Strategy'[77] and the legislative proposals for a

---

[72]   Proposal for a Regulation of the European Parliament and of the Council on European data governance (Data Governance Act) COM/2020/767final; Proposal for a Regulation of the European Parliament and of the Council on contestable and fair markets in the digital sector (Digital Markets Act) COM/2020/374 final.

[73]   The platform-to-business (P2B) regulation of the European Union has provided, since 2019, an encompassing legal framework for the relations of digital platforms and businesses. The rules require online intermediation services and online search engines to follow certain restrictions regarding their behaviour in the internal market. In particular, the P2B regulation requires a higher degree of transparency from platforms on their terms and conditions, the ranking parameters, the differentiated treatment of their own products and products of third parties (self-preferencing), access to data, exclusivity clauses or price parity agreements. The rules primarily require transparency, but do not prohibit specific behaviours. The P2B-regulation is to be reviewed as early as 2022, only a short period of time after its implementation.

[74]   The Commission is about to adopt a Proposal for a Regulation on new complementary tool to strengthen competition enforcement.

[75]   Proposal for a Regulation on European Data Governance (Data Governance Act), COM(2020) 767, 25 November 2020. As well as this proposed regulation, the European strategy for data intends to adopt legislative measures on data governance, access and reuse.

[76]   Communication from the Commission to the European Parliament, the Council, the European Economic and Social Committee, and the Committee of Regions on a Digital Finance Strategy for the EU, COM/2020/591 final.

[77]   Communication from the Commission to the European Parliament, the Council, the European Economic and Social Committee and the Committee of the Regions, on a Retail Payments Strategy for the EU, COM/2020/592 final.

'DLT Pilot Regime'[78] and for more 'digital resilience' in the financial sector (including a proposal for 'Markets in Crypto-Assets Regulation' – MiCA).[79]

Legislative initiatives are about to be launched by the Commission to ascribe the responsibilities in the artificial intelligence ecosystem (below, section 6) by applying the principles of subsidiarity and proportionality, but also of precaution.[80]

So much for the Commission. The EU Council and therefore the EU member states provide development policy support to the Commission's regulatory instruments. For example, it launches the initiative for a European cloud,[81] which among the various objectives also aims at guaranteeing the territoriality of data and therefore the application of Union welfare, since the 'Brussels effect' alone cannot guarantee extraterritoriality and prevents exceptions to jurisdiction (and the Court of Justice has now clarified this on several occasions).[82]

The European Parliament and the Council have passed the rules for European collective action, thus legitimizing consumer representatives as active players in the regulatory circle.[83]

The European Central Bank (ECB) also plays its part, and develops rules and standards for the digital euro and, as we shall see later, for private crypto-currencies.[84]

In the United States, existing antitrust instruments are used and refined. The two paths seem diametrically opposed but, as we shall see, in some cases they converge (below, section 3).

---

[78] Proposal for a Regulation of the European Parliament and of the Council on a pilot regime for market infrastructures based on distributed ledger technology, COM/2020/594 final.

[79] Proposal for a Regulation of the European Parliament and of the Council on Markets in Crypto-assets, and amending Directive (EU) 2019/1937, COM/2020/593 final.

[80] For a general investigation on the precautionary principle see: F. Bassan (2006), *Gli obblighi di precauzione nel diritto internazionale*, Iovene.

[81] GAIA-X is a project for the development of a federation of data infrastructure and service providers for Europe, which is supported by representatives of business, science and administration from European countries. The project was first presented to the general public at the Digital Summit 2019 in Dortmund (Germany) and has been continuously developed since then.

[82] Below, section 4.

[83] Directive (EU) 2020/1828 of the European Parliament and of the Council of 25 November 2020 on representative actions for the protection of the collective interests of consumers and repealing Directive 2009/22/EC.

[84] ECB, Report on a digital euro, October 2020.

2.20   Twenty: Regulatory Discontinuity and Market Codification

The evolutionary process – traditionally, the legislative process – that provides for the application of existing rules to new challenges, becomes revolutionary when placed on the path started by the new European Commission: general principles and rules, implementation by 'market codification'. As in the case of the Payment Services Directive 2 (PSD2), both recently[85] and following the standard of liberalization of the 1990s, in the era of crisis of the system or technological discontinuity, regulation stops chasing innovation (if the turtle chases Achilles the paradox does not work anymore) and rushes forward, dictating the new perimeter of the game in which operators can compete. It is an act of courage that defines the European industrial policy (*recte*: necessary sustainable and inclusive growth policy) and deserves support. Today, we are in a *terra incognita*.

However, something seems to escape the regulatory evolution that I summarized above, interpreting it. What is missing, more than what is there, is the subject of investigation in this book.

Ecosystems (according to the technological and economic definitions) do not allow for a regulation totally imposed from the outside. Recent practice shows that digital platforms are partially porous.

This is why I have emphasized in this section the profiles of co-regulation, a negotiated discipline, an intersection between private and public regulation. If these tools and the resulting methodology are always valid, they must be

---

[85]   M. Polasika, A. Huterskaa, R. Iftikharb, Š. Mikulac (2020), The impact of Payment Services Directive 2 on the PayTech sector development in Europe, *Journal of Economic Behavior & Organization*, 178, 385–401; D. Humphrey (2019), Payments, in A.N. Berger, P. Molyneux, J.O.S. Wilson (eds), *The Oxford Handbook of Banking*, Oxford University Press, 285–321; A. Brener (2019), Payment Service Directive II and its implications, in T. Lynn, J.G. Mooney, P. Rosati, M. Cummins (eds), *Disrupting Finance FinTech and Strategy in the 21st Century*, Palgrave Macmillan, 103–121; I. Romānova, S. Grima, J. Spiteri, M. Kudinska (2018), The Payment Services Directive 2 and competitiveness: the perspective of European FinTech companies, *European Research Studies Journal*, 21(2), 5–24; I.H. Chiu (2017), A new era in FinTech payment innovations? A perspective from the institutions and regulation of payment systems, *Law, Innovation and Technology*, 9(2), 190–234; European Commission, Payment Services Directive (PSD2): Regulatory Technical Standards (RTS) enabling consumers to benefit from safer and more innovative electronic payments, Brussels, 27 November 2017; M. Donnelly (2016), Payments in the digital market: evaluating the contribution of Payment Services Directive II, *Computer Law & Security Review*, 32(6), 827–839; P. Valcke, N. Vandezande, N. Van de Velde (2015), The evolution of third party payment providers and cryptocurrencies under the EU's upcoming PSD2 and AMLD4, Swift Institute Working Paper No. 2015/001, 12–23.

taken, in legal terms, from the level of market regulation to a higher level, of general theory. I shall do so in Chapters 2, 3 and 4.

3.   DIGITAL PLATFORMS AND THE REGULATED COMPETITION

Competition law (in the EU) and antitrust law (in the US) have moved from an economic approach that starts from the definition of a digital platform as a two-sided market (above, section 1), with certain substantial differences, which I shall briefly illustrate here. As for the competition law of the European Union, I shall restrict the review to the European Commission, since the national cases show more specific but also partially contradictory approaches.

The focus is not on illustrating in detail all the elements of digital platforms that are relevant for the purposes of antitrust law (in the USA) and competition law (in the EU). Rather, my intention is to verify whether the direction taken by states and regulators is correct, and whether it is exhaustive or can be integrated, and possibly whether this integration, aimed at filling possible gaps, allows a partially different approach, not just regulatory.

The issue mentioned in the previous section is that of the communicating vessels between private and public regulation. From this basic approach, the relationship between regulation and competition is inserted within public regulation.

3.1   Abuses of Dominant Positions by Digital Platforms

By implementing the practice and the case law on multiverse markets, the European Commission has sanctioned Google (Google shopping,[86] Google

---

[86]   Commission Case No. COMP/AT.39740 of 27 June 2017 – *Google Search* (Shopping). The EC considered Google to be leveraging from the dominated market for general search services into markets for comparison shopping services. Conversely, the FTC closed (in 2013) a similar investigation concluding that Google did not change its search results primarily to exclude actual or potential competitors but to improve the quality of its search results: see Statement of the FTC Regarding Google's Search Practices, In the Matter of Google Inc., FTC File Number 111-0163, 3 January 2013, available at http://ftc.gov/os/2013/01/130103googlesearchstmtofcomm.pdf (accessed 24 December 2016).

Android,[87] Google AdSense[88]), launched investigations against Amazon[89] and
Apple[90] on the basis of what had already happened, in the digital innovation
sector, with Microsoft.[91] Contiguity of the markets, extension of the dominant
position on contiguous markets, 'leveraging strategy' and economic depend-
ency are the tools used to sanction abuses and bring digital platforms back to
a path that is, if not virtuous, at least consistent with the typical protections of
a non-inclined plane.

In the wake of the European tradition, the investigations launched (and the
fines imposed) by the Commission start from the evaluation of the effects of
the conduct on the market, not the way in which they are produced, nor the
intentions of the platforms. Therefore, not only the subjective element (intention) but also the tool (algorithm) remain outside the perimeter of the analysis.

The toolbox has proved to be only partially effective for surveillance of the
digital platform markets, and the need for reform, on a legislative or executive
level, is unanimously felt.

---

[87]   The EC fined Google for abuse of its dominant position: (i) in the national
markets for general search services; (ii) in the worldwide market for licensable smart
mobile OSs, and (iii) in the worldwide market for app stores for the Android mobile OS.
Commission decision of 18 July 2018 in Case No. COMP/AT.40099 – *Google Android*.
Conversely, in the US – *Feitelson v. Google Inc.*, 80 F. Supp. 3d 1019, 1022 (N.D.
Cal., 20 February 2015) – the California District Court rejected the complaint because
the plaintiff was unable to demonstrate the foreclosure effect due to the exclusivity
agreements concerning the pre-installation of Google's apps. On this topic, see J.M.
Newman (2016), Antitrust in zero-price markets: applications, *Washington University
Law Review*, 94(2), 101. For a comment on the European decision, see V. Kathuria
(2019), Greed for data and exclusionary conduct, *Computer Law & Security Review*,
35, 89–102.
[88]   Commission decision of 20 March 2019 in Case No. COMP/AT.40411 – *Google
Search (AdSense)*. According to the EC, Google abused its dominant position in the
EEA-wide market for online search advertising intermediation.
[89]   On July 2019 the Commission launched an investigation against Amazon to
assess whether the online marketplace, in its dual role of online platform and retailer,
had put in place (along with independent sellers that are part of its network) anticompetitive agreements under Art. 101 Treaty on the Functioning of the European Union
(TFEU) and/or had abused its (alleged) dominant position (in the market for online
intermediation of e-commerce) under Art. 102 TFEU (Case AT.40462 – *Amazon
Marketplace*, started on 17 July 2019).
[90]   The EC investigation announced on 3 June 2019 started from a complaint lodged
by Spotify, according to which Apple allegedly: (1) unfairly limits competitors in their
access to the Apple Music streaming service; and (2) imposed a 30% fee levied on
content-based service providers for using Apple's in-app purchase system (IAP) for any
subscriptions sold in its Apple store.
[91]   Great Chamber, 17 September 2007, Case T-201/04, *Microsoft v. Commission*,
§ 1088, dismissing the appeal on Commission Decision 2007/53/EC of 24 March 2004
(Case COMP/C-3/37.792 – *Microsoft*).

Hence, as in the case of abuse by exclusion, the economic tests on predatory prices are useless when the service is sold for an economic consideration that is, however, non-monetary (hence the superstition about services that are free of charge).[92] On the one hand, there is an undeniable advantage for the consumer, which can only be measured following an economic evaluation of the data transferred by the consumer in exchange for the service: an analysis which is still imperfect. On the other hand, the difficulty of shifting price discrimination from abuse by exclusion (in respect of competing companies) to exploitation (in respect of consumers) when the price is 'reserved', is tailored to the availability and attitude of the individual, as profiled up to that point.[93]

On the other hand, again, the presumed irrationality of predatory prices in the face of the difficulty of recovering losses (in the USA), or the objective assessment of the non-coverage of average variable costs or the avoidable average and incremental long-term cost (in the European Union)[94] can hardly be brought more up to date, there being no adequate checks, although they clearly contrast with the world of digital innovation: Amazon has built an entire philosophy and a consequent business strategy (even included in its by-laws) on losses in the medium term.

Furthermore, the qualification of the markets is cumbersome, but this is normal in the evolution of the case law that pursues the market. Thus, the European Commission considered the 'search engine market for general surveys' to be relevant,[95] but has and will have difficulty in grasping the relevance of data acquisition and data management. Moreover, new criteria for assessing dominance in multiverse and networked markets on digital

---

[92]   The foundation of the US antitrust law theory, which protects competition, not competitors and even less consumers, applied to the digital sector is effectively summarized by R.H. Bork, E.F. Sidak (2012), What does the Chicago School teach about internet search and the treatment of Google?, *Journal of Competition Law & Economics*, 8(4), 663–700. As for the presumption of free services, see: J.M. Newman (2015), Antitrust in zero-price markets: foundations, *University of Pennsylvania Law Review*, 164, 202.

[93]   Unless we transform price discrimination into legal discrimination: A. Ottolia (2017), *Big Data e innovazione computazionale*, Giappichelli, 317, or we consider personalized prices as exploitation prices because they are able to extract from consumers all their willingness to pay: S. Mannoni, G. Stazi (2018), *Is Competition a Click Away?*, Editoriale Scientifica, 40, and M. Maggiolino (2018), *Big Data e il diritto antitrust*, Diritto dell'economia, 320.

[94]   M. Libertini (2014), *Diritto della concorrenza dell'Unione europea*, Giuffrè, 330.

[95]   European Commission, Case AT.39749, p. 28.

innovation have only been outlined in Germany, and it is significant that the intervention was legislative.[96]

The theory of the absence of true barriers to access to markets characterized by technological innovation, which in the United States too, above all, takes pride in recognized and unanimous practice and jurisprudence, yields to the evidence of economies of scale and self-powered network effects. The aggressive, all-US strategy of start-up acquisitions that made it completes the picture.[97]

Moreover, qualifying the infrastructure used by digital platforms as essential, as has been authoritatively supported[98] (as well as, in the future, DLTs or blockchains) to force their opening with non-discriminatory conditions and reasonable prices, appears to be a complex operation, since it requires (in Europe, from Bronner onwards),[99] in addition to the evidence of dominance on the upstream and downstream markets, the proof of the essentiality of the infrastructure and therefore of the absence of alternative platforms or, at least, the proof that the platform constitutes a bottleneck because it holds a product or service that it does not sell (*IMS Health*).[100]

Finally, it appears objectively difficult to impose data sharing (another authoritative proposal[101]) because the data are only partially relevant – it is the ability to process them that is crucial. Data processing leads to the algorithm

---

[96]   The German legislator has listed five criteria for determining dominance in multiverse or networked markets: direct and indirect network effects; parallel use of multiple services costs of migrating from one to another (the so-called multi-homing); economies of scale in relation to network effects; access to competitively sensitive data; pressure exerted by innovation on competition (Neuntes Gesetz sur Anderung des Gesetzes gegen Wettbewerbeschrankungen, 2017, chapter 2, para. 18.3a).

[97]   Difficulties made evident by the Commission's investigation, European Commission, Case AT.39740, *Google Search (Shopping)*, 27 June 2017, p. 67.

[98]   L. Kahn (2018), What makes tech platforms so powerful?, in G. Rolnik (ed.), *Digital Platforms and Concentration*, Chicago Booth School of Business, 15.

[99]   According to Bronner, refusal to deal can violate Article 102 TFEU under the three exceptional circumstances that the refusal concerns an indispensable input; that no objective justification excusing such refusal exists; and that the refusal eliminates competition downstream. See among others: R. Nazzini (2011), *The Foundations of European Union Competition Law. The Objective and Principles of Article 102*, Oxford University Press, 262 ff.; J. Temple Lang (2000), The principle of essential facilities in European Community competition law. The position since Bronner, *Journal of Network Industries*, 1, 375–405.

[100]   The *IMS Health* judgment specifies that where the refusal relates to access to intangible property protected by IP rights it must show the ability to prevent the emergence of new product(s) for which there is consumer demand. See: N. Dunne (2020), Dispensing with indispensability, *Journal of Competition Law & Economics*, 16(1), 77.

[101]   V. Mayer-Schönberger, T. Range (2018), *Reinventing Capitalism in the Age of Big Data*, Hachette, 169.

and transparency operates within certain limits (constrained by industrial property rights) and is also ineffective, since what is relevant is the ability to generate data. This is also a dead end.

Hence, there are sanctions for abuses but they remain marginal. In the Google Search case, the Commission found classic abuses by discrimination (leverage and tying), similar to those that Microsoft had faced a decade earlier and always connected to the browser.[102] No different are the abuses claimed by the Commission against Qualcomm to guarantee the exclusivity of chips on Apple products,[103] against Apple, which rejected a version of Spotify IOS in favour of an Apple Music one,[104] or against Amazon, which imposed on publishers contracts with a most favourable treatment clause, which allowed Amazon to control the market,[105] to the point of forcing the counterparties to the paradox of a defensive agreement, itself sanctioned because it was anti-competitive.[106]

However, the real moves on the market remained outside the scope of the Commission's intervention, relating for example to proprietary APIs (application programming interfaces) which make the migration of advertisers between platforms sticky if not impossible, and it is a paradox, if even the American Federal Trade Commission (FTC) intervened on the point.[107] This tells a lot about the difficulty of struggling in retrospect against the walled garden, the *hortus conclusus* enclosed by proprietary terminals and platforms.

Nor can the protection of personal data become a discriminating criterion, for abuses and concentrations, despite the attempt by the German

---

[102] Namely, the abuses would consist in having forced manufacturers to pre-install the Google Search application and its browsing application (Chrome) as a condition for granting the licence relating to the Google application sales portal (Play Store); in having paid some large manufacturers and mobile network operators to pre-install the Google Search application on their devices exclusively; and in preventing manufacturers who wanted to pre-install Google applications from selling even a single smart mobile device running on alternative versions of Android not approved by Google (Android forks). For comments, on both sides, about the correctness of the analysis, see: M. Granieri, V. Falce (2016), La search neutrality tra regolazione e abuso di posizione dominante, *Mercato Concorrenza Regole*, 2, 305–306; S. Mannoni, G. Stazi, (2018), *Is Competition a Click Away?*, Editoriale Scientifica, 37 ff.

[103] European Commission, Antitrust: Commission Fines Qualcomm 997 million euros for Abuse of Dominant Market Position, 24 January 2018.

[104] European Commission, Cases AT.40437 (*Apple – App Store Practices – music streaming*) and AT.40652 (*Apple – App Store Practices – e-books/audiobooks*).

[105] European Commission, Press Release, Antitrust: Commission Accepts Commitments from Amazon on E-books, 4 May 2017.

[106] Case COMP/AT.39847 *E-Books*.

[107] H. Shelanski (2013), Information, innovation, and competition policy for the internet, *University of Pennsylvania Law Review*, 161, 1697.

Bundeskartellamt, which has taken it as one of the parameters of abuse.[108] There is no damage and, in this case too, there are no tests (quantitative parameters, output and price). If the value of the data is not scientifically defined and the price in monetary terms is zero, the tools developed by the practice so far and the jurisprudence produced by the Court of Justice and the national courts can build the perimeter walls but fail to protect, for the roof is uncovered.[109]

Unless the system is modernized, its inadequacy emerges even more clearly when measured in relation to the blockchain. This technology decentralizes consensus and facilitates exchanges and, by distributing information, tends to eliminate asymmetry and reduce access barriers, supporting competition. This, however, in addition to raising relevant issues for the protection of personal data, makes the market extremely transparent to the nodes of the blockchain which, especially in private markets often constituted of important financial institutions, can be a small number, due to the high costs of node management and of the necessary authorization. The number of operators is limited, the market is transparent, the barriers are high: the perfect environment for tacit collusion. Measures that also prevent network nodes from accessing information that generates consent are difficult to imagine with current tools, if not a posteriori, in case of abuse; a priori, preventive measures may only apply in cases of mergers and acquisitions. European regulation, in this case, must help.

In conclusion, the *ex post* nature of the intervention by the competition authorities, which is by definition backward looking, and the power to impose only financial sanctions, are the structural and procedural limits of the Commission's action. Hence the need, on the one hand, for greater coordination with regulation (with what until recently constituted vertical silos), and on the other hand, for a steady use of the 'regulatory instruments' typical of European competition law: behavioural and structural obligations that can be imposed not only in case of concentrations but also of abuses of dominant position.

3.2　　Mergers and Acquisitions

As for the rules on concentration, the 2007 *Google/Double Click* case (concentration in the search engine market) was a mistake by the European

---

[108]　See: M.E. Stucke, A.P. Grunes (2016), *Big Data and Competition Policy*, Oxford University Press, 2016.

[109]　The irrelevance of privacy – but, one would argue today, not of data protection – has been clearly sanctioned by the Court of Justice in the *Asneft-Equifax* judgment of 23 November 2006 (C-238/05): 'since any questions relating to the confidential nature of personal data do not fall, as such, under competition law, they can be resolved on the basis of the relevant provisions on data protection'.

Commission,[110] and even shared by the FTC.[111] Similarly, the EU Commission did not consider the Microsoft/LinkedIn,[112] Apple/Shazam[113] and Facebook/WhatsApp[114] mergers to be dangerous for competition.

---

[110] Case COMP/M.4731 – *Google/DoubleClick*. See: S.Y. Esayas (2019), Privacy-as-a-quality parameter of competition. Some reflections on the scepticism surrounding it, in B. Lundqvist, M.S. Gal (eds), Competition Law for the Digital Economy, Edward Elgar Publishing, 126–172; M. Cave, H.P. Williams (2011), Google and European Competition Law, TPRC 2011, available at SSRN: https://ssrn.com/abstract=1992974; M.C. Wasastjerna (2019), The implications of Big Data and privacy on competition analysis in merger control and the controversial competition–data protection interface, *European Business Law Review*, 30(3), 337–365.

[111] Federal Trade Commission, 20 December 2007, Case 071-0170 – *Google/Double Click*. The main argument which led to the approval was the competitive pressure exerted on Google:

> [A] number of Google's competitors have at their disposal valuable stores of data not available to Google. For instance, Google's most significant competitors in the ad intermediation market, Microsoft, Yahoo!, and Time Warner have access to their own unique data stores. These firms own popular search engines, and will have access to consumer information from their internal ad servers, ad intermediation services, other web properties, and software. The entry and expansion of these well-financed competitors has transformed the ad intermediation marketplace over the last six months. All of these firms are vertically integrated, and all appear to be well-positioned to compete vigorously against Google in this new marketplace. (pp. 12–13)

As to privacy-related concerns (Double Click possessed highly personalized datasets, specializing in targeted advertising), the FTC concluded that their assessment in the context of merger review was neither possible nor desirable: 'not only does the Commission lack legal authority to require conditions to this merger that do not relate to antitrust, regulating the privacy requirements of just one company could itself pose a serious detriment to competition in this vast and rapidly evolving industry' (p. 2). In her dissenting opinion, Commissioner Pamela Harbour feared that the transaction would have combined not only the two firms' products and services, but also their vast troves of data about consumer behaviour on the internet. Thus, the transaction reflected an interplay between traditional competition and consumer protection issues. The FTC was uniquely situated to evaluate the implications of this kind of data merger, from a competition as well as a consumer protection perspective. Therefore, the FTC should have maximized its opportunity to do so, given that, following the transaction, the merged firm would have been capable of dominating the 'Database of Intentions' (p. 4). Absent intervention, she expected data foreclosure as a result of the merger (§ 359). See: D. Srinivasan (2020), Why Google dominates advertising markets. competition policy should lean on the principles of financial market regulation, *Stanford Technology Law Review*, 24(1), 55–175; P.J. Harbour, T.I. Koslov (2010), Section 2 in a Web 2.0 world: an expanded vision of relevant product markets, *Antitrust Law Journal*, 76(3), 769 ff.

[112] Case COMP/M.8124, *Microsoft/LinkedIn*, 6 December 2016.

[113] Case COMP/M.8788, *Apple/Shazam*, 6 September 2018,

[114] Case COMP/M.7217, *Facebook/WhatsApp*, 3 October 2014.

Yet, the one relating to concentrations is the only a priori intervention by competition authorities and allows up-to-date assessment of the market. It also allows the imposition of measures and the monitoring of compliance. In a market based on innovation, the acquisition of competitors who have developed the right idea or technology is one of the main tools of market control, in which the big corporations usually stumble.

Nevertheless, so far the concentration of data has not constituted a threat to competition, and this can be admitted for the 2008 case of *Google/Double Click*,[115] less so for the acquisition of WhatsApp by Facebook (2014), authorized in the United States but also by the European Commission and without conditions.[116] The errors in that decision, relating both to the relevant markets (online advertising, communications between users and social networking, but what about the data?) and to the existence of alternative (potential?) platforms emerged with evidence when, three years later (2017), the aggregation of the two databases led to minor consequences for Facebook (financial penalties imposed by the European Commission and national authorities).[117]

The proposed solutions, i.e. lower the threshold of the relevant turnover for notification, or parameterize it to the value of the transaction (as the German legislator imposed) fail to hit the mark, because they encounter the difficulty, on one hand, of identifying the relevant market data processing and management, which constitutes a secondary, indirect, slippery, hypothetical market,[118] and on the other, of imposing the transparency of the algorithm that processes the data.[119] Only in 2020 did the Commission impose behavioural conditions on Google in relation to an acquisition operation.[120]

---

[115] Case COMP/M.4731, *Google/DoubleClick*.

[116] Case COMP/M7217, *Google/Facebook*.

[117] In Italy: AGCM, Provvedimento n. 26597, 11/5/2017, WhatsApp-Trasferimento dati a Facebook, with which the Competition Authority considered the imposition of the modification of the contractual conditions of WhatsApp as an aggressive practice, instrumental in consenting to the integration of the two platforms.

[118] I. Graef (2018), When data evolves into market power – data concentration and data abuse under competition law, in M. Moore, D. Tambini (eds), *Digital Dominance. The Power of Google, Amazon, Facebook, and Apple*, Oxford University Press, 77; I. Graef (2016), *EU Competition Law, Data Protection and Online Platforms. Data as Essential Facility*, Kluwer Law International, 347; P.J. Harbour, T.I. Koslov (20), Section 2 in a Web 2.0 world: an expanded vision of relevant product market, *Antitrust Law Journal*, 76(3), 784–785.

[119] C. Sandvig, K. Hamilton, K. Karahalios, C. Langbort (2014), Auditing algorithms: research methods for detecting discrimination on internet platforms, Conference Paper; V. Mayer-Schönberger, K. Cukier (2013), *Big Data. A Revolution That Will Transform How We Live, Work and Think*, John Murray, 178–182.

[120] Case COMP/M9660 – *Google/Fitbit*. These obligations will clearly determine 'how Google may use the data collected for advertising purposes', 'how interopera-

'Killer acquisitions' or 'platform envelopment' strategies, the balance between *ex ante* and *ex post* assessments, theories of 'balance of harms' and jurisdictional thresholds proved to be only partially effective, due also to the digital platforms' strategy of purchasing small start-ups with initially low turnover but a quickly growing user base and a high future market potential (i.e., Facebook/Instagram and Google/Waze mergers originally escaped the Commission's scrutiny). In all these cases, it is difficult to distinguish pro-competitive or neutral deals from anti-competitive ones. Old assumptions, such as efficiencies from vertical transactions, should be abandoned and new ones, such as the unlawfulness of a merger between dominant platforms and substantial competitors, or uniquely likely future competitors, should be implemented.

3.3   The Path towards the Modernization of Competition Law

Hence the need, alternatively or cumulatively, for a 'modernization' of competition rules and their integration with complementary *ex ante* regulation. As for the first, both the market definition and the assessment of market dominance should change in order to address properly not only the multi-sided nature of digital platforms but also the transactions conducted in this market, which often do not involve the transfer of monetary consideration.[121]

3.4   Competition and Regulation, and Regulatory Competition

As for the second need, symmetric or asymmetric *ex ante* regulatory models are often invoked as complementary tools to address competition concerns and provide for competition *for* the market, when competition *in* the market is unachievable (due to market failure, customer inertia or abusive strategic

---

bility between wearable devices of other suppliers and those with the Android operating system will be safeguarded' and how users can continue to share health and fitness data if they wish. Another very strong concern was related to the processing of personal data. The issue is part of the package of obligations undertaken by Google, which in fact will have to ensure compliance with the provisions and principles of the European regulation on data processing, the GDPR, according to which the processing of personal data relating to health is not allowed, unless the person concerned has given explicit informed consent. With regard to advertisements, however, Google has agreed not to use the data collected through wearable technologies and other Fitbit devices used by users.

[121] Above, note 74. The typical instruments of competition remain, but with a limited burden of proof for the Commission.

market behaviour).[122] Again, the participatory design of remedies involves a co-regulatory pattern (*ex ante* guidelines) based on the regulatory circle.

The two European Commission regulation proposals of December 2020, the Digital Market Act (DMA) and the Digital Services Act (DSA), propose a combination of regulation and competition, *ex ante* and *ex post* intervention, entrusting both to the European Commission. The DMA and the DSA thus resolve in a pragmatic way an issue that dates back to the relationship between competition law and regulation and between their respective competent authorities.[123]

The DMA accurately lists the criteria for identifying the gatekeepers, recipients of the rules of regulated competition (operating systems, platforms,

---

[122] P. Alexiadis, A. de Streel (2020), Designing an EU intervention standard for digital platforms, EUI Working Papers RSCAS 2020/14, at p. 17; J. Crémer, Y. de Montjoye, H. Schweitzer (2019), *Competition Policy for the Digital Era*, European Commission; O. Lynskey (2017), Regulating 'platform power', LSE Law, Society and Economy Working Papers 1/2017. See also J.E. Cohen (2019), *Between Truth and Power*, Oxford University Press; Common Understanding of G7 Competition Authorities on 'Competition and the Digital Economy', June 2019. ARCEP, the French telecommunications authority, in Systemic digital platforms, December 2019, proposes a test of systemic digital platforms based on three main criteria: the existence of bottleneck power, a certain number of users in the EU, the existing integration of that firm into an ecosystem enabling leverage effects. The proposed 10th Amendment of the German competition law (new Section 19a(1) of the German Act against Restraints of Competition) introduces the concept of an undertaking of paramount significance, which would be determined on the basis of six criteria: a dominant position on one or more markets; financial strength or access to other resources; vertical integration and activities on otherwise related markets; access to data relevant for competition; importance of activities for third parties' access to supply and sales markets; and related influence on third parties' business activities.

[123] The discussion was initially on the prevalence of competition over regulation, or vice versa. The theses are well known: from the US 'supermandate', for which the general discipline of competition prevailed over regulation, which in any case had to be interpreted in a manner consistent with the first (and, in case of conflict, yielded); to the thesis of regulation limited in time as it is functional to compensate for market asymmetries that regulation had to help eliminate; to the opposite thesis according to which regulation remained in every competition policy, as it was aimed at addressing the economic issues that competition leaves unresolved and the social problems that competition cannot solve. The failure of the theses that started from the assumption of incompatibility has shifted the debate on the methods of exercising control: *ex ante* and prognostic for regulation; *ex post* for competition. The implicit consequence was a diversity of purposes: the restoration of the violated legality for the first, the repression and punishment of the violation for the second. The refrain of *ex ante – ex post*, however rough (the nuances are lost in this kind of analysis, but they do not cease to exist) has long framed the debate.

clouds and search services) and put into three lists (black, grey, white[124]) the actions that they must take to prevent investigations for abuse of dominant position, adding to this the abuse of economic dependence.[125] The remedies plan is also improved in terms of penalties (up to 10% of the turnover) and of the behavioural and structural measures (up to a typical US break-up) that the Commission can impose.

The DSA, on the other hand, qualifies the responsibility of digital platforms in terms of content, imposing the removal of illegal content (but only by recommendation of third parties) with responsibility in case of non-compliance, as well as protection of third-party content (traditional media) and transparency of system profiling to counter fake news.[126]

3.5   The Intent to Monopolize, Reloaded

Overseas, the reforms under discussion are those of a regulatory authority with specific competence in digital matters, which could enforce remedies for antitrust violation, and a reform of antitrust law through a common law-like process or new legislation (through a general tightening).[127] Furthermore, the assessment of an intent to monopolize led the US Department of Justice to sue

---

[124] The black list indicates prohibited behaviours. The white list illustrates positive behaviours, such as data sharing. The grey list concerns the most sensitive measures for the activity of the platforms (for example, the interoperability of the systems), which can be negotiated, in advance, between undertakings and the Commission.

[125] The abuse of economic dependence, adopted as a criterion by some member states, was opposed by the European Commission (under the Barroso Presidency: 2004–2009) and has now become instead a useful tool on a European level; another example of the virtuous functioning of the regulatory circle.

[126] Proposal for a Regulation of the European Parliament and of the Council on a Single Market for Digital Services (Digital Services Act) and amending Directive 2000/31/EC, Articles 16–33.

[127] Stigler Center (2019), Committee for the Study of Digital Platforms – Market structure and Antitrust Subcommittee, Report, 1 July 2019, Chicago. According to this study new answers should be given to old questions, among others: how to assess consumer welfare in a two-sided market; how to assess potential competition from new or small firms or not-yet-identified future innovators and entrants; how to assess the quality-adjusted price paid for a good or service sold in a barter transaction with zero or close to zero monetary price. Again, ancient doctrines should be changed, such as: the circumstances under which a refusal to deal can be prohibited; the paradigm of predatory pricing law; the harms theories; the proof requirements imposed upon antitrust plaintiffs, etc. See also: J. Furman et al. (2019), *Unlocking Digital Competition, Report of the Digital Competition Expert Panel*, HM Treasury, 10 and 55; Stigler Center (2019), Digital Platforms, Markets and Democracy: A Path Forward, Conference, Chicago.

Google[128] in October 2020; in December 2020, in an independent initiative, ten US states also sued Google, and the Federal Trade Commission sued Facebook.[129] All these cases were initiated after a document of Congress at the end of the legislature (October 2020)[130] identified paths and defined constraints and which, reasonably, the new administration will follow.

3.6   What Is Lacking

Again, however, as already seen on the level of regulation (above, section 2), something seems to be lacking. In this case, it is the notion of the ecosystem, which is also the basis of the economic definition of digital platform (above, section 1) and is consistent with a legal definition of order (see Chapter 3). As an ecosystem, independent from the others (other platforms, but also artificial intelligence), but in an increasingly strict relationship with them, the digital platform cannot be considered, in a traditional way, a company that operates in a market competing with other companies.

The ecosystem can include integrated services: the operating system, a marketplace for applications, a payment system, a cloud service, a range of smart home applications, online services (videos, emails, books, games, storage, maps, communications systems), some complementary, connected through private APIs.

---

[128] US Department of Justice suit against Google LLC, of October 2020. The DoJ accused Google of illegally protecting its monopoly over search and search advertising, by locking up deals with giant partners like Apple and throttling competition through exclusive business contracts and agreements.

[129] The Federal Trade Commission sued Facebook, alleging that the company is illegally maintaining its personal social networking monopoly through a years-long course of anticompetitive conduct. Following a lengthy investigation in cooperation with a coalition of attorneys general of 46 states, the District of Columbia, and Guam, the complaint alleges that Facebook has engaged in a systematic strategy – including its 2012 acquisition of up-and-coming rival Instagram, its 2014 acquisition of the mobile messaging app WhatsApp, and the imposition of anticompetitive conditions on software developers – to eliminate threats to its monopoly. According to the FTC, this course of conduct harms competition, leaves consumers with few choices for personal social networking, and deprives advertisers of the benefits of competition.

[130] House Report, Investigation of Competition in Digital Markets, Majority Staff Report and Recommendations – Subcommittee on antitrust, commercial and administrative law of the committee on the judiciary, 2020. The subcommittee investigated the following markets: online search; online commerce; social networks and social media; mobile app stores; mobile operating systems; digital mapping; cloud computing; voice assistant; web browsers; digital advertising.

3.7   Digital Platform as a Market

As an independent ecosystem, each platform is a market.[131] The combination of economies of scale and scope and indirect network effects allows digital platforms to aggregate and match massive amounts of users on both sides of the market, reaching a tipping point where, in the light of the winner-takes-all situation and of the existing barriers to entry, dislodging the Big Tech becomes very difficult.[132] It is a common statement that, when such conditions are met, platforms: (i) become the market (competition for the market); (ii) constitute the point of access to that market (platforms as gatekeepers); (iii) contribute, at least de facto, to setting the rules for operating within that market (platforms as regulators). Platforms are often vertically integrated and, in addition to providing the intermediation service, offer products and/or services on the business side of the market. This dual role is quite insidious because it might lead to conflict of interest and to neutrality problems, broadly defined as 'self-preferencing'.[133]

---

[131] This is demonstrated by the economic theory on the costs of leaving a social network and supported by some scholars: A. Gebicka, A. Heinemann (2014), Social media & competition law, *World Competition*, 37(2), 159; S. Weber Waller (2012), Antitrust and social networking, *North Carolina Law Review*, 90, 1771–1806; C.S. Yoo (2012), When antitrust met Facebook, *George Mason Law Review*, 19, 1147–1162. This feature of social networks comes from two-sidedness and indirect network effects: J. Farrell, P. Klemperer (2007), Coordination and lock-in: competition with switching costs and network effects, in M. Armstrong, R.H. Porter (eds), *Handbook of Industrial Organization*, Vol. 3. North-Holland, 1967–2072.

[132] M. Cappai (2019), Doctoral dissertation in Economic and Consumer Law, Governing markets in the Data Driven Economy (DDE). An analysis of the Digital Single Market (DSM) strategy through theory of regulation: a critical approach, Roma Tre University.

[133] I. Graef (2019), Differentiated treatment in platform-to-business relations: EU competition law and economic dependence, *Yearbook of European Law*, 448–499. A more sophisticated analysis separates 'pure self-preferencing', 'pure secondary-line self-preferencing' and hybrid self-preferencing. Pure self-preferencing occurs when a vertically integrated platform treats its affiliated services more favorably than non-affiliated services (e.g. the more prominent display of Google's comparison shopping service in its general search results as compared to rival comparison shopping services). A secondary line self-preferencing occurs when a non-vertically integrated platform engages in differentiated treatment among non-affiliated services in a market in which it is not active itself (e.g. a hotel booking platform providing hotels that pay higher commission fees with a higher ranking). Finally, a hybrid self-preferencing occurs when a platform engages in differentiated treatment among non-affiliated services in an effort to favour its own business (e.g. a platform blocking an app that interferes with its ability to gain revenues through advertising would be an example).

3.8   From a Market to a System

Hence, according to EU competition case law, one should shift from the definition of the market to that of a 'system'.[134] In a 'system', primary and secondary
markets are by definition strictly correlated, and the digital platform operator
(as system operator) should guarantee a minimum set of rules or a certain level
of competition *in* the markets of the system.

The issue is therefore to ensure that the rules of the market constituted by
each platform (system) are, if not fully compatible, at least consistent with the
rules that guarantee full competition,[135] and that are different in the national
orders in which the digital platforms operate: the comparison between US
antitrust and European competition law is only the simplest one.

3.9   Digital Platforms' Internal System/External Market

Once the problem has been identified, the analysis plan is twofold, internal and
external. The one internal to the platform (as a system), and of which whoever
manages and regulates it must ensure the consistency with the general principles of competition, and the external one, of the relationship between platforms, which must compete with each other in a way that is not only consistent
with, but in compliance with competition law – including the new regulated
competition – applicable in the countries in which they operate.

3.10   Current Practice and System Framework Mismatch

The misalignment between practice, case law, and reality consistent with
the theoretical reconstruction elaborated here, is thus evident. As for the
internal plan, of the platform as a market in itself (as a system), the European
Commission has so far investigated trying to apply multiverse market case
law and jurisprudence on exclusionary and exploitative abuses in 'innovation
markets', looking also at conglomerate effects (and related theories of harm),

---

[134] *Confédération européenne des associations d'horlogers-réparateurs (CEAHR)
v. Commission*, (T-427/08) EU T:2010:517, para. 105.

[135] A proposal, related to the introduction of an EU Market Investigation Regime
(P. Marsden, R. Podszun (2020), *Restoring Balance to Digital Competition – Sensible
Rules, Effective Enforcement*, Konrad-Adenauer-Stiftung) provides for the following remedies applicable to digital platforms: interoperability; data portability; access
to data; open APIs; transparency regarding nodes or algorithmic patterns; prohibition
of certain dark patterns; standards for consumer choice; code of conduct for the use of
default menus or drop-down menus; ranking parameters; digital sandboxes for innovative activities; opening up of public sector information.

imposing, with little success, compliance with – and not mere consistency with – competition law. As for the external level of the relationship between platforms, in which this compliance should instead be imposed (as well as interoperability between platforms, via APIs, protocols, standards, data), the Commission has not yet investigated.

The 'regulated competition' pictured with the DMA and the DSA offers a limited evolution and a partial solution in this regard. The DMA proposes a regulation in support of the instruments of competition, and the DSA reinforces the autonomous regulatory constraints (not functional to competition). Both, however, refer – in equal measure and with the same force – to both the inner plane and the outer plane. But, as we have seen, the degree of coercion that can be imposed on digital platforms when they operate on the market (external level) and when they operate in their own system (internal level) is different.

An evolution that the DMA (especially) and the DSA could enable is to make the self-assessment tools of digital platforms more refined, to verify compliance with regulated competition. This is a relevant point for the autonomous development of the platform as a 'system' consistent with – not necessarily compliant with – the 'external' regulation. This solution highlights the 'regulatory circle', strengthens the self-assessment of platforms for compliance purposes, enhances the function of platforms as ecosystems (on an economic level) and – we shall see – of legal orders, on a legal level.

However, it is necessary to bring the rules back to the level of systems, and bring these into unity. I shall try to do that in Chapters 2, 3 and 4, to draw later in Chapter 5 the consequences of the conclusions.

4. DIGITAL PLATFORMS BETWEEN DATA ACCESS AND DATA PROTECTION

The protection of personal data in the digital environment is one of the most controversial and constantly evolving issues, on both a regulatory and judicial level. I do not claim to examine its relevant aspects here. In line with the approach I have proposed, I shall focus on seeking, on the one hand, if not a lowest common denominator, at least a line of consistency in the regulation, i.e. in the relationship between states and digital platforms, and, on the other, a continuity also in the gaps and in the errors (if any) occurring the regulatory approach.

Algorithm-based data management is the core business of digital platforms, their lowest common denominator and, at the same time, what differentiates them most from all other companies, for which data management is only one of the ways of developing business, an additional tool – and not even a necessary one until a few years ago.

4.1   Regulation and the Market

It is therefore not surprising that data protection has been one of the main battlegrounds between regulation and the market. The most advanced regulatory frontier is obviously the European Union, and the applicable discipline is the GDPR.[136] The European regulation focuses on the fundamental rights of the individual: because incorrect data management might violate them, and because data are themselves considered fundamental rights, when personal.[137] Hence the need to separate personal and non-personal data, subject to different rules: the former are protected, the latter are mostly not regulated. Therefore, the debate is still ongoing and based on the economic value of the data, and the possibility of granting monetary consideration (not only the supply of a service) to those who generate personal data (data subjects). A possibility that is denied, though, if we consider personal data as a fundamental right inalienable by the individual and subordinate only to a 'more fundamental' right; public health, for example, as the pandemic has shown.

The European regulation on personal data was initially opposed by digital platforms, to be then used at a later stage – especially by closed platforms – as a shield, not to share data. That was until the paradox, highlighted by the notification of exposure to Covid-19, of the agreement between Google (Android) and Apple which, through an interoperable software, allowed all mobile terminals to interface with each other to send notifications, managing data in a decentralized way, in full compliance with the constraints of the GDPR which, on the contrary, some European governments risked violating.[138]

This demonstrates that while data protection rules affect the costs of providing a service, being burdened by the weight of rights, they can be used as any other lever on the market, for competitive purposes or for providing a more complete or higher-quality service, transforming the regulatory risk into an opportunity (see above, section 2).

---

[136] Regulation (EU) 2016/679 of the European Parliament and of the Council of 27 April 2016 on the protection of natural persons with regard to the processing of personal data and on the free movement of such data, and repealing Directive 95/46/EC (General Data Protection Regulation).

[137] The right to the protection of personal data is provided for by Article 8 of the Charter of Fundamental Rights, incorporated into the Treaties since 2009, with the relative competence attributed to the Union by Article 16 of the TFEU. This fundamental right is today a protection no longer of the private sphere but of the identity of the individual, as guaranteed by the Charter of Rights, a rule of primary European law. We have gone from the I-fortress to the I-controller.

[138] Above, note 30.

4.2   From Ownership to Control

The lawfulness of data processing under the regulation in force (GDPR) is based on principles that, if correctly implemented, appear adequate for regulating the circulation of data and their processing by digital platforms. This is also due to the partial change of the proprietary vision of data (strictly connected to the protection of the personal dignity and identity) in favour of a guarantee, for data subjects (and indeed for any natural person), of having control over the data concerning them, regardless of and even before any acquisition and processing of data.

Hence the new centrality of consent and the functional remodelling of the rights of access, rectification, opposition, deletion (oblivion), restricted processing, data portability, the right to learn about the automated decision-making processes, including profiling, which can also be communicated by the data controller by means of standardized icons and applications, which should be submitted in advance to the national competent authorities and to the European Data Protection Board (EDPB)[139] for preventive assessment.

4.3   Privacy by Design and by Default

Among the *ex ante* remedies, there are privacy by design and privacy by default. Through the first, the controller undertakes to set the parameters for data processing in the preparatory phase, in order to collect only the relevant data and only for the necessary period. With the second, the controller implements appropriate technical measures to ensure that, by default, only the personal data necessary for the specific purpose for which they are collected are processed, according to the principles of necessity and proportionality. Furthermore, the Data Protection Regulation governs the data subjects' right to revoke consent and delete the data, the right to be forgotten, and the right to the pseudo-anonymization of data (and their not being re-identified): algorithms are the basis of digital identity, profiling, and self-determination of information, all connected to fundamental rights, the essential core of European welfare.

---

[139] The European Data Protection Board is composed of representatives of the national data protection authorities, and the European Data Protection Supervisor (EDPS). It contributes to the consistent application of data protection rules throughout the European Union and promotes cooperation between the EU's data protection authorities.

4.4   Data Protection Compliance

The Data Protection Regulation operates within the context of integrated risk management (Article 24 of the GDPR expressly deals with prevention) which is one of the focal points of the multisectoral regulatory perspective. The risks borne by the data controller – who is required to carry out a preventive and updated assessment consistent with a dynamic vision of protection – are different from those borne by the data subject. The latter is allowed to control not only his data but also the risks generated by their processing by the controller or controllers, within the algorithmic chain of digital circulation. Risks that affect, among other things, the freedom of choice. In this perspective, the data subject's right (Article 22 of the GDPR) to not be subject to a decision based solely on automated processing, including profiling, which produces legal effects concerning him, or affects him significantly, applies.[140]

The notion of personal data is extended to new cases, some of which are subject to enhanced protection (subject to prior notification to the national supervisory authority: i.e. biometric and genetic data, or health services): however, this list is not exhaustive and atypical cases are allowed. The quality of the data is then highlighted in the GDPR for the purposes of rectification and deletion – which extends to implying for the controller the obligation to advise all those to whom the data have been transferred during processing – but it will probably constitute one of most relevant issues, being a measure of the processing.

4.5   Protection and Free Movement of Personal Data

The intersection, evident in the *ex ante* remedies, between protection of personal data and competition is direct: the rules are two-sided. This is also why they seem so ponderous to US operators and regulators, accustomed to a market freedom limited only by the intent to monopolize. Therefore, the principle of accountability emerges as a cornerstone of the new European regulation, in the broad sense of the taking of responsibility (and risks) by the company, which is no longer required to notify the processing of data to the supervisory authority but to independently assess the risk (by means of a preventive impact assessment) and manage it. Such an approach based on risk assessment in advance implies a dynamic, and no longer static, data pro-

---

[140] This has become standard enough to be a guideline for artificial intelligence as well.

tection.[141] The transition from mere bureaucratic compliance to efficient data processing is the objective of the reform, which imposes a true obligation in terms of results and not of means.

Such a step is not dissimilar, *mutatis mutandis*, from the one taken in competition law for the notifications of concentrations, originally mandatory, and then entrusted to the undertaking's autonomous assessment of the anti-competitive effects. Similarly, the European reform proposal (DMA)[142] operates by listing areas of actions (black, grey, white) that undertakings can use as a parameter to evaluate (self-evaluate) in advance the legitimacy of their behaviours and actions on the market. The law of digital platforms starts from self-regulation.

4.6 Remedial Safeguard

A key role, as the necessary counterpart of accountability, is thus taken by remedial safeguard, which guarantees the compliance of self-regulation with the regulatory principles and with the approach – widely used in competition law and at the basis of privacy by design – of compatibility tests, aimed at allowing compliance with GDPR protocols (Articles 40–41) and already tested in vertical regulations. The new environment is also consistent with the new powers granted to national data protection supervisory authorities, who can now not only adopt sanctions but also impose behavioural or structural remedies.

4.7 Data Protection and Algorithms

It is difficult to assess the degree of applicability of the European regulation to the protection of personal data when it comes to the algorithm, one of the main tools used by digital platforms. The effectiveness of the protection will depend on the extension of the notion of personal data and on the application of the rules on data subject consent that will be established by national supervisory authorities and by national and European judges.

---

[141] See on the risk-based dynamic approach provided by Art. 35 (data protection impact assessment – DPIA): R. Gellert (2018), Understanding the notion of risk in the General Data Protection Regulation, *Computer Law & Security Review*, 34, 279–288; C. Quelle (2017), The 'risk revolution' in EU data protection law: we can't have our cake and eat it, too, in R. Leenes, R. van Brakel, S. Gutwirth, P. De Hert (eds), *Data Protection and Privacy: The Age of Intelligent Machines*, Hart Publishing, Chapter 2. See also Article 29 Working Party, Guidelines on Data Protection Impact Assessment (DPIA).

[142] Above, note 46.

The 'Charter of Digital Rights' currently applicable in the EU guarantees to data subjects the right to: (i) get information relating to the processing of their data in a concise, transparent, intelligible and easily accessible form (Article 12); (ii) know how their personal data will be used and for how long they will be kept (Articles 13 and 14); (iii) access the personal data that are processed by the controller and by third parties (Article 15); (iv) rectify their personal data (Article 16) and obtain from the controller their deletion (Article 17); (v) restrict the processing when the accuracy of the personal data is challenged by the data subjects, the processing is unlawful, or the controller no longer needs the personal data for the purposes of the processing (Article 18); (vi) rectify or delete their personal data or restrict their processing, when the data subjects have objected to the processing (Article 19); (vii) receive the personal data concerning them provided to a controller, in a structured, commonly used and machine-readable form (Article 20); (viii) object to the processing (Article 21).

4.8   Rights and Principles

One should interpret and apply the data subjects' rights in compliance with certain principles. The first consists of restricting the purpose of the processing of personal data, which prevents their secondary use if incompatible; each purpose requires a specific collection of data and the consequent consent from the data subject, so retaining data for future purposes is prohibited. This principle is functional to the circulation of high-quality data and is therefore aimed at providing a guarantee to both the data subjects (who have the right to verify and review the accuracy and quality of the data concerning them) and to the data controllers, who risk processing data that are flawed in their original form.

The second is the principle of data minimization, according to which the data processed must be adequate, relevant and limited.

The third is the right to data portability, whereby data subjects can transfer their data from one data controller to another. Individual identity is protected against the acquisition of information, which is an allowed activity, and the data subject's consent operates as an authorization, a removal of the obstacle for the exercise of the activity. The data subject has therefore the right to object, even after having given consent, and that right is absolute when the data is processed for marketing or profiling purposes. Again, the enforcement of the rule requires guidelines to be issued by the national supervisory authorities, and market standards.

4.9   Data Protection and Blockchain

The Data Protection Regulation appears scarcely compatible with blockchain technology, for the latter shows a disruptive function and represents a qualitative break with the past (market) and the present (regulatory) systems.

The Data Protection Regulation seems to be only partially compatible with the blockchain, which: (i) discloses the participants' personal data (starting from the public key) to each node in the chain (regardless of the reason for which they were collated), (ii) does not allow deletion or modification, (iii) does not provide for centralized control (nor for a Data Protection Officer) and (iv) is based on a fully automated procedure of data management processes.[143] The definitions of data subject, data controller and processor are not applicable in either a permissioned or permissionless blockchain. The nodes of the chain may be considered as controllers in a permissioned blockchain, while it is difficult not to consider them as mere processors in a permissionless chain, in which the prohibitive costs of the operations required to identify the participants are such as to restrict the group of controllers. The purpose of using the blockchain also affects the qualifications as data subject and controller, as the purpose of an investor is different from that of whoever merely concludes transactions. One should therefore find ways of applying the rules that allow their useful effect, for example through anonymization or pseudo-anonymization techniques consistent with GDPR constraints.

Furthermore, the centrality of informed consent, the main novelty of the GDPR, seems to yield in the face of practice, which already highlights a collection of personal information obtained through the analysis of reprocessed

---

[143] See: Blockchain and the General Data Protection Regulation. Can distributed ledgers be squared with European data protection law?, European Parliamentary Research Service, European Parliament, July 2019; M. Kianieff (2019), *Blockchain Technology and the Law: Opportunities and Risks*, Routledge, 151–184; L. Moerel (2019), Blockchain and data protection, in L.A. Di Matteo, M. Cannarsa, C. Poncibò (eds), *The Cambridge Handbook of Smart Contracts, Blockchain Technology and Digital Platforms*, Cambridge University Press, 213–232; M. Finck (2019), *Blockchain Regulation and Governance in Europe*, Cambridge University Press, 88–116; C. Kuner, F. Cate, O. Lynskey, C. Millard, N. Ni Loideain, D. Svantesson (2018), Blockchain versus data protection, *International Data Privacy Law*, 8(2), 103–104; M. Finck (2018), Blockchains and data protection in the European Union, *European Data Protection Law Review*, 4(1), 17–35; M. Mainelli (2017), Blockchain could help us reclaim control of our personal data, *Harvard Business Review*, available at https://hbr.org; G. Zyskind, O. Nathan, A. Pentland (2015), Decentralizing Privacy: Using Blockchain to Protect Personal Data, IEEE CS Security and Privacy Workshops, available at https://ieeexplore.ieee.org, accessed 6 March 2021.

data: restricting the purposes and minimizing the data looks like sandbags along the banks of a flooding river.

4.10   Data Protection and Jurisdiction

A potentially relevant aspect, not only for the protection of personal data but also for the law of digital platform ecosystems, is the qualification in the GDPR of the right of establishment for the purposes of attributing the responsibility for data processing. The competence (of the supervisory authorities) and the jurisdiction (of the European courts) are based on the establishment of the company in the EU, both the place (EU or extra-EU) of the processing and the nationality of the data controller being irrelevant, provided that (this is the objective limit of application) the processing relates to the offer of goods, or the provision of services, or the monitoring of behaviour (the so-called targeting principle, already elaborated by the EU Court of Justice in the *Google Spain* and *Schrems I* and *II* judgments).[144] No extraterritorial claim to the rule, therefore; only the application of the general principles of the EU, modernized.

But the GDPR goes so far as to apply the principle of jurisdiction of the country of destination of the service and therefore of the data subject, even in the absence of any payment for the service. A correct application of this principle would allow the establishing of a compliant practice of the main operators

---

[144] On 16 July 2020, the Court of Justice of the EU (CJEU) issued its judgment in *Data Protection Commissioner v. Facebook Ireland Limited, Maximillian Schrems* (Case C-311/18, '*Schrems II*'). The case is a companion to the Court's 2015 ruling in *Maximillian Schrems v. Data Protection Commissioner* (Case C-362/14, '*Schrems I*'), in which the Court invalidated the Commission's adequacy decision underlying the EU–US Safe Harbour arrangement. The literature on the subject is extensive. On *Schrems I*, among others, see: T. Ojanen (2016), Making the essence of fundamental rights real: the Court of Justice of the European Union clarifies the structure of fundamental rights under the Charter (ECJ 6 October 2015, Case C-362/14), *European Constitutional Law Review*, 12(2), 318–329; M.L. Flórez Rojas (2016), Legal implications after Schrems case: are we trading fundamental rights?, *Information & Communications Technology Law*, 25(3), 292–309; L. Azoulai, M. van der Sluis (2016), Institutionalizing personal data protection in times of global institutional distrust: Schrems, *Common Market Law Review*, 53(5), 1343–1371. On *Schrems II*, see: S. Fantin (2020), Data Protection Commissioner Facebook Ireland Limited, Maximillian Schrems: AG discusses the validity of standard contractual clauses and raises concerns over privacy shield, *European Data Protection Law Review*, 6(2), 325–331; X. Tracol (2020), 'Schrems II': The return of the privacy shield, *Computer Law & Security Review*, 39(105), 484; A. Chander (2020), Is data localization a solution for Schrems II? *Journal of International Economic Law*, 23(3), 771–784; J.X. Dhont (2019), Schrems II. The EU adequacy regime in existential crisis?, *Maastricht Journal of European and Comparative Law*, 26(5), 597–601.

and the overcoming of the competition between legal systems that is inherent in the right of establishment, which risks attributing competence and entrenching jurisdiction over these issues to the Irish supervisory authority and judges, respectively, entrusting harmonization to the collaboration among national supervisors and, ultimately, to the Court of Justice of the European Union.

The lack of approval, at present, of the e-privacy regulation proposal also prevents the principle from being applied (at a subjective level) to the manufacturers of devices (smartphones, PCs, etc.) and – on an objective level – to metadata; however, it is probable that, as for the latter, the broad notion of personal data will allow an extension of protection to metadata.

4.11   Data Circulation and Regulatory Circle

In the digital environment, personal data deserve protection, their anonymization must be implemented at every stage, their portability becomes a decisive competitive tool but is based on the data subjects' right to consent (revocable), which is not a hindrance but a guarantee. Personal data must circulate but are also a fundamental right, and protection cannot be compressed by a legitimate interest in the processing. This is a part of the European welfare that the Union shares with extra-EU countries in an inclusive way.

When it comes to data protection, the regulatory approach is uniform, as regards both the internal and external action of digital platforms. It is always the data subject's consent that is the pivot around which the use of the data by the platform (internal level) and the transmissibility of the data to other subjects (external level) rotate.

The role of national supervisory authorities is decisive for a correct and effective digital circulation of the data. Not only in terms of sanctions (now the authorities' powers of investigation and sanction are expanded), but also in terms of prevention, because the national authorities can assess the techniques and conditions of the controllers' data processing and launch guidelines, approve standards, give opinions, fostering or endorsing codes of conduct or certification tools. They will probably also differentiate the compliance requirements related to the platforms' internal activity from those relating to their external activity.

The reforms, implemented through directly applicable European regulations, reduce the autonomy of the member states. To comply with the revolutionary speed of the markets is then up to the national supervisory authorities, which decide on the changing balances between use and reuse, protection and freedom, in ascending and descending subsidiary links with the European authority, the European Protection Board.

4.12   Data Protection and the Digital Platform Ecosystem

The protection of personal data has clear limits, both in terms of territoriality (as highlighted by the two *Schrems* judgments of the Court of Justice), and of keeping pace with the technological evolution: we have already seen how the rules, when not embedded in technology, risk being poorly effective or, at worst, illusory (section 2).

As for the first limit, geo-blocking tools make it possible to adapt compliance to the legal patchwork in which the digital platforms operate; but they can do little when the data are transferred from one regulatory area to another.

As for the second limit, technology allows the use of forever new and refined tools, functional to the achievement of new and changing objectives, and/or created to circumvent a particular regulation.

When efficient, regulations (see section 2) go at linear speed, while technology runs at exponential speed. The consequence is that the platforms develop an internal law of their own that provides users with other protections than those granted by the public national regulation. Sometimes, after scandals (Facebook and Cambridge Analytica) or disruptive events (the pandemic), a true 'competition between ecosystems' arises which, at the end of this book, we shall qualify as a 'relationship between legal orders'.

5.   DIGITAL PLATFORMS AND DEMOCRACY

If we apply the outline and principles that are beginning to take shape in relation to all aspects of the organization and activity of digital platforms and their impact on democratic principles, the topic must also be divided into two different lines of research.[145]

---

[145] P. Cavaliere (2019), Digital platforms and the rise of global regulation of hate speech, *Cambridge International Law Journal*, 8(12), 282; S. Zuboff (2019), *The Age of Surveillance Capitalism*, Profile Books; S.T. Roberts (2019), *Behind the Scene: Content Moderation in the Shadows of Social Media*, Yale University Press; J.M. Balkin (2011), Free speech is a triangle, *Columbia Law Review*, 118, 2011–2056; T. Gillespie (2018), *Custodians of the Internet: Platforms, Content Moderation, and the Hidden Decisions that Shape Social Media*, Yale University Press; Jack Balkin (2018), Free speech in the algorithmic society: Big Data, private governance, and new school speech regulation, *University of California Davis Law Review*, 51; E. Benvenisti (2018), Upholding democracy amid the challenges of new technology: what role for the law of global governance?, *European Journal of International Law*, 29(1), 9–82; L. Casini (2018), Googling democracy? New technologies and the law of global governance: Afterword to Eyal Benvenisti's Foreword, *The European Journal of International Law*, 29(4), 1071–1077; ICO, Democracy disrupted? Personal information and political influence, 11 July 2018, available at https://ico.org.uk/media/

The first concerns the internal part, the ecosystem of the platform, closed or partially open depending on the type, qualified according to the proposed taxonomy. This topic is generally approached in terms of freedom of speech, and of how the platforms respect rules and principles which, to date, are not mandatory, even if based on different rules, on both sides of the Atlantic.

The second concerns the external part, the relationship between platforms, and between these and the national legal systems. The theme has very broad contents and boundaries. As I have already made clear, I shall limit myself here to highlighting the relevant aspects for the purposes of our investigation. I shall look closer at the two profiles on the legal level in Chapters 2 and 3 with reference to the relationship between legal systems and (in Chapter 4) to legal subjectivity.

5.1 Digital Platforms and Democracy: The Internal Face

The first issue, relating to the impact of digital platforms on the democratic structure within the platforms, does not arise in abstract terms: digital platforms are private ecosystems, hierarchically organized and not subject to democratic principles. Nevertheless, the evolution of the platforms highlights their progressive implementation of principles typical of public law, from the rule of law to the separation of powers (see Chapter 2, section 3) to strengthen their accountability.[146] The issue that various authors – mainly American – have investigated, becomes therefore that of public laws enacted and enforced by private lawmakers, which undermines fundamental constitutional principles such as the 'state action doctrine' and the separation of powers, as well as the 'no-delegation doctrine', based on the distinction between private and governmental functions and on the limits of congressional power to delegate its legislative power directly to the private sector, for private actors are not sufficiently bound by constitutional principles of accountability, transparency and legitimacy and may not adequately represent the public interest.[147]

---

action-weve-taken/2259369/democracy-disrupted-110718.pdf; M. Moore, D. Tambini (eds) (2018), *Digital Dominance. The Power of Google, Amazon, Facebook and Apple*, Oxford University Press, 265 ff.; R. van Loo (2017), The rise of the digital regulator, *Duke Law Journal*, 66, 1267; J. Cheney-Lippold (2017), *We Are Data*, New York University Press.

[146] N. Elkin-Koren, M. Perel (2020), Separation of functions for AI: restraining speech regulation by online platforms, *Lewis and Clark Law Review*, 857–898; J. Balkin (2018), Free speech is a triangle, *Columbia Law Review*, 2018, pp. 2011 ff.

[147] K. Klonick (2018), The new governors: the people, rules, and processes governing online speech, *Harvard Law Review*, 1598; K. Brown (2016), Public laws and private lawmakers, *Washington University Law Review*, 615 ff.; M. Birnhack, N. Elkin-Koren (2003), The invisible handshake: the reemergence of the state in the digital

This freedom is now partially limited in the United States by a Presidential Executive Order,[148] and challenged by legislative proposals, both in the United States and in the European Union,[149] which point out that when the platforms' activity (i.e. content moderation) is pursued through a system of artificial intelligence, public/private classifications largely lose their distinctive power.

In terms of their 'internal' law (platform law), digital platforms apply international law rather than domestic law – meaning the law of the place where the community member has registered. So it happens, for example, with regard to the protection of human rights, and also in relation to freedom of expression.[150]

5.2   Digital Platforms and Democratic States: The External Face

As for the second issue, which concerns the external part (relationships between platforms and between platforms and states), while digital platforms are impermeable to obligations imposed from the outside, they can, however, accept them, to an extent that depends on many factors, the first of which is certainly the degree of sharing of the rules. And therefore, what can be achieved through co-regulation (and this is the direction chosen by the European Commission) is, for example, with reference to the principle of a rule of law, to require online platforms to work with independent, certified dispute settlement bodies where users can lodge complaints when they believe their contents have been wrongfully removed. Users should go through the

---

environment, *Virginia Journal of Law and Technology*, 8, 6 ff.; N. Elkin-Koren, E. Haber (2016), Governance by proxy: cyber challenges to civil liberties, *Brookings Law Review*, 105 ff.; D. Keller (2019), Who do you sue? State and platform hybrid power over online speech, Hoover Institution, Aegis Series Paper No. 1902, 29 n. 9, available at www.hoover.org/ sites/default/files/research/docs/who-do-you-sue-state-and-pla tform-hybrid-power-over-onlinespeech_0.pdf; J. Boyle (2000), A nondelegation doctrine for the digital age?, *Duke Law Journal*, 5 ff.; J. Boyle (1997), Foucault in cyberspace: surveillance, sovereignty, and hardwired censors, *University of Cincinnati Law Review*, 177 ff.

[148] Executive Order No. 13925, Preventing Online Censorship, 85 Fed. Reg. 34079 (28 May 2020). The order instructs several federal agencies to take actions that threaten to limit the legal immunity of platforms for user-generated content and jeopardize the economic strength of platforms.

[149] I am referring to the proposals to reform Section 230 of the Communications Decency Act, which grants internet platforms legal immunity for most of the content posted by their users in US, and to the Proposals for a Digital Services Act and for the Digital Markets Act in the EU.

[150] The states' regulatory power to change the digital platforms' internal rules is limited. The transnational operation of digital platforms has moved them beyond traditional regulatory accountability, particularly where speech and content moderation are concerned (see Chapter 2, section 3).

platforms' internal complaint procedures before being entitled to call upon an independent dispute settlement body.[151]

Thus, as for the 'external' profile of the relations between platforms and between platforms and states, the impact is there and it is often associated with the influence of social media on election campaigns. This is what the European Commission said recently, affirming that the digital revolution has transformed democratic politics.[152]

Yet, although this is the most obvious aspect, it is not the only one. However, economists and jurists often question what level of regulation would be the most apt to govern the way in which platforms operate, and which rules and principles they should follow within their own community, when these rules and principles would potentially affect the democratic life of state systems.[153] Recent examples have been provided by the use of social networks

---

[151] The Digital Services Act provides for a mechanism similar to that of the 'prior exhaustion of internal remedies' (below, Chapter 3, section 1.3)

[152] Communication from the Commission to the European Parliament, the Council, the European Economic and Social Committee of the Regions, on the European democracy action plan, COM(2020) 790 final, 3 December 2020. The Commission states that digital innovation gives political actors new opportunities to reach out to voters. It also brings new opportunities for civic engagement, making it easier for some groups – in particular young people – to access information and participate in public life and democratic debate. However, the rapid growth of online campaigning and online platforms has also opened up new vulnerabilities and made it more difficult to maintain the integrity of elections, ensure a free and plural media, and protect the democratic process from disinformation and other manipulation. Digitalization enabled new ways to finance political actors from uncontrolled sources, cyber-attacks can target critical electoral infrastructure, journalists face online harassment and hate speech, and false information and polarizing messages spread rapidly through social media, and also through coordinated disinformation campaigns. The impact of some of these steps is amplified by the use of opaque algorithms controlled by widely used communication platforms.

[153] Among lawyers, see P. Alexiadis, A. de Streel (2020), Designing an EU intervention standard for digital platforms, EUI Working Paper RSCAS 2020/14, available at https://cadmus.eui.eu//handle/1814/66307; T. Flew, F. Martin, N. Suzor (2019), Internet regulation as media policy: rethinking the question of digital communication platform governance, *Journal of Digital Media & Policy*, 10(1), 33–50; K. Langvardt (2018), Regulating online content moderation, *Georgetown Law Journal*, 106, 1353–1388; O. Lynskey (2017), Regulating 'platform power', LSE Law, Society and Economy Working Papers 1/2017, available at http://eprints.lse.ac.uk/73404/1/WPS2017-01_Lynskey.pdf; T. Gillespie (2018), Regulation of and by platforms, in J. Burgess, A. Marwick, T. Poell (eds), *The SAGE Handbook of Social Media*, SAGE, 254–278. Among economists, see Y. Zhang, L. Yuchen, J. Jingjing, T.W. Tong (2020), Platform governance matters: how platform gatekeeping affects knowledge sharing among complementors, *Strategic Management Journal*; D.S. Evans (2012), Governing bad behavior by users of multi-sided platforms, *Berkeley Technology Law Journal*, 27(2), 1201–1250; K. Boudreau, A. Hagiu (2009), Platform rules: multi-sided plat-

(Twitter, Facebook) by the President of the United States, Donald Trump, both during the 2020 election campaign and on 7 January 2021, before and during the attack on Capitol Hill. In the first case, the policies adopted by Twitter and Facebook differed,[154] while in the second case – given the seriousness of the events – both platforms blocked the President's account.[155] The censorship in the second case was interpreted, by the parties involved, respectively as a limitation of a fundamental freedom (of expression) and as an intervention to safeguard public order and, ultimately, democracy. Hence the open debate about the opportunity to amend Section 230 of the Communication Decency Act of 1996, which guaranteed to digital platforms an exemption from editorial liability.

We have therefore seen, even in these recent cases, that the degree of pervasiveness and enforcement of state regulations is different with respect to the external activity of the platforms (in relation to other platforms and states) and their internal policy.

The question is evident in practice, and we shall deal with it on a juridical level in the following chapters (2, 3 and 4). A few clarifications, however, must be made at the outset.

The traditional dynamics that see industrial and intellectual property opposing (and prevailing over) competition, are now transformed into more complex dynamics between property (secrecy of the algorithm, directly proportional to its accuracy and precision) and democracy, and this time the former cannot prevail, since the values of the latter are constitutionally protected. The error in the assessment, however, lies in bringing the friction between the two rights back into a single ecosystem (for economists) or a single legal order (for jurists). As we have seen so far, the rules within the private system of platforms are one thing, while the effects that the relations within the platforms can produce externally, in state systems, for example, by influencing voting choices, are quite another.

---

forms as regulators, in A. Gawer (ed.), *Platforms, Markets and Innovation*, Edward Elgar Publishing, 163–191.

[154] In May 2020, as Twitter executives waded into a confrontation with President Trump, Facebook kept its head down. As a matter of fact, Twitter added a fact-check link to one of President Trump's tweets criticizing mail-in voting. The company said the president violated rules regarding voter suppression. President Trump posted the same words on Facebook, which has similar rules around voter suppression. But Facebook didn't do anything about it.

[155] D. Ghosh (2021), Are we entering a new era of social media regulation?, *Harvard Business Review*, https://hbr.org/2021/01/are-we-entering-a-new-era-of-social-media -regulation.

5.3   What Practice Is Teaching Us

For this reason, the mainly regulatory issues of algorithm transparency are, in my opinion, wrongly placed.[156] And so are, from another point of view, those of data access, which are also regulatory issues, but which have arisen recently and with precise arguments on a supranational level, of international law.[157]

If we separate the internal from the external sphere, what state systems can impose on platforms concerns the effects that their behaviour and those of their members produce in state systems (external profile). States can therefore prescribe the achievement of certain objectives through the application of principles: accountability and transparency, among others. However, states cannot determine how these are to be achieved. In other words, they cannot affect digital platforms on the internal level in the same way and with the same force by which they are allowed to impose behaviours on the external level, in the platforms' relations with other platforms and with states. The issue here is not so much the degree of extension of private autonomy, because the internal law of digital platforms escapes in many ways the legal system of the state that regulates it (or attempts to do so); partly due to the original choice of states not to regulate, partly due to the subsequent autonomy conquered by the platforms via technology (in which, as mentioned earlier, the rules are now embedded).

This requires, on the one hand, a new declination of the very notion of democracy and of the elements that constitute it – if we really want to apply this paradigm to the internal law of digital platforms – and, on the other, the creation of new tools, adequate to protect it, in terms of the internal law of platforms, of the (public and private) law of states, and finally of transnational and international law, as we shall see (Chapters 2, 3 and 4).

---

[156] See: F. Di Porto, M. Zuppetta (2020), Co-regulating algorithmic disclosure for digital platforms, *Policy and Society*, 40(2), 272–293; C. Coglianese, D. Lehr (2019), Transparency and algorithmic governance, *Faculty Scholarship at Penn Law*, 2123; F. Di Porto, M. Maggiolino (2019), Algorithmic information disclosure by regulators and competition authorities, *Global Jurist*, 19(2), 1–17; M. Ananny, K. Crawford (2016), Seeing without knowing: limitations of the transparency ideal and its application to algorithmic accountability, *New Media & Society*, 20(3), 973–989.

[157] E. Benvenisti (2018), Upholding democracy amid the challenges of new technology: what role for the law of global governance?, *European Journal of International Law*, 29, 76 *et seq*. The author points out that international law governs cyberspace, which becomes an accessible global commons. According to the author, 'social networks and other internet service providers, such as Facebook and Google ... invoking their private nature and their contractual relations with their users, expect to be exempted even from the discipline of domestic public law and envision a private cyberspace where they, and only they, make the rules'. The author argues that 'it is entirely possible to argue that cyberspace is not only a private or domestic space but also simultaneously a global space and, hence, subject to international law'.

5.4   Digital Platforms, Fundamental Rights and the Rule of Law

Starting from 2020, the European Commission has set foot on this path, radically modifying the direction, previously followed, of a 'stand alone' development of the digital single market and its regulation, shifting the aim towards the relationship between digital technologies, fundamental rights and the rule of law. On the one hand, this entanglement explains the complexity; on the other, it allows the proposal for regulation of platform activity that is consistent with continental European welfare, as well as with the democracy protection tools that the European Union is adopting. This approach, consistent with the more comprehensive reform of digital regulation, provides for the intervention of national authorities and of the European Commission in terms of co-regulation, as opposed to the US model, which is still anchored to self-regulation. Co-regulation is consistent and compatible with the analysis that I have proposed, of a differentiated regulatory intervention with regard to the internal sphere of the platforms and to the external one.

Therefore, the relational plan of the relationship between digital platforms and state systems finds concrete application in the transition from a system of self-regulation to one of co-regulation, in which traditional cooperation between companies (market) and regulators, the prevailing instrument of European regulation in the last two decades, turns into a cooperation between legal systems (see Chapter 2).

Therefore, it is not only the platforms that have to evolve, paying greater attention to the effects of their activity 'externally', but state systems too, and these must do so in a way that is consistent with the protection of rights.

Such evolution is often misunderstood, and the cooperation between digital platforms and state systems is reduced to ethical principles, which involve aspects of the evolution of artificial intelligence. However, the two levels must be distinguished.

6.   DIGITAL PLATFORMS, AI AND ETHICAL CONSTRAINTS

6.1   Ecosystems and their Intersection

Artificial intelligence (AI) constitutes an ecosystem in itself, which produces many applications and which is only partially used by the existing digital platforms; the intersection between the two systems produces a third ecosystem, not independent, but autonomous with respect to the two that generate it. This is the aspect of our interest here, since AI is relevant to the extent that it is used by digital platforms.

However, the 'artificial intelligence' ecosystem must be examined in itself first, and then in its interaction with the platforms and therefore in the subset it produces with them.

The topic is extremely broad and already investigated in the literature,[158] but still unclear in its regulatory and also social developments. The intent here is to understand whether and to what extent the relationships between these ecosystems can take some legal significance; whether the approach I have proposed is consistent with the current evolution of a differentiation, in terms of regulations, between the internal and external law of the platforms, and finally, whether this internal law applies norms and principles of international law rather than domestic (national) law. Any positive outcome in this direction would strengthen the premises of the investigation which, in subsequent chapters, will move on to the topic of legal systems and legal subjectivity.

The goal is to understand not only which are the applicable rules but also which of these are ethical and which instead are legal norms that we can reduce to general principles.[159] According to the mainstream, when it comes to

---

[158] W. Hoffmann-Riem (2020), Artificial intelligence as a challenge for law and regulators, in T. Wischmeyer, T. Rademacher (eds), *Regulating Artificial Intelligence*, Springer, 1–33; V. Dignum (2020), Responsibility and artificial intelligence, in M.D. Dubber, F. Pasquale, S. Das (eds), *The Oxford Handbook of Ethics of AI*, Oxford University Press, 215–233; J. Turner (2019), *Robot Rules: Regulating Artificial Intelligence*, Palgrave Macmillan, 81–133; M. Chinen (2019), *Law and Autonomous Machines*, Edward Elgar Publishing, 52–103; Independent High-Level Expert Group on Artificial Intelligence (2019), A Definition of AI: Main Capabilities and Disciplines, European Commission, available at https://ec.europa.eu/futurium/en/ai-alliance -consultation/guidelines, accessed 9 March 2021; A. Agrawal, J. Gans, A. Goldfarb (2018), *Prediction Machines. The Simple Economics of Artificial Intelligence*, Harvard Business Review Press; S. Bayern (2018), Artificial intelligence and private law, in W. Barfield, U. Pagallo (eds), *Research Handbook on the Law of Artificial Intelligence*, Edward Elgar Publishing, 144–155.

[159] Article 5 of the European Parliament Resolution for a 'Regulation on ethical principles for the development, deployment and use of artificial intelligence, robotics and related technologies' (2020/2012-INL), states as follows:
> Ethical principles of artificial intelligence, robotics and related technologies
> Any artificial intelligence, robotics and related technologies, including software, algorithms and data used or produced by such technologies, shall be developed, deployed and used in the Union in accordance with Union law and in full respect of human dignity, autonomy and safety and other funda-mental rights set out in the Charter.
> Any processing of personal data carried out in the development, deployment and use of artificial intelligence, robotics and related technologies, including personal data derived from non-personal data and biometric data, shall be carried out in accordance with Regulation (EU) 2016/679 and Directive 2002/58/EC.

artificial intelligence, rules and regulations yield to ethical constraints. From a non-superficial examination, the reference to ethics, with the consequent renunciation of positive law, is perhaps unnecessary.

6.2   Regulatory Definitions for AI

Again, I propose to start from the definitions of AI, including the one on which the European regulatory perspective is based.

Niels J. Nilsson defined AI as 'that activity devoted to making machines intelligent, and intelligence is that quality that enables an entity to function appropriately and with foresight in its environment'.[160] AI can be also defined simply as a collection of technologies that combine data, algorithms and computing power.[161]

The definition accepted by the European Commission is more precise:

> Artificial intelligence refers to systems that display intelligent behaviour by analysing their environment and taking actions – with some degree of autonomy – to achieve specific goals. AI-based systems can be purely software-based, acting in the virtual world (e.g. voice assistants, image analysis software, search engines, speech and face recognition systems) or AI can be embedded in hardware devices (e.g. advanced robots, autonomous cars, drones or Internet of Things applications).[162]

> The Union and its Member States shall encourage research projects intended to provide solutions, based on artificial intelligence, robotics and related technologies, that seek to promote social inclusion, democracy, plurality, solidarity, fairness, equality and cooperation.

It seems clear that although the Article is titled 'ethical principles', it rather refers to compliance with legal rules. Likewise, Article 16 provides for the establishment of a 'European Certificate of Ethical Compliance'.

[160] N.J. Nilsson (2010), *The Quest for Artificial Intelligence: A History of Ideas and Achievements*, Cambridge University Press.

[161] European Commission (2020), White Paper on Artificial Intelligence – A European approach to excellence and trust, COM(2020)65 final.

[162] European Commission (2018), Communication on AI for Europe, COM(2018) 237 final, p. 1. According to Article 3 of the Proposal for a Regulation of the European Parliament and of the Council laying down harmonised rules on Artificial Intelligence (Artificial Intelligence Act) and amending certain Union legislative acts (Com(2021) 206 final, April 21 2021), '"artificial intelligence system" (AI system) means software that is developed with one or more of the techniques and approaches listed in Annex I and can, for a given set of human-defined objectives, generate outputs such as content, predictions, recommendations, or decisions influencing the environments they interact with'.

Again, according to the High Level Expert Group of the European Commission,

> Artificial intelligence systems are software (and possibly also hardware) systems designed by humans that, given a complex goal, act in the physical or digital dimension by perceiving their environment through data acquisition, interpreting the collected structured or unstructured data, reasoning on the knowledge, or processing the information, derived from this data and deciding the best action(s) to take to achieve the given goal. AI systems can either use symbolic rules or learn a numeric model, and they can also adapt their behaviour by analysing how the environment is affected by their previous actions.[163]

Various authors offer many other definitions of AI, and each captures relevant aspects of AI activity.[164] Again, however, the definitions serve a primarily regulatory objective. They highlight the features (software or hardware) and the activities that AI can carry out, more or less autonomously, and also in relation to the relevance of machine learning in those activities. The European Commission's attempt to bring AI back to a system is more ambitious: it intends to classify AI as an ecosystem in itself, and regulate it according to fundamental principles, compatible with those of the democratic systems of European Union member states, starting from the principle of the rule of law.

---

[163] High Level Expert Group, A Definition of Artificial Intelligence, p. 8. When it comes to AI implementation, AI is already being massively used in a number of areas and can be broken down into many sub-domains and techniques. These include search and planning; knowledge representation and reasoning; machine learning, which has led to AI breakthroughs in fields such as search and product recommendation engines, speech recognition, fraud detection, image understanding, etc.; multi-agent systems; robotics; machine perception, including computer vision and natural language processing; and more: see A. Renda (2019), Artificial intelligence ethics, governance and policy challenges – Report of a CEPS Task Force Centre for European Policy Studies (CEPS), p. 14.

[164] A. Bertolini (2020), Artificial intelligence and civil liability, study for Legal affairs, Policy department for citizen's rights and constitutional affairs Directorate-General for Internal Policies (European Parliament, July 2020) available at www.europarl.europa .eu/RegData/etudes, accessed 7 March 2021, pp. 15–33; J.J. Bryson (2020), The artificial intelligence of the ethics of artificial intelligence: an introductory overview for law and regulation, in M.D. Dubber, F. Pasquale, S. Das (eds), *The Oxford Handbook of Ethics of AI*, Oxford University Press, 3–27; J. Turner (2019), *Robot Rules: Regulating Artificial Intelligence*, Palgrave Macmillan, 1–36; C. Misselhorn (2018), Artificial morality. Concepts, issues, and challenges, *Society*, 55(2), 161–169; S.J. Russell, P. Norvig (2016), *Artificial Intelligence: A Modern Approach*, 3rd edn, Pearson, 1–34; J. Kaplan (2016), *Artificial Intelligence: What Everyone Needs to Know*, Oxford University Press, 1–13; N. Nilsson (2010), *The Quest for Artificial Intelligence. A History of Ideas and Achievements*, Cambridge University Press, 13; J. McCarthy (2007), What Is Artificial Intelligence, available at http://jmc.stanford.edu, accessed 7 March 2021.

6.3   AI and Ethics: The Origin of a Misunderstanding

When we talk about AI and ethical rules, we often refer to the choices that machines have to make as a result of machine learning and the processing of algorithms for this purpose. The textbook case is the self-driving vehicle that must choose the lesser evil when it is impossible to avoid the death of one or more people, and the choice is reduced to which one (life or death decisions).[165]

In this perspective machines could be trained to be utilitarian (Bentham, Mill), and thus focus on the ultimate result of their action and the rationality of their behaviour. Alternatively, a deontology-focused approach (Kantian) would focus on the law, as well as on moral imperatives and actions that are considered to be ethical or unethical, regardless of the result. Conversely, virtue ethics[166] (Aristotle) focus on motives and are relational rather than rational, in that they focus on following virtuous examples. Deontology and virtue ethics focus on individual decision-makers, while teleology considers all affected parties. None of these approaches provides uncontroversial, definitive ways to resolve conflicts.[167] There are numerous lists of principles which, starting from the various approaches, are considered relevant for the purpose of solving the case.[168]

---

[165]   R. Freedman, J. Schaich Borg, W. Sinnott-Armstrong, J. Dickerson and V. Conitzer (2018), Adapting a Kidney Exchange Algorithm to Align with Human Values, in *Proceedings of the Thirty-Second AAAI Conference on Artificial Intelligence* (AAAI-18), New Orleans, LA; E. Awad, S. Dsouza, R. Kim, J. Schulz, J. Henrich, A. Shariff, J.-F. Bonnefon, I. Rahwan (2018), The moral machine experiment, *Nature*, 563, 59–64; L. Floridi (2012), Big Data and their epistemological challenge, *Philosophy and Technology*, 25(4), 435–437.

[166]   N. Berberich, K. Diepold (2018), Virtous Machine – Old Ethics for New Technology?, available at https://arxiv.org/pdf/1806.10322.pdf; V. Dignum et al. (2018), Ethics by Design. Necessity or Curse?, Conference Paper, AIES '18, 2–3 February 2018, New Orleans, LA.

[167]   A. Renda (2019), Artificial intelligence ethics, governance and policy challenges – Report of a CEPS Task Force Centre for European Policy Studies (CEPS), p. 34.

[168]   European Group on Science and New Technologies (2018), EGE statement on artificial intelligence, robotics and 'autonomous' systems; L. Floridi et al. (2018) compare the EGE statement with five other documents: the Asilomar AI principles; the Montréal Declaration for Responsible AI; the General Principles offered in the second version of the IEEE 'Ethically Aligned Design: A Vision for Prioritizing Human Well-Being with Autonomous and Intelligent Systems'; the five overarching principles for an AI code developed by the UK House of Lords (2018); and the Tenets of the Partnership on AI (2018). Already these documents lead to a total of 47 different principles, although with significant overlaps.

The European Parliament Resolution for a 'Regulation on ethical principles for the development, deployment and use of artificial intelligence, robotics and related technologies' (2020/2012-INL) builds on the following principles: human-centric,

As fascinating as it is, the matter relating to the philosophical approach to algorithms – and to the lists of principles that follow from it – can, in my opinion, arise only at the end of a complex process that concerns the possibility, legitimacy and enforcement of a verification (*ex ante* or *ex post*) of the algorithm, of its setting and of the degree of autonomy of machine learning which, based on the set algorithm, makes the choices. Yet, the process must differ according to the degree of danger, measured in relation to both industry area and activity.

6.4   AI Ethical Constraints and the Risk-Based Approach

The regulatory solutions to regulate AI in the EU are indeed those of a level of risk-based system of regulation that would go from no regulation for the most innocuous AI systems to a complete ban for the most dangerous ones. A risk-based approach ensures that the regulatory intervention is proportionate. However, it requires clear criteria for the differentiation between the various AI applications, in particular in relation to the question whether they are 'high risk' or not.

According to the European Commission, a given AI application should generally be considered high risk in the light of what is at stake, considering whether both its industry and its intended use involve significant risks.[169] Again, the EU Commission is creating a 'matrix' with vertical silos (industries) and horizontal ones (intended use).

---

human-made and human-controlled artificial intelligence, robotics and related technologies; mandatory compliance assessment of high-risk artificial intelligence, robotics and related technologies; safety, transparency and accountability; safeguards and remedies against bias and discrimination; right to redress; social responsibility and gender equality in artificial intelligence, robotics and related technologies; environmentally sustainable artificial intelligence, robotics and related technologies; respect for privacy and limitations on the use of biometric recognition; good governance relating to artificial intelligence, robotics and related technologies, including the data used or produced by such technologies.

[169] See the Proposal for a Regulation of the European Parliament and of the Council laying down harmonised rules on Artificial Intelligence (Artificial Intelligence Act) and amending certain Union legislative acts (Com(2021) 206 final, April 21 2021); the European approach to Artificial Intelligence: the final Ethics Guidelines for Trustworthy Artificial Intelligence prepared by the High-Level Group on Artificial Intelligence, published on 8 April 2019; Expert Group on Liability and New Technologies (2019), Liability for Artificial Intelligence and Other Emerging Digital Technologies, published on 21 November 2019; the Declaration on Cooperation on Artificial Intelligence, signed by 25 European countries on 10 April 2018; the Proposal for a Regulation of the European Parliament and the Council on Artificial Intelligence, published on 21 April 2021.

As for industries, health care, transport and energy are among the most sensitive ones in a longer list that should be gradually updated. As for high-risk AI applications, the requirements could consist of such key features as: training data;[170] data and record-keeping;[171] information to be provided;[172] robustness and accuracy;[173] human oversight;[174] and specific requirements for certain particular AI applications, such as those used for purposes of remote biometric identification.[175]

---

[170] Requirements aimed at providing reasonable assurances that: (i) the subsequent use of the products or services that the AI system enables is safe; (ii) it does not lead to outcomes entailing prohibited discrimination; (iii) privacy and personal data are adequately protected during the use of AI-enabled products and services.

[171] The regulatory framework will prescribe that the following should be kept: accurate records regarding the dataset used to train and test the AI systems, including a description of the main characteristics and how the dataset was selected; in certain justified cases, the datasets themselves; documentation on the programming and training methodologies, processes and techniques used to build, test and validate the AI systems, including where relevant in respect of safety and avoiding biases that could lead to prohibited discrimination.

[172] Firstly, clear information should be provided as to the AI system's capabilities and limitations, in particular the purpose for which the systems are intended, the conditions under which they can be expected to function as intended, and the expected level of accuracy in achieving the specified purpose. Secondly, citizens should be clearly informed when they are interacting with an AI system and not a human being.

[173] These requirements should ensure that: (i) the AI systems are robust and accurate, or at least correctly reflect their level of accuracy, during all life cycle phases; (ii) the outcomes are reproducible; (iii) AI systems can adequately deal with errors or inconsistencies during all life cycle phases; (iv) AI systems are resilient against both overt attacks and more subtle attempts to manipulate data or algorithms themselves; and (v) mitigating measures are taken in such cases.

[174] The objective of trustworthy, ethical and human-centric AI can only be achieved by ensuring an appropriate involvement of human beings in relation to high-risk AI applications. Examples of human oversight manifestations are as follows: the output of the AI system does not become effective unless it has been previously reviewed and validated by a human (e.g. the rejection of an application for social security benefits may be decided only by a human); the output of the AI system becomes immediately effective, but human intervention is ensured afterwards (e.g. the rejection of an application for a credit card may be processed by an AI system, but human review must be possible afterwards); monitoring of the AI system while in operation and the ability to intervene in real time and deactivate (e.g. a stop button or procedure is available in a driverless car when a human determines that the car operation is not safe); in the design phase, by imposing operational constraints on the AI system (e.g. a driverless car shall stop operating in certain conditions of low visibility when sensors may become less reliable or shall maintain a certain distance in any given condition from the preceding vehicle).

[175] The gathering and use of biometric data for remote identification purposes, for instance through the deployment of facial recognition in public places, carries specific

6.5   AI Risks and Liabilities

The European matrix is also useful to define, qualify and attribute liability for damages created by the use of AI.

The issue is that of AI responsibility and sustainability (social, environmental and now also by reallocating entitlements as close as possible to where value is generated). Generally, advocating responsibility implies acknowledging the potential risks of AI, and acting accordingly to mitigate them in the design, development and use of AI. Essentially, the idea of responsible AI stems from the acknowledgment of possible unintended consequences of AI development and use, acting on essential aspects of AI such as fairness, accountability, transparency and explicability.

The approach followed by the European Union – again, an example of the most advanced regulation, based on rules embedded in technology – is to extend the existing regulation on product responsibilities to artificial intelligence, updating it to specific needs.[176] Such a regulatory evolution is consistent with the classic path of legislation, which advances by applying the rules that have proved effective to the new, and updating the old. But this is only partially useful when it comes to AI, as there are many cases in which it is difficult to attribute responsibility to a given AI system.[177]

---

risks for fundamental rights. Hence, in accordance with the current EU data protection rules and the Charter of Fundamental Rights, AI can only be used for remote biometric identification purposes where such use is duly justified, proportionate and subject to adequate safeguards.

[176] The current EU rules on the liability of AI systems is mostly related to the Product Liability Directive (Directive 85/374/EEC) and the Machinery Directive (Directive 2006/42/EC).

An update of the Directive is expected on certain aspects of it, such as the concepts of 'defect', 'damage', 'product' and 'producer'. In this respect, key aspects will have to be clarified, including: (i) how to interpret damage predictability; (ii) how to construe the so-called 'state-of-the-art' liability exception; (iii) whether to include 'as a service' the use of AI within the scope of the Directive; and (iv) how to ensure that the definition of misuse of an AI product does not place too much risk on the side of the end users. On the other hand, the Machinery Directive sets general health and safety requirements for products, such as robots or 3D printers. Finally, the future EU liability regime will also have to be designed in combination with a suitable insurance framework.

[177] This can happen due to any of the following scenarios: (i) a system causes given damage, but the specific contribution of AI to causing the damage is impossible to prove; (ii) an AI system does not incur any malfunction, but its interaction with human behaviour leads to damage; (iii) an interaction between two or more AI-enabled algorithms causes damage to third parties (e.g. the so-called 'flash crashes'); (iv) the combination of two or more AI systems from different vendors in a single product leads to damage, where it is not easy to correctly distribute the liability between the system

A path to identify a responsible entity for the damage caused by AI is linked to an ethical principle: the 'human in the loop' or the 'human in control' requirement should be replaced by a 'human responsible' requirement, to avoid imposing excessively burdensome obligations on AI developers, vendors and distributors in circumstances in which it is virtually impossible or useless to have a human in immediate control of the system, and at the same time guarantee that end users will be compensated for the damage caused and will therefore be more likely to accept and use the new systems.[178]

This approach to responsibility inevitably leads to the identification of a strict (not fault-based) liability regime. But questions still arise on whether such a regime would be absolute or relative; whether there would be one entity in the entire value chain that is primarily responsible vis-à-vis the end user; and whether there would be joint and several liability in case of joint participation in causing an accident.

Again, answers can differ depending on many elements. According to the 'one-stop shop' procedure, a single entity is responsible for consumer redress: the producer in the case of product liability, the vendor in the case of contractual guarantees in the sale of goods.[179] The 'one-stop shop' allows the first responsible entity to sue other entities in the value chain to obtain redress.

Liability would be mitigated by the fact that end users have misused the product, or in any way taken insufficient care while using an AI-enabled system; coupling strict liability with contributory negligence can provide optimal incentives for both parties involved in a dangerous activity,[180] pro-

---

vendors; or (v) it is difficult to prove who, among the AI vendor, the distributor, or the OEM (original equipment manufacturer), has caused the damage.

[178] A. Renda (2019), Artificial intelligence ethics, governance and policy challenges – Report of a CEPS Task Force Centre for European Policy Studies (CEPS), p. 84.

[179] A. Bertolini (2020), Artificial Intelligence and civil liability, study for Legal affairs, Policy department for citizen's rights and constitutional affairs Directorate-General for Internal Policies (European Parliament, July 2020), available at www.europarl .europa.eu/RegData/etudes, accessed 7 March 2021, pp. 99–103; Expert Group on Liability and New Technologies(2020), Liability for Artificial Intelligence and Other Emerging Digital Technologies, European Commission, available at https://ec.europa .eu/transparency/regexpert, accessed 7 March 2021, pp. 57–63; A. Arnbak, W. Geursen, S. Yakovleva (2020), Kaleidoscopic data-related enforcement in the digital age, *Common Market Law Review*, 57(5), 1461–1494; A. Bertolini (2016), Insurance and risk management for robotic devices: identifying the problems, *Global Jurist*, 2, 1–2; E. Palmerini, A. Bertolini (2016), Liability and risk management in robotics, in R. Schulze, D. Staudenmayer (eds), *Digital Revolution. Challenges for Contract Law in Practice*, 225–259.

[180] M. Bashayreh, F.N. Sibai, A. Tabbara (2021), Artificial intelligence and legal liability: towards an international approach of proportional liability based on risk sharing, *Information & Communications Technology Law*, 30(2), 169–192; A. Renda

vided that consumers receive sufficient information and advice on how to handle a given AI product.

But in the case of a 'flash crash', or when damage is caused by the interaction between algorithms and the external environment, including other algorithms, it may be difficult to apportion liability among two or more entities.[181] In these cases, the answer to the question 'who is responsible, and for how much?' depends on how AI is considered. Obviously, since AI is many things, the answer may differ depending on the type of AI. A few examples follow.

If the specific implementation of AI is considered as an extension of the human being, or a part thereof (as could occur in the case of augmented intelligence), then the liability rules applicable to humans would also apply to the AI system.[182] Conversely, if AI is considered equivalent to an object, negligence can be presumed if one's property causes harm to a third party.[183] But where

---

(2019), Artificial intelligence ethics, governance and policy challenges – Report of a CEPS Task Force Centre for European Policy Studies (CEPS), available at www .ceps.eu, accessed 7 March 2021, pp. 86–88; Expert Group on Liability and New Technologies (2019), Liability for Artificial Intelligence and Other Emerging Digital Technologies, pp. 25–29; F.P. Hubbard (2011), Do androids dream? Personhood and intelligent artifacts, *Temple Law Review*, 83(2), 405–474; B.-J. Koops, M. Hildebrandt, D.O. Jaquet-Chiffelle (2010), Bridging the accountability gap: rights for new entities in the Information Society?, *Minnesota Journal of Law, Science & Technology*, 11(2), 497–561; L.B. Solum (1992), Legal personhood for artificial intelligences, *North Carolina Law Review*, 70(4), 1231–1287.

[181] S. Van Uytsel (2021), Different liability regimes for autonomous vehicles: one preferable above the other, in S. Van Uytsel, D. Vasconcellos (eds), *Autonomous Vehicles: Business, Technology and Law*, Springer, 67–93; C. Martins Pereira (2020), Unregulated algorithmic trading: testing the boundaries of the European Union algorithmic trading regime, *Journal of Financial Regulation*, 6, 270–305; A. Renda (2019), Artificial intelligence ethics, governance and policy challenges – Report of a CEPS Task Force Centre for European Policy Studies (CEPS), pp. 82–85; H. Zech (2019), Liability for autonomous systems: tackling specific risks of modern IT, in S. Lohsse, R. Schulze, D. Staudenmayer (eds), *Liability for Artificial Intelligence and the Internet of Things*, Hart Publishing, 187–201; N.E. Vellinga (2019), Automated Driving and the Future of Traffic Law, in L. Reins (ed.), *Regulating New Technologies in Uncertain Times*, T.M.C. Asser Press/Springer, 67–83.

[182] S. Wojtczak (2021), Endowing artificial intelligence with legal subjectivity, *AI & Society*, available at https://link.springer.com, accessed 7 March 2021; B. Bennett, A. Daly (2020), Recognising rights for robots: Can we? Will we? Should we?, *Law, Innovation and Technology*, 12(1), 60–80; J. Chen, P. Burgess (2019), The boundaries of legal personhood: how spontaneous intelligence can problematise differences between humans, artificial intelligence, companies and animals, *Artificial Intelligence and Law*, 27, 73–92; C.D. Stone (2010), *Should Trees Have Standing? Law, Morality, and the Environment*, Oxford University Press, 4–23.

[183] D. Fairgrieve, G. Howells, P. Møgelvang-Hansen, G. Straetmans, D. Verhoeven, P. Machnikowski, A. Janssen, R. Schulze (2016), Product Liability Directive, in P.

no negligence is found on the part of the custodian, owner, or user, liability can be transferred to the manufacturer of the AI-enabled system. The alternative approach would be outright no-fault (strict) liability, which is construed by some authors also as a fault-based system, configuring a duty to exercise care in monitoring the objects under custody (*culpa in vigilando*).[184]

If a specific implementation of AI is used 'as a service', and causes damage, the question is whether the resulting responsibility should be of a contractual nature (i.e. provision of a service that does not conform to sufficient security requirements), which does not exonerate the purchasing party from liability towards the damaged parties, or of non-contractual nature (tort liability), which would then have to be extended to services.[185]

If an AI system is considered to be similar to an animal (when it displays a certain degree of autonomy) it means that AI systems have no legal personhood, and that strict liability applies only in case of damage caused by dangerous AI.[186]

Machnikowski (ed.), *European Product Liability: An Analysis of the State of the Art in the Era of New Technologies*, Intersentia, 17–108; N.M. Richards, W.D. Smart (2016), How should the law think about robots?, in R. Calo, A.M. Froomkin, I. Kerr (eds), *Robot Law*, Edward Elgar, 3–22; J.M. Balkin (2015), The path of robotics law, *California Law Review Circuit*, 6, 45–60; A. Bertolini (2013), Robots as products: the case for a realistic analysis of robotic applications and liability rules, *Law, Innovation & Technology*, 5(2), 214–247.

[184] G. Spindler (2019), User liability and strict liability in the Internet of Things and for robots, in S. Lohsse, R. Schulze, D. Staudenmayer (eds), *Liability for Artificial Intelligence and the Internet of Things*, Hart Publishing, 125–145; R.H. Weber, D.N. Staiger (2017), New liability patterns in the digital era, in T.-E. Synodinou, P. Jougleux, C. Markou, T. Prastitou (eds), *EU Internet Law: Regulation and Enforcement*, Springer, 197–217; U. Pagallo (2013), *The Laws of Robots: Crimes, Contracts, and Torts*, Springer, 29–35.

[185] M. Bashayreh, F.N. Sibai, A. Tabbara (2021), Artificial intelligence and legal liability: towards an international approach of proportional liability based on risk sharing, *Information & Communications Technology Law*, 30(2), 169–192; H.-Y. Liu, M. Maas, J. Danaher, L. Scarcella, M. Lexer, L. Van Rompaey (2020), Artificial intelligence and legal disruption: a new model for analysis, *Law, Innovation and Technology*, 12(2), 205–258; S. Chopra, L.F. White (2011), *A Legal Theory of Autonomous Artificial Agents*, University of Michigan Press, 123–127.

[186] D.G. Johnson, M. Verdicchio (2018), Why robots should not be treated like animals, *Ethics and Information Technology*, 20, 291–301; S.M. Solaiman (2017), Legal personality of robots, corporations, idols and chimpanzees: a quest for legitimacy, *Artificial Intelligence and Law*, 25(2), 155–179; K. Hogan (2017), Is the machine question the same question as the animal question?, *Ethics and Information Technology*, 19, 29–38; M. Coeckelbergh (2011), Humans, animals and robots: a phenomenological approach to human–robot relations, *International Journal of Social Robotics*, 3, 197–204. R. Kelley, E. Schaerer, M. Gomez, M. Nicolescu (2009), Robots as Animals: A Framework for Liability and Responsibility in Human–Robot Interactions, 18th

If AI is considered to be a 'slave', its master will be liable for any damage.[187] If AI is considered to be an employee, it will be given legal personhood as well as the duty to exercise due care. Strict liability would still be attributed to their owners, but the AI system would be given legal personhood and could, in principle, be asked to compensate for the damage.[188] Finally, AI systems (and robots in particular) might not be considered as employees but as outright legal persons, with no link to an 'owner' or developer.[189]

Therefore, in the opinion of the European Commission, by operating in this direction, and considering the various possible applications of AI, the existing rules may apply from time to time, possibly 'modernizing' them to make them consistent with the evolution of AI. Therefore, those who believe that not AI itself but its applications should be subject to regulation, and that the existing

---

IEEE International Symposium on Robot and Human Interactive Communication, available at https://ieeexplore.ieee.org, accessed 6 March 2021; D.J. Calverley (2006), Android science and animal rights, does an analogy exist?, *Connection Science*, 18(4), 403–417.

[187] V.A.J. Kurki (2019), *A Theory of Legal Personhood*, Oxford University Press, 175–189; J.J. Bryson (2010), Robots should be slaves, in Y. Wilks (ed.), *Close Engagements with Artificial Companions*, John Benjamins Publishing Company, 63–75; R. Gamauf (2009), Slaves doing business: the role of Roman law in the economy of a Roman household, *European Review of History*, 16(3), 331–346.

[188] G. Teubner (2018), Digital personhood? The status of autonomous software agents in private law, available at https://ssrn.com/abstract=3177096, accessed 6 March 2021; R. van den Hoven van Genderen (2018), Legal personhood in the age of artificially intelligent robots, in W. Barfield, U. Pagallo (eds), *Research Handbook on the Law of Artificial Intelligence*, Edward Elgar Publishing, 213–250; F.P. Hubbard (2011), Do androids dream? Personhood and intelligent artifacts, *Temple Law Review*, 83(2), 405–474; G. Teubner (20), Rights of non-humans? Electronic agents and animals as new actors in politics and law, *Journal of Law and Society*, 33(4), 497–521; N. Naffine (2003), Who are law's persons? From Cheshire cats to responsible subjects, *Modern Law Review*, 66(3), 346–367; C.E.A. Karnow (1994), The encrypted self: fleshing out the rights of electronic personalities, *Journal of Computer & Information Law*, 13(1), 1–16; L.B. Solum (1992), Legal personhood for artificial intelligences, *North Carolina Law Review*, 70(4), 1231–1287.

[189] J. Chen, P. Burgess (2019), The boundaries of legal personhood: how spontaneous intelligence can problematise differences between humans, artificial intelligence, companies and animals, *Artificial Intelligence and Law*, 27, 73–92; R. Dremliuga, P. Kuznetcov, A. Mamychev (2019), Criteria for recognition of AI as a legal person, *Journal of Politics and Law*, 12(3), 105–112; T. Pietrzykowski (2018), *Personhood beyond Humanism. Animals, Chimeras, Autonomous Agents and the Law*, Springer, 7–24; T. Pietrzykowski (2017), the idea of non-personal subjects of law, in V.A.J. Kurki, T. Pietrzykowski (eds), *Legal Personhood: Animals, Artificial Intelligence and the Unborn*, Springer, 201749–69; M. Radin (1932), The endless problem of corporate personality, *Columbia Law Review*, 32, 643–667.

regulation allows for a solution to be found to all the possible questions regarding AI responsibility, would be right.

Therefore, if we take this approach to a systematic reconstruction, there would be no 'AI ecosystem', as AI would be nothing more than a tool, not an end, and least of all a 'system'.

6.6   AI as a System and Liability

On the other hand, we can reconstruct the system if we adopt the presumptions that apply to cases in which, using the tools indicated above, it is not possible, in the specific case, to attribute responsibility to one or more operators in the value chain. In other words, we need a presumptive criterion of responsibility, be it objective or fault-based.

The approaches to these cases are many and divergent from each other. In the United States, the main one – due also to the numerous jurisprudential applications – is that of the 'most efficient choice' of the liability regime. According to this theory, the key criteria in designing an efficient liability regime are the identification of the 'cheapest cost avoider' (i.e. the entity that can avoid the emergence of system failures at the lowest cost); and/or the 'superior insurer' (i.e. the entity that can buy insurance most effectively and cheaply, thereby offering relief to the damaged party also due to voluntary or mandatory insurance – 'deep pocket theory').[190]

This paradigm distinguishes reciprocity and reasonableness of risk. If the risk is not reciprocal, the person who imposes it is liable for the damage (general principle of fairness). In that case, strict liability is justified.

Only partially different – and not opposed – is the European approach, which has developed (in its proposed regulation on AI) the principle of proximity of risk.

An assessment of law and economics in the US; and a legal assessment based on position responsibility in the European Union.[191] Although starting

---

[190] J.C.P. Goldberg (2020), Torts, in A.S. Gold, J.C.P. Goldberg, D.B. Kelly, E. Sherwin, H.E. Smith (eds), *The Oxford Handbook of the New Private Law*, Oxford University Press, 269 ff.; R.A. Posner, W.M. Landes (1980), The positive economic theory of tort law, *Georgia Law Review*, 15, 851–924; G. Calabresi (1975), Concerning cause and the law of torts, *University of Chicago Law Review*, 43, 69–108; G. Calabresi, J.T. Hirschoff (1972), Toward a test for strict liability in torts, *Yale Law Journal*, 81(6), 1055–1085; G. Calabresi (1970), *The Cost of Accidents. A Legal and Economic Analysis*, Yale University Press, 135–174; G. Calabresi (1961), Some thoughts on risk distribution and the law of Torts, *Yale Law Journal*, 70(4), 499–553.

[191] White Paper on Artificial Intelligence. A European Approach to Excellence and Trust (European Commission, Brussels, 19 February 2020, COM(2020) 65 final), pp. 12–13; Report on the safety and liability implications of AI, the Internet of Things

from different models, legal traditions, objectives and instruments, the US and European paths converge in the practice: in most cases they lead to univocal solutions.

6.7   AI Risks and the 'Cloud Regulatory Jump'

We have seen that the solutions provided by researchers and legislators in the field of AI are in continuity with a past that needs to be modernized, and that, however, the diversity of approaches on the two sides of the Atlantic tends to reduce, if we qualify AI as a system.

In relation to another system contiguous to that of digital platforms, the European legislator was more courageous. Rather than applying the old to the new, adapting it, the European Commission proposed a 'regulatory leap', consistent with the technological discontinuity, certainly running the risk of directing the market, but not waiting for it to pass through evolution. I am referring to the cloud environment, in which the regulation anticipated the technological evolution from the current centralized cloud to a distributed one and then a decentralized one (edge), consistently supporting the industrial evolution of European companies that converges towards this outcome (above, section 2).

The direction traced for cloud regulation is that of a corpus of general rules indicating fundamental rights and general principles, and allowing specific applications that go well beyond vertical and horizontal 'silos' and depend on individual applications (above, section 2). A corpus that should be consistent and compatible with those of other ecosystems, starting with that of digital platforms and that of AI. Only in this way would the discipline applicable in the intersection between the ecosystems resolve (at least in abstract terms) conflicts, gaps and overlapping rules.

We would also have expected a similar regulatory 'leap' with reference to AI, based on a corpus of general rules and differentiated specific applications. This doesn't seem to be the case at present, but could be the result of the dual path followed (regulatory in the EU versus jurisprudential in the United States).

This 'system solution' would find (at least) the following justifications. First of all, the current European regulation of product liability is not adequate for AI, in which the use of algorithms and machine learning produces a progressive fracture between manufacturer and end product which often goes beyond, if not the assumptions, at least the intentions of its creator. There is indeed an

---

and robotics (European Commission, Brussels, 19 February 2020, COM(2020) 64 final), pp. 8 ff.; M.C. Buiten (2019), Towards intelligent regulation of artificial intelligence, *European Journal of Risk Regulation*, 10(1), 41–59.

inverse relationship between the degree of precision and accuracy of the AI and its explicability.

Secondly, when it comes to AI, the final product is so composite that it is particularly difficult to distinguish the responsibilities in the different phases of the chain, and also because in many of these it is not the man who intervenes, but the machine. The different forms of anthropocentrism of law, which put man at the centre on the level of responsibility (summarized in the principle of complementarity with humans – 'human-centric AI' – and which are resolved in the responsible human requirement) provide an instrument of useful interpretation, but which has not yet been transformed into norms.

Thirdly, product liability works in an extremely partial way when a service is connected to the product, as often happens in the IoT and, certainly, in digital platforms.

In relation to the object and tools of a specific regulation, in the event of a (desirable) 'regulatory leap', a subsidiary intervention by the European legislator and the regulators would be reasonable – and proportional – with respect to the contents of the contracts stipulated between the (numerous) parties involved in the production, distribution and use of products and services that make use of AI to some extent. Here, too, it is a question of applying the 'regulatory circle' and the subsidiarity relationship between public and private regulation (above, section 2), mainly to protect the user (intermediate or final).

Following this path, public rules should in any case attribute responsibility to one of the parties in the supply chain that produces, distributes, uses the algorithm and delivers the product based on AI, in the absence of a precise definition of responsibility in contractual relationships.

Such a provision would constitute an incentive for the clear definition in the contracts of the limits of liability of each 'component of the chain', and would be consistent with the multiplicity of jurisdictions involved in the contractual relationships typical of these systems. Furthermore, it would encourage a uniform law codification that would allow the reuniting of different typical contractual relationships under a shared contractual regime to a broader degree than the one relating to European Union law (see Chapter 5, section 3). Finally, and with reference to the use of AI in digital platforms, this solution would constitute an incentive for the harmonization of contracts, which represents the main engine for developing relations within the platform.

6.8   Intersection between AI and Digital Platforms

When the AI is used by digital platforms, an additional entry is added to the table of the original AI matrix (consisting of sectors – vertical silos – and applications – horizontal silos): that of the subjects. When digital platforms qualified as gatekeepers (above, section 3) use AI, further constraints apply on a subjective basis.

The intersection between the two ecosystems (digital platforms and AI) therefore sees the application of both regulations, which must remain consistent in their overlap. This consistency is jeopardized if we consider the rules on AI which are of an ethical nature, rather than a legal nature. Even the 'ethical principles', the guidelines, the lists, can be traced back to general legal (often constitutional) principles, norms and rights. The connection with positive law is not the basis for abandoning an alleged contemporaneity, if this is confused with an autonomous *lex mercatoria* of platforms.

Furthermore, the consistency of the two ecosystems should be investigated, taking into account the difference between the internal and external faces of digital platforms, or at least differentiating the use of AI in the ecosystem of platforms and the effects that AI produces externally, in relation to domestic law, or to transnational or international law. It is up to digital platforms, in principle, to create an environment and a system compatible with the standards applicable to AI in state and regional or international organizations. But digital platforms cannot do the job of coordinating these rules, or making a synthesis of them. However, the issue needs to be further explored. I shall do so in Chapter 2.

7. DIGITAL PLATFORMS AND THE BLOCKCHAIN PATH

When the digital platform ecosystem meets the DLT ecosystem, the intersection between the two becomes a 'strongbox'. Distributed ledger technology has several applications in fact, the blockchain being the most interesting and relevant for digital platforms. The blockchain is 'closed' by definition and makes the digital platform that uses it (whether closed or partially open) even more impermeable. This also applies to blockchain-specific applications, including cryptocurrencies and smart contracts. These two applications have a certain relevance for both the legal classification of digital platforms and the law applicable to them (Chapters 2, 3 and 4). It is therefore appropriate to provide an overview, albeit brief, as it is functional to this sole objective: to measure both its application by digital platforms and the effects produced, within the digital platform ecosystem and in the relationships between this and the other ecosystems or, as we shall better see in the following chapters, of the other legal orders.[192]

---

[192] Recently: T. Marwala, E. Hurwitz (2017): *Artificial Intelligence and Economic Theory: Skynet in the Market*, Springer.

7.1   Blockchain

Distributed ledger technologies are commonly used and, among these, block-chains: private or public networks (permissioned and permissionless, respectively) made up of nodes (the servers of the participants) that contain blocks of information organized in a database. Each activity – a transaction, for example – is effective only if approved by all the blocks in the network, which therefore record and store it, automatically verifying (mining) its legitimacy and certifying its origin from an authorized subject (broadcast and consensus). Hence the characteristic of decentralization (the network does not have a centre and therefore a clearing house is not needed), security (it is not possible to trace the generating algorithms), transparency (the governance of the blockchain is shared and each exchange is visible from every node), immutability (of the data), confidentiality (the 'wallet keys' guarantee user pseudo-anonymization, a necessary counterpart to the transparency of the operations), reduction of costs (operational, transactional, counterparty). In a nutshell, the full implementation of the myth of control without government, of the efficiency of the self-regulated market, of legal certainty, of risk control.

All these advantages have been appreciated by the European Parliament which, however, after having listed them, highlighted their criticisms (scalability of control, volatility and uncertainty in the long term, technical limitations of the infrastructure, data confidentiality, absence of adequate governance structures which produces different consequences in the private blockchain, subject to the risk of control without accountability, and in the public one, where decentralization reduces the effectiveness of a reaction to a crisis). Many of these criticisms are a counterweight to the typical characteristics of DLT, and suggested a regulatory moratorium until a more mature stage of development, in compliance with the principle of proportionality and subject to an impact assessment.[193]

---

[193] The European Parliament Resolution of 26 May 2016 on virtual currencies (2016/2007(INI)), after pointing out (para. 18) that 'key EU legislation, such as EMIR, CSDR, SFD, MiFID/MiFIR, UCITs and AIFMD, could provide a regulatory framework in line with the activities carried out, irrespective of the underlying technology, even as VCs and DLT-based applications expand into new markets and extend their activities' observes, however, 'that more tailor-made legislation might be needed'. Similarly, and more specifically on DLT, the European Parliament Resolution of 3 October 2018 on distributed ledger technologies and blockchain: building trust with disintermediation (2017/2772(RSP)) in which the Parliament also recalls the principle of neutrality, both technological and of business models. The inadequacy of the system appears evident if we look at the electronic signature systems and the double keys provided by the CAD system, not applicable in a permissionless blockchain (where authentication is subject only to the verification of the credentials and not also of the identity

The market then acts alone and offers solutions to limit risks and strengthen trust: self-regulation, by applying tools created for other purposes and in other markets. A good example is trust service providers (TPS), who are subject to strong regulation in terms of long-term data retention, business continuity, compliance with high security standards, confidentiality of data and information;[194] the TPS blockchain networks as trust-by-design platforms are an interesting entry point for future regulation. Another example, again from contiguous regulated markets: the repos (repurchase agreements) typical of overnight markets, in which smart contracts reduce – almost to zero – operational and counterparty risks, and to which the regulation on high frequency trading and therefore the Markets in Financial Instruments Directive II (MiFID II) might apply.[195]

Apparently, the playing field on which to measure the resilience of blockchain technology will be that of financial transactions, both because it amplifies and enhances the advantages and opportunities offered by the blockchain but also because it highlights its limits (transparency versus confidentiality, for example), and because it brings out the contrast between a highly regulated sector – that of financial services – and another in which regulation is suspended. It is the classic Drake Passage, where the perfect storm rises, against which emergency regulations are trying to fight.

Born for financial transactions (i.e., electronic money), the blockchain pattern is applicable to all cases of traded assets, certified by public and shared registers, as they are based on distributed (or distributable) databases.

---

of the user) and applicable only in an interpretative way in the permissioned one. It is therefore necessary to modify (also) this regulation to recognize legal effects on documents circulating on the blockchain. The only alternative is to resign oneself to evaluating them according to different rules and principles. See: K. Yeung (2019), Regulation by blockchain: the emerging battle for supremacy between the code of law and code as law, *Modern Law Review*, 82, 207; R. Brownsword (2019), Smart contracts: coding the transaction, decoding the legal debates, in Philipp Hacker et al. (eds), *Regulating Blockchain. Techno-Social and Legal Challenges*, Oxford University Press; M. Finck (2018), Blockchains: regulating the unknown, *German Law Journal*, 19, 665, 687.

[194] Trust service providers (TSP) are authorized pursuant to EU Regulation 910/2014-eIDAS and create, check and validate electronic signatures, digital certificates, digital archives, etc. The eIDAS regulation makes the authorization of TSPs subject to compliance with stringent conditions and requirements in the provision of services and high security standards, as well as internal audits for the prevention and management of risks, compliance with consumer protection regulations, with data security measures, etc.

[195] Namely, Directive 2014/65/EU (MiFID II) governs, in Article 17, algorithmic trading, to which Regulatory Technical Standards (RTS) adopted by ESMA must apply. RTS can therefore modify the rules in the application, to make them flexible and consistent with market and technology changes.

The exchange is based on the token, a set of digital information over which a subject exercises the right of ownership, as it is registered on the blockchain and therefore transferable through a protocol.[196]

On the other hand, there are the smart contracts, self-executing digital transactions that use decentralized cryptographic tools (the blockchain, of which they are one of the terminals) to guarantee their enforcement – clear and precise because there is no room for interpretation.[197] Hence the importance of semantics for the management of future payments, made by the tokens automatically upon the occurrence of conditions that the token itself monitors, or for standardized or periodic payments, or for the provision of services, or again, simply, as an asset itself, with its own specific value (the ownership of the information collected in the token). What distinguishes these contracts from others that also circulate in the digital environment (data-oriented or computable contracts) is

---

[196] There are various classifications: utility tokens are those that allow the use of services; asset-based are those that guarantee a future payment linked to a real asset; investment tokens are comparable to financial instruments as they are transferable, negotiable and standardized. Other tokens are mere virtual currencies (cryptocurrencies). Among the recent evolutions is the so-called token +, with associated Big Data, indivisible, and traceable in its history (chain of ownership). Obviously, different types of tokens match with different applicable disciplines, each with different rights and obligations.
Among the most used applications are, on the one hand, the multiple signature (multi-signature or multi-sig) which allows the completion of the transaction without transferring the availability of the asset (tangible or intangible) upon positive verification by a third party, acting almost like an internal arbitrator to the relationship.

[197] O. Meyer (2020), Stopping the unstoppable: termination and unwinding of smart contracts, *Journal of European Consumer and Market Law*, 9(1), 17–24; M. Kianieff (2019), *Blockchain Technology and the Law: Opportunities and Risks*, Routledge, 35–72; R. De Caria (2019), The legal meaning of smart contracts, *European Review of Private Law*, 26(6), 731–752; M. Cannarsa (2019), Interpretation of contracts and smart contracts: smart interpretation or interpretation of smart contracts?, *European Review of Private Law*, 26(6), 773–786; L.-D. Muka Tshibende (2019), Smart contracts, in L.A. Di Matteo, M. Cannarsa, C. Poncibò (eds), *The Cambridge Handbook of Smart Contracts, Blockchain Technology and Digital Platforms*, Cambridge University Press, 240–250; R. Unsworth (2019), Smart contract this! An assessment of the contractual landscape and the Herculean challenges it currently presents for 'self-executing' contracts, in M. Corrales, M. Fenwick, H. Haapio (eds), *Legal Tech, Smart Contracts and Blockchain*, Springer, 17–63; M. Djurovic, A. Janssen (2018), The formation of blockchain-based smart contracts in the light of contract law, *European Review of Private Law*, 26(6), 753–771; E. Mik (20), Smart contracts: terminology, technical limitations and real world complexity, *Law, Innovation and Technology*, 9(2), 269–300; J. Fairfield (2014), Smart contracts, bitcoin bots and consumer protection, *Washington and Lee Law Review Online*, 71(2), 35–50.

that the digital code in smart contracts does not constitute a representation of the agreement: it is the agreement (the code is law).[198]

7.2   Smart Contracts

Currently, the objectivity of a smart contract, software programmable to automatically execute the coded functions when certain conditions occur, can be admitted on the level of execution, but not on that of the elaboration of the code that is executed, which is the result of a deterministic algorithm (identical results in identical conditions) but programmed and therefore never neutral.[199] Hence the need for the immutability of the contractual data, the certification and reliability of the sources and methods of controlling behaviour. In short, all the guarantees that a blockchain can provide.[200]

---

[198]   This issue is the subject of vibrant discussion. An author against this idea is A. Kolber (2018), Not-so-smart blockchain contracts and artificial responsibility, *Stanford Technology Law Review*, 198–234. The definitions of smart contracts (especially in the US) are endless. The first and most significant is by N. Szabo (1996), Smart contracts: building blocks for digital markets, *EXTROPY: The Journal of Transhumanist Thought*, 16, also available at www.fon.hum.uva.nl/rob/Courses/InformationInSpeech/ CDROM/Literature/LOTwinterschool2006/szabo.best.vwh.net/smart_contracts_2 .html; A. Rosic (2020), Smart contracts: the blockchain technology that will replace lawyers, available at http://blockgeeks.com/guides/smart-contracts/.

[199]   An already common example is insurance contracts for motor vehicles equipped with electronic devices that provide data on driver behaviour, which automatically activate advantage or disadvantage clauses. Or again, the sales and purchases of shareholdings when certain price thresholds or other conditions included in the contract are exceeded.

[200]   Some early investigation work may be found in: M. Raskin (2017), The law and legality of smart contracts, *Georgetown Law Technology Review*, 306–341. See also: P. Sirena, F.P. Patti (2020), Smart contracts and automation of private relationships, Bocconi Legal Studies Research Paper Series, 3662402, July 2020; L.H. Scholz (2017), Algorithmic contracts, *Stanford Technology Law Review*, 20, 128; S. Williams (2019), Predictive contracting, *Columbia Business Law Review*, 621; A. De Franceschi, R. Schulze (eds) (2019), *Digital Revolution – New Challenges for the Law*, C.H. Beck; P. De Filippi, A. Wright (2018), *Blockchain and the Law. The Rule of Code*, Harvard University Press, 74; G. Gitti (2018), Robotic Transactional Decisions, *Osservatorio di Diritto Civile Commerciale*, 619, 622; M. Durovic, A. Janssen (2018), The formation of blockchain-based smart contracts in the light of contract law, *European Review of Private Law*, 26, 753–771; J.G. Allen (2018), Wrapped and stacked: 'smart contracts' and the interaction of natural and formal language, *European Review of Contract Law*, 14, 307–343; K. Werbach, N. Cornell (2017), Contracts ex machina, *Duke Law Journal*, 67, 313, 318; E. Mik (2017), Smart contracts: terminology, technical limitations and real world complexity, *Law, Innovation and Technology*, 9, 269; K.D. Betts, K.R. Jaep (2017), The dawn of fully automated contract drafting: machine learning breathes new life into a decades old promise, *Duke Law & Technology Review*, 15, 216.

There are many other applications in contexts in which the role of the intermediary becomes superfluous, since the activity or transaction can be regulated directly by the parties who, by inserting the smart contract in a block-chain, overcome the distrust that limits the circulation of wealth.[201]

The instruments of competition law in Europe appear to be of little use in dealing with the phenomenon (above, section 3), but also the regulations in the various industry sectors seem (some indeed more than others) not very suitable to regulate this game change (section 2).

Smart contracts, included in the blockchain and therefore not only irrev-ocable but also able to automatically evolve the contractual relationship by regulating all the negotiations (and therefore also pre-contractual ones) and application phases,[202] seem at first sight incompatible not only with the insti-tutions of the civil codes of continental Europe (think of the requirements of form, effectiveness, binding nature, underwriting, etc.) but also with external regulatory instruments. Compliant with the case law of common law, these contracts provide for all possible developments and can prevent, even before

---

[201] From the land register to copyright protection, to brand protection, to the man-agement of original spare parts; from the Internet of Things to the traceability of the production and distribution chain (at the basis not only of food safety but also of the circular economy); from data retention to voting mechanisms and public affairs man-agement; from insurance to trading platforms; from banking and financial markets to payment systems; from peer-to-peer (loans, energy exchange, etc.) to regulatory com-pliance; from logistics (identification of customers and suppliers) to the tracking of industrial chains; from health care (management of patient data shared by medical facilities) to public administration (to build digital identities, reduce tax evasion, fight crime, automate procurement processes by means of tenders, etc.).

We continue to refer to national markets, as the European strategy for a digital single market does not contain specific rules. Again, there is room to increase compe-tition between the legal systems in the EU through regulation, or to transform it into a sustainable inclusive growth. After all, with more than 25 billion interconnected objects in 2020, smart contracts will allow these terminals to operate autonomously, share resources and information, and exchange data without the need for centralized management.

[202] As for the costs of inflexibility, see: E. Seidel, A. Horsch, A. Eickstädt (2020), Potentials and limitations of smart contracts: a primer from an economic point of view, *European Business Law Review*, 31, 169, 176–179; D. D'Onfro (2020), Smart contracts and the illusion of automated enforcement, *Washington University Journal of Law & Policy*, 61, 173; E. Mik (2020), The resilience of contract law in light of technologi-cal change, in M. Furmston (ed.), *The Future of the Law of Contract*, Routledge, 112; O. Meyer (2020), Stopping the unstoppable: termination and unwinding of smart con-tracts, *Journal of European Consumer and Market Law*, 17, at 20–24; L.A. Di Matteo, C. Poncibó (2018), Quandary of smart contracts and remedies: the role of contract law and self-help remedies, *European Review of Private Law*, 26, 805; J.M. Sklaroff (2017), Smart contracts and the cost of inflexibility, *University of Pennsylvania Law Review*, 166, 263.

regulating, flaws that are eliminated at the root, together with the subjective and discretionary elements in the application of the contract (software is by definition trustless).

Therefore, being self-executing but also self-enforcing, smart contracts represent, each separately, a reproposal of that medieval 'common law', a unique *ius mercatorum* for all legal systems, outside and with no need for any legal system. Self-sufficient, as if it were a 'private legal system', it does not require rules other than those encoded in the software, nor a judicial review, or tools for resolving disputes, because non-compliance is simply impossible.[203]

Many tend to reduce the scope and impact of this possible innovation and believe, even on the basis of the first applications, that smart contracts are nothing more than tools to simplify and certify the formation of the agreement, strengthen its evidentiary effects, guaranteeing its execution within the framework of the codes. To regulate this new structure of the agreement, a similar supervisory procedure would therefore be sufficient.[204]

However, on closer inspection, the juridical categories slip and the legal institutes do not hold firm. The capacity of the parties does not matter. The blockchain does not verify the validity of a contract, but only that a transaction has taken place (not even that this constitutes execution of the contract). And how can consent be certified, when it is between two machines?[205] And what is the meaning of consent, given that the distinction between the pre-contractual and contractual phases, both potentially integrated in smart contracts, disappears? And then, the flawed consent becomes irrelevant for the algorithm, which does not care about the intention and is not required to interpret.[206] Even fulfilment is no longer part of the relationship of the algorithm, so non-fulfilment (by the parties, of course) becomes impossible. No breach exists any longer, except that of the integrity of the algorithmic code (hence the necessary protection and possibly insurance measures) or of the verification of the external data entered (off-chain events, the occurrence of which affects the relationship ascertained by third parties, the 'oracle' that the parties choose

---

[203] M. Raskin (2017), The law and legality of smart contracts, Georgetown Law Technology Review, 1, 305.

[204] See: A. Janssen (2019), Demystifying smart contracts, in C.J.H. Jansen et al. (eds), *Onderneming en Digitalisering*, Wolters Kluwer, 15–29, at 22–23.

[205] For two opposing theses, represented at the origin of the debate, about the need to create new legal categories for the formation of consensus between computers, see: F. Easterbrook (1996), Cyberspace and the law of the horse, *University of Chicago Legal Forum*, 207, and L. Lessig (1999), The law of the horse: what cyberlaw might teach, *Harvard Law Review*, 113, 501.

[206] M. Cannarsa (2018), Interpretation of contracts and smart contracts: smart interpretation or interpretation of smart contracts?, *European Review of Private Law*, 26, 773.

together with the external databases from which the relevant information must be collected).

A bitter debate followed the DAO affair, about whether theft is legitimate when it constitutes correct execution of an algorithmic code.[207] Furthermore, smart contracts no longer present the asymmetries that justify the protection of the weak party (i.e., the consumer), guarantees that the proponent will eventually be able to use as a competitive asset, and here the role of the regulatory authorities can be relevant. And what about the cause of the contract, which is irrelevant and has no lawfulness of its own, if not inserted in a legal system that qualifies it? And finally, if the legal system cannot impose the execution of a smart contract (because there is no need for it, but even more so because the relationship goes beyond the legal system) one can seriously doubt that we are still faced with a contract.

It is therefore evident that the use of smart contracts by digital platforms, and within their ecosystem, constitutes a further step that distances them from the law of the states, which smart contracts can free themselves from almost completely, if the territorial constraint of jurisdiction is lost.

7.3   Current Misunderstandings on Smart Contracts

However, it is necessary to avoid a misunderstanding on which supporters and critics are currently clashing: smart contracts do not find universal application, since their characteristics allow the overcoming of the problems inherent in many contractual relationships (e.g. international trade, financial markets, insurances, etc.), but their rigidity advises against their use in many others, where flexibility and even efficient violation are a primary requirement. Smart contracts therefore do not revolutionize contract law and do not replace it.

Instead, we can imagine a regulation of smart contracts based on those shared rules that constitute the lowest common denominator (a rule of law)

---

[207] In 2016, a system bug allowed one or more subjects to subtract 50 million from the total of 160 million US dollars that the DAO had raised via crowdfunding. The action was not prohibited by the algorithmic code and the debate among lenders who participated in the crowdfunding campaign focused on how to qualify the act (lawful or illegal) and therefore on what actions to take. The issue ended with the classic child split in half: in the absence of an agreement, the code was modified and the participants who updated their system obtained the return of their funds, which in the meantime had been frozen, while those who considered making the principle prevail (the code is law) maintained the old code (both are still in force today). See, among others: A. J Kolber (2018), Not-so-smart blockchain contracts and artificial responsibility, *Stanford Technology Law Review*, 21, 198; B. Carron, V. Botteron (2019), How smart can a contract be?, in Daniel Kraus et al. (eds), *Blockchains, Smart Contracts, Decentralised Autonomous Organisations and the Law*, Edward Elgar Publishing, 101.

elaborated by international organizations or institutions that deal with contractual harmonization (UNCITRAL and UNIDROIT above all). It is public law that affects smart contracts, not private law (the *lex cryptographia*, a new *lex mercatoria* also authoritatively envisaged, being still utopic); however, we have already said that such distinction is useless, now that the two are communicating vessels.

Hence the urgency of further research on the compatibility and coherence of the regulation of the markets, with vertical silos not communicating with each other, with the technological revolution that integrates the markets and does not care about the regulation, because, if it is applied at all, it is only on the terms accepted by the parties. It is no longer a question of defining the boundary between regulated and non-regulated activities, or of regulating their hybridization with classic tools (precedence, with a focus on the activity and not on the subjects); the issue is more radical and concerns the defence of the legal system, the survival of which depends – like everything in nature – on its necessity.

Now, given the speed of technological evolution, the wariness of international and European institutions, the still largely incomplete and partially inadequate nature of the rules governing digital negotiations,[208] the progressive irrelevance of the member states, which have delegated the necessary competences to the European Union and are now almost completely disintermediated in the implementation phase that the EU has reserved to independent national authorities, either coordinated with each other or with the European agencies, or with the Commission as appropriate, it is clear that in the European Union a possible regulatory response can only come from the national regulatory authorities. With the typical instruments of vertical subsidiarity, national regulatory authorities will have to transform interventions on the markets into best practices, and then into benchmarks and into rules that become executive acts or legislative proposals of the European Commission approved by the Parliament and the Council (above, section 2). The 'regulatory circle' exists and works, and we shall soon see whether it is sufficient and adequate, since we know the limits of the evolution of regulation: it is linear, while technological growth, via the blockchain, appears exponential. Therefore, a 'regulatory leap' is needed, from the current field of comparison (the code is law) to a potential one (the law is code) and the intent of this research is to understand in which direction this should move.[209]

---

[208] See the Regulation of the European Parliament and the Council of 23 July 2014, n. 910/2014 (Regulation eIDAS).

[209] See P. De Filippi, A. Wright (2018), *Blockchain and the Law: The Rule of Code*, Harvard University Press. Some rules are beginning to be seen above all, at state level, in the USA. For a first list see: M. Dell'Erba (2018), Demystifying technology. Do smart

7.4   Artificial Responsibility

When the algorithm is elaborated or used within a DLT, in one of its implementation procedures (the blockchain with its applications: smart contracts, cryptocurrencies) the liability attribution mechanism does not differ from that illustrated in the previous paragraph on AI. The solutions are also the same, and lead to determining risk categories in relation to which instruments and responsibilities are ranked. This also governs the case in which the algorithm is processed by another algorithm, in an algorithmic chain that becomes independent from the initial programmer, to whom a causal link cannot be attributed. The system of algorithms processes the data, organizes them in various ways, uses them for a series of purposes, allows some developments and prevents others, according to an objectively abstract model, but which is actually functional to the goal it is intended to achieve, which is different each time.

The nuances are many and find numerous applications in the blockchain environment. Think of the advice of robot advisors, the progressive automation of the intellectual professions, crowdfunding (the case of the DAO is emblematic), alternative bonds, stock exchange contracts (futures, swaps, derivative transactions, if they govern cash flows), consumer contracts, cases in which the algorithm not only executes but decides (in home automation, automatic driving, etc.).

A further question arises for public blockchains, in which transparency and sharing would lead, in terms of responsibility, to the opposite short-circuit (collective co-responsibility of the participants), which is also unreasonable, even applying different jurisdictions to the nodes of the network.

It is therefore about separating and classifying, with the old methods of jurists, and looking for new solutions. What is visible (in nautical terms, the topsides of the web) is different from what remains unseen (the hull). For the first, the previously codified and traditional tools are valid and can still play an important role: transparency, information, consent, self-discipline, tools and practices for the prevention and management of risks, and through regulatory compliance, etc.

For the hull, on the other hand, it is necessary to separate legitimate and illegal activities, fundamental rights and economic interests. Only afterwards

---

contracts require a new legal framework? Regulatory fragmentation, self-regulation, public regulation, available at https://papers.18ssrn.com/sol3/papers.cfm?abstract_id= 3228445, 33–36. For a specific case in the derivatives market: R. Surujnath (2017), Off the chain! A guide to blockchain derivatives markets and the implications on systemic risk, *Fordham Journal of Corporate and Financial Law*, 257 ff., and the White Paper by the International Swaps and Derivatives Association (ISDA) and Linklaters (2017): Smart contracts and distributed ledger – A legal perspective.

can one attempt to provide solutions, which can also go in the direction of creating an 'artificial responsibility', attributable to decentralized autonomous organizations (DAO) – open-source organizations consisting of a set of smart contracts that operate absent a centralized organization and, this is the issue, presently often without legal personality – to which the security of the infrastructure, of the data and values that pass through it (blockchain, smart contracts but also cryptocurrencies) is delegated.[210] And here separation is again necessary, since a violation of public blockchains such as Bitcoin or Ethereum appears extremely complex, as their hacking requires – considering their development – a computational capacity that is currently unavailable, while a private blockchain (permissioned) is subject to greater risks, inversely proportional to its diffusion.

7.5 The Intersection between the Digital Platforms' and the Blockchains' Ecosystems

The intersection area between the two ecosystems of DLT and digital platforms, seems still completely unexplored, however.

If, on the one hand, the regulatory gap can be justified, due to the fact that the possible evolutions of technology have not yet had evident developments and have not yet consolidated, on the other hand the absence of specific research by experts and regulators raises more questions. Via DLT (smart contracts, cryptocurrencies) digital platforms can indeed close the environment hermetically (the ecosystem, for economists, the legal system, for jurists), in the case of closed platforms (social networks), or they can lock parts of them in watertight compartments, in the case of partially open platforms. It seems to me that, in this case too, the error – from which the current underestimation originates – lies in considering DLTs not for what they are (ecosystems) but as tools, worthy of attention only in relation to the goals that they achieve. Basically, the path started with 'the code is law' was not brought to its final conclusion, which is more than the mere slogan with which it was reclassified, and reveals a world behind it: that of the new matrix, which is replacing the regulatory matrix (section 2). This error, if placed in the right legal perspective, could prove to be fatal. We shall address these issues in Chapter 2, section 4.

---

[210] See A. Kolber (2018), Not-so-smart blockchain contracts and artificial responsibility, *Stanford Technology Law Review*, 198–234.

8. CURRENT MISUNDERSTANDINGS ABOUT DIGITAL PLATFORMS

So far, we have examined some of the main issues usually raised in relation to digital platforms. Competition, regulation, data protection, impact on democratic principles, ethical rules, DLT and blockchain. We have seen the interconnection between the rules applicable to platforms and those of other ecosystems (those of AI, DLT and within it, the blockchain) and the need for these rules to be compatible with each other (interoperability, engineers would say), to make them consistent with the environment that is created at their intersection.

We have seen some misunderstandings that are slowing down the race in the necessary direction and sometimes diverting the path. Examples of those misunderstandings are: that the regulatory matrix is still existing and adequate, and that a few modernization adjustments are sufficient; that competition policy is still an adequate tool for those that are thought to be nothing more than multinational companies, and potential gatekeepers; that the protection of personal data is an adequate tool to guarantee data sovereignty; that it is possible (and sufficient) to impose specific governance rules on digital platforms to ensure that they will not interfere with the democratic processes of state systems; that public laws cannot fully regulate the evolution of AI and in that case, ethical rules and principles are necessary; and that the blockchain and its applications (smart contracts, cryptocurrencies) are subject to current, modernized regulation.

However, we have also seen that, in this overall perspective, the regulatory issues assume a different importance and can be looked at from a different perspective. The convergence of regulation, regulated competition, protection of personal data, defence of democratic principles and ethics becomes a tool and an end towards new regulatory developments.

As a matter of fact, if the internal side (the relations within the platform) and the external one (the relations between the platform and the other platforms and the states) are clearly distinct, as this research seems to highlight, the regulatory development should tend towards self-regulation of the platforms (private regulation), and forms of co-regulation (public regulation), differently scaled, as regards the internal and external sides. The intervention of public regulation should be allowed on a subsidiary basis, where self-regulation is inadequate, measured by the tools of compliance based on the outcome of preventive checks, according to the principles of subsidiarity and proportionality and to accountability rules.

This evolution is consistent with the notion of the platform 'as a system', according to the technical definitions given by economists, as well as jurists (even if limited, for the time being, to regulatory issues).

So far, we have investigated markets and regulation. The conclusions reached require further insight, in legal terms, on the level of internal law of the platforms and on the level of external law, relating to the relationships between platforms, state legal systems, transnational law, international law. This approach still seems to me not sufficiently investigated, or in any case not in a unified way. It is possible that this derives from an excessive compartmentalization of the law, which makes the approach to the issues that the platforms propose, which are evidently cross-disciplinary, too complex. It is also probable that the technological component constitutes a barrier, if its legal qualification is a topic that is placed on the level of the theory of legal systems.

Whatever the reasons for the gap, the aim of this research is to study these aspects further. I shall start from an overall vision, which requires bringing the analysis to the highest level of transnational law and international law, of legal subjectivity and of the relationship between legal systems. This is the direction towards which the traces we have found on the markets are leading, sometimes directly and sometimes as a reflection (and a consequence) of the regulators' actions.

2. Digital platforms as private transnational legal orders

We now move from the realm of ecosystems and the regulatory matrix settled to face it, to the relationships between orders. We start by evaluating the impact of the digital revolution on the development of the transnational law that is generated by or that is addressed to multinational or transnational companies. We try to understand if there are qualitative differences between transnational companies (section 1) and digital platforms (section 2) and what consequences these differences may have in terms of legal order.

1. TRANSNATIONAL COMPANIES AND TRANSNATIONAL LAW

The model of the multinational companies, characterized by a centralized organization, is now overtaken by the more efficient one of transnational corporations.

A company is transnational when its subsidiaries operating in different countries, although part of the group, enjoy a degree of autonomy sufficient to adapt to the markets of the host countries, and are therefore subject to coordination, rather than centralized control, by the parent company.

Such recognized autonomy translates into the flexibility that allows each company in the group to relate to the peculiar context in which it operates.

1.1 Transnational Corporations

Transnational corporations operate within, outside and beyond state legal systems. They are recipients of standards, placed on a scale graded from hard to soft law (from the technical rules of the standard-setting bodies to the rules of self-regulation[1] and codes of conduct[2]), which originate both from the state systems (those of incorporation and those in which they operate[3]) and from transnational law (state and non-state, the latter developed also thanks to the action of the companies themselves). Transnational law is undergoing today, due to the evolution of the digital economy, the most dynamic development, and tests the institutions historically assigned to the production of uniform law.[4]

1.2   *Lex Mercatoria*

This evolution, slow but constant in case law and practice, has led many in the literature and some national supreme courts to believe that a *lex mercatoria*, a non-state transnational law applied by a multiplicity of enterprises, states and courts (national and transnational), produces standard contracts and general contract conditions (such as UNIDROIT, UNCITRAL and The Hague Permanent Conference on Private International Law), standard clauses (e.g.

---

[1]   The reference is to the OECD models, in the form of declarations or guidelines (OECD Declaration on International Investment and Multinational Enterprises; OECD Guidelines for Multinational Enterprises) and the action of the United Nations (UN Global Compact), founded on the will of the acceding states, and on the shared commitment of economic operators, respectively. The degree of enforcement of the two systems is obviously different, but the differences are diminishing over time and with the evolution of the practice, which makes the rules which apply spontaneously (almost self-binding a company that adopts them) voluntary and not coercive. Then there are the numerous global legal standards, adopted by atypical bodies, which do not (or do not only) represent states, but also trade associations, national and international organizations, public or private operators, and which produce market regulation rules that, even if not binding, become such when followed by the states or by the national regulatory authorities. Among the most obvious examples: the rules of the financial and banking markets, dictated by the Financial Stability Board or by the Basel committee (under the coordination of the Bank for International Settlements).

[2]   The taxonomy of codes of conduct is instrumental to the function. In relation to the source, the codes of conduct of governmental and intergovernmental origin are distinguished from those of private origin (the latter being individual or collective). As for the objects, there are both specific and detailed ones and others that indicate general principles. As for the purpose, the most enlightening perspective is that which identifies them as forms of self-regulation.

[3]   State orders are those which still produce the norms that transnational companies must comply with, because transnational companies have no international legal personality and consequently the international law cannot address them.

[4]   UNCITRAL, UNIDROIT and The Hague Permanent Conference of Private International Law, which through conventions, model laws and legislative guides have consolidated and oriented the behaviour of companies in international markets for a century and more.

INCOTERMS, or the UNIDROIT Principles of International Commercial Contracts), conciliation procedures or disputes (e.g. the ICC Conciliation and Arbitration Rules) which also end up affecting the content and effectiveness of this specific transnational law. To the point that today, the assumption that the *lex mercatoria* is not only law but a real transnational legal order,[5] based on a customary norm, is increasingly widespread.[6]

1.3   Transnational Law

The notion of transnational law dates back to the 1950s and was originally intended to provide a framework in which to find a place for non-state law that was neither attributable to public nor to private international law, but to 'other rules' which were emerging, mainly of private nature.[7] Starting from the ways in which transnational legal ordering is created, the most recent debate has

---

[5]   The main reference in Italy is the decision of the Court of Cassation of 8 February 1982 n. 722 (*Foro Italiano*, 1982, I, c. 2285, and *Rivista di diritto internazionale privato e processuale* (*RDIPP*), 1982, 835) which qualifies the *opinio necessitatis* for economic operators for some rules of conduct with changing but, *pro tempore*, determined contents. Relevant is also the CCI award n. 9875 of 2000, in which the arbitrators defined the *lex mercatoria* as 'a set of rules and uses of international trade originating from economic operators, from arbitration jurisprudence and from international bodies such as UNIDROIT'.

For a systematic reconstruction of the arguments underlying the thesis of a *lex mercatoria* qualified as a legal system, see: F. Marrella (2017), Protection internationale des droits de l'homme et activités des sociétés transnationales, *Le Recueil des Cours de l'Académie de Droit International de La Haye* (*RCADI*), 385; F. Marrella (2003), La nuova lex mercatoria: principi unidroit ed usi dei contratti del commercio internazionale, in *Trattato di diritto commerciale e di diritto pubblico dell'economia*, Vol. 30, Cedam; B. Goldman (1983), *Lex mercatoria, Forum Internationale on Commercial Law and Arbitration*, 3, 20–23; K.P. Berger (2010), *The Creeping Codification of the New Lex Mercatoria*, 2nd edn, Kluwer, 146–147; K.P. Berger (2017), The *lex mercatoria* as a legal system, in O. Toth, *The Lex Mercatoria in Theory and Practice*, Oxford University Press, 161–194. On the contrary, as they define the *lex mercatoria* as a rudimentary and incomplete body of rules that does not constitute an autonomous legal order: F.E. Klein (1977), De l'autorité de la loi dans les rapports commerciaux internationaux, in W. Flume (ed.), *Internationales Recht und Wirtschaftsordnung*, C.H. Beck; A. Kassis (1984), *Théorie Génerale des Usages du Commerce*, Librairie générale de droit et de jurisprudence. The recent debate starts from assumptions developed by the literature over the past seventy years: the first supporter of the thesis of a transnational system in formation was P. Jessup (1956), *Transnational Law*, Yale University Press.

[6]   The 'mercantile law' arises when the belief in binding values is consolidated, intended as rules of conduct with changing but, *pro tempore*, determined contents, on which operators base their behaviour.

[7]   P. Jessup, *Transnational Law*, 1956, was the first to define transnational law as 'all law which regulates actions or events that transcend national frontiers', which

allowed the development of the notion of 'transnational legal order', qualified as 'a collection of rules and an organization that regulates the interpretation and application of the law in a binding way'.[8]

Both these definitions of transnational law and transnational legal order – the second, evidently derived from the first – arise from the need to interpret a reality that does not find answers in the mere interrelation and contrast of state systems with each other and with the international law, and calls for the identification of a legal basis for the production of the transnational rules brought to light by the practice.[9]

This approach arises from practice and is confronted with significant objections – overcome or not, from time to time, due to the evolutionary power of the law – ranging from: the absence, at the basis of the legal system, of a sufficiently identifiable, autonomous and independent social circle;[10] to confusing the mere existence of the *lex mercatoria* with the recognition of its legality

---

included public international law, private international law and 'other rules which do not wholly fit into such standard categories'.

[8]   T. Halliday, G. Shaffer (2015), Transnational legal orders, in T. Halliday, G. Shaffer (eds), *Transnational Legal Orders*, Cambridge University Press, 5, defined transnational legal orders as 'a collection of formalized legal norms and associated organizations and actors that authoritatively order the understanding and practice of law across national jurisdictions'. The system becomes legal when 'it involves international or transnational legal organizations or networks, directly or indirectly engages multiple national and local legal institutions, and assumes a recognizable legal form'. Similarly: R. Michaels (2007), The true *lex mercatoria*: law beyond the state, *Indiana Journal of Global Legal Studies*, 14, 447. On the effects of the development of the lex mercatoria in globalization see: P. Verkuil (2007), *Outsourcing Sovereignty: Why Privatization of Government Functions Threatens Democracy and What We Can Do About It*, Cambridge University Press.

[9]   For a general overview of the phenomenon see: G.P. Calliess, P. Zumbansen (2010), *Rough Consensus and Running Code: A Theory of Transnational Private Law*, Hart Publishing, but also R. Michaels, N. Jansen (2006), Private law beyond the state? Europeanization, globalization, privatization, *American Journal of Comparative Law* 54, 843–890. On this point see: P. Glenn (2003), A transnational concept of law, in P. Cane, M.V. Tushnet (eds), *The Oxford Handbook of Legal Studies*, 839–862. L.C. Baker (2016) (The emerging normative structures of transnational law: non-state enterprises in polycentric asymmetric global orders, *Brigham Young University Journal of Public Law*, 31) identifies four characteristic and constitutive elements of the transnational system: '(1) scope of authority, (2) institutional autonomy, (3) regulatory authority, (4) effectiveness of power to settle disputes. ... Such principles include the constitution of a government apparatus and the rules for the operation of the governance power vested in this organization.'

[10]   M. Giuliano (1967), Quelques problèmes en matière de conflits de lois et de jurisdictions dans la vente commerciale, *Rivista di diritto internazionale privato e processuale (RDIPP)*, 237; M. Giuliano, T. Scovazzi, T. Treves (1991), *Diritto Internazionale – Parte generale*, Giuffrè Editore, 545. Equally critical is C. Scott

in the uses of international trade (hence the so-called 'empirical paradox'[11]); to founding a horizontal, 'widespread' legal order on the (uncertain) custom alone, a legal order where, as in international law, not only are the legislators also the recipients of the rules, but arbitral awards are at the same time proof of the existence and only source of the *lex mercatoria*; to a non-centralized judicial control, based on the *lex mercatoria* as a contract law, applicable only on the terms in which the arbitrators deem it independent ('de-localized arbitration', independent from the *lex loci arbitri*, which remains the law of a national system); in essence, to requesting a 'paradigm shift' in identifying a non-national order, which does not identify with that of a state, or with an order made up of states (international organizations) or with the international order. To the point that some believe transnational law is nothing but a legal methodology, like comparative law.[12]

1.4   Towards a Transnational Legal System

The prospect of a real transnational legal system is therefore still uncertain since it is based on practice – the origin is necessarily customary – and this still appears to be neither univocal nor consolidated. However, states actively participate in the formation of transnational law, which is therefore not entirely autonomous, not even in its formation and evolution.[13] At the same time, acts

---

(2009), 'Transnational law' as a proto-concept: three conceptions, *German Law Journal*, 10, 859, 876.

[11]   In fact,

[T]he lex mercatoria rules prescribe certain human conduct to be followed by group members. However, the lex mercatoria rules do not only prescribe human conduct, they are also *derived* from human conduct. What is more, the conduct from which they are derived is empirically the *same* as the conduct that they prescribe. The primary rules of the lex mercatoria therefore give rise to what we have called the empirical paradox. (K.P. Berger, The *lex mercatoria* as a legal system, above, note 6, at 166).

[12]   P. Zumbansen (2006), Transnational law, evolving, in J.M. Smits (ed.), *Elgar Encyclopedia of Comparative Law*, Edward Elgar Publishing, 899.

[13]   T. Halliday, G. Shaffer, Transnational legal orders, above, note 9:

TLOs are thus typically connected at some point to nation-state law and practice, including through the enforcement of private contracts and undertakings. It would be a mistake to develop a concept of transnational law that is wholly autonomous from national law and legal institutions. Private lawmaking is facilitated and structured by public lawmaking. The nation-state participates in its own transformation in transnational legal ordering. Transnational legal orders are thus not wholly autonomous of nation-state legal institutions.

K.P. Berger (The *lex mercatoria* as a legal system, above, note 6, at 163) admits that:

Even Goldman acknowledged that [*lex mercatoria*] is a system which 'perhaps is fragile, and which to some extent depends on national orders, but is distinct

of transnational law – qualified as hard or soft law according to the case (codes of conduct, ethical codes, principles, rules and standards) – can be implemented by state laws.[14] The legal orders are therefore permeable and evolve; there are no centres and suburbs.[15]

2. DIGITAL PLATFORMS AS PRIVATE TRANSNATIONAL LEGAL SYSTEMS

2.1 Digital Platforms as Special Transnational Companies

If compared with traditional transnational companies, digital platforms have their own characteristics, which, if on the one hand do not differentiate them from the former in general terms (they belong to the same genus), on the other hand they make it possible to identify completely peculiar profiles (as a species in itself). These are, in the first place, transnational companies which, like the others, operate through companies set up in several states, are subject to their

---

from them.' The autonomy of the lex mercatoria is best described by its 'distinct' character, rather than by its 'total independence' from national laws. The issue is therefore not *whether* the lex mercatoria depends on national laws, but the *extent* to which it must rely on domestic legal systems.

[14] To give examples, UNCITRAL's 2007 Legislative Guide on Secured Transactions is directed to legislatures across the world with the aim of facilitating the granting of credit. The World Bank and International Monetary Fund (IMF) use diagnostic instruments, such as Reports on the Observance of Standards and Codes (ROSCs) to provide legal norms regarding financial standards to be enacted by national lawmakers. The Codex Alimentarius Commission adopts food safety standards that member states are encouraged to adopt nationally, further incentivized by WTO rules. The UN Human Rights Commission promotes the Paris Principles for national adoption to improve human rights practices. The World Bank and World Justice Project design rule of law indicators to spur change through domestic legal institutions. In addition, at the level of private lawmaking, there are the Uniform Customs and Practices or the INCOTERMS of the International Chamber of Commerce, and the product standards approved by the International Organization for Standardization or by the International Electrotechnical Commission.

[15] G. Teubner (2009, The corporate codes of multinationals: company constitutions beyond corporate governance and co-determination, in R. Nickel (ed.), *Conflict of Laws and Laws of Conflict in Europe and Beyond: Patterns of Abovenational and Transnational Juridification*) defines it as a polycentric globalization where 'corporate codes are no longer mere public relations strategies; instead, they have matured into genuine civil constitutions – in the fashion of constitutional pluralism'. Teubner indicates five conditions for this to occur: juridification, constitutionalization, judicialization, hybridization, intermeshing. The concept of juridification is relevant, because it 'begs the same question as lex mercatoria, internet law and other global regimes in which private actors make rules, the binding nature of which is not guaranteed by state power, yet which display a high normative efficacy'.

rules as regards conduction of business, taxation, and lobbying on local regulations in order to streamline compliance obligations, and are therefore among the main promoters of the *lex mercatoria*. As digital platforms, however – in the sense referred to in the definition that I propose[16] – these companies exercise, within the framework of the freedom granted to them by state laws (both those of incorporation and those in which they operate), but also beyond this, an independent regulatory, executive and judicial power.[17]

2.2   The Regulatory Power of Digital Platforms

First of all, digital transnational companies are legal systems, whose social circle is easily identifiable, autonomous and unitary, as well as spontaneous in its formation. They apply their own rules, partly originating from their state of incorporation order, partly created by the companies themselves, and sometimes also conforming to rules and principles originating from states or international organizations, which are not binding (they are located at various levels of the scale ranging from soft to hard law) but become so when integrated into the legal order of the transnational company.[18] The process of integration between public (international, state) and private (arbitration chambers, standards and codes of conduct, among others) systems is in progressive formation; digital transnational companies, which are part of this evolution, then take on peculiar characteristics.

Secondly, digital transnational companies now regulate within their community – of their legal order, therefore – all physiological or pathological relations

---

[16]   See Chapter 1, section 1.

[17]   As for free speech, 'online intermediaries are effectively performing three roles at the same time: they act like a legislature, in defining what constitutes legitimate content on their platform, like judges who determine the legitimacy of content in particular instances, and like administrative agencies who act on these adjudications to block illegitimate content': N. Elkin-Koren, M. Perel (2020), Guarding the guardians: content moderation by online intermediaries and the rule of law, in G. Frosio (ed.), *Oxford Handbook of Online Intermediary Liability*, 669–678. According to the authors, content moderation by online intermediaries challenges the rule of law in three ways: it blurs the distinction between private interests and public responsibilities; it delegates the power to make social choices about content legitimacy to opaque algorithms; and it circumvents the constitutional safeguard of the separation of powers.

[18]   As for freedom of speech, platforms exercise regulatory power when they filter, block, and remove content, at the request of government agents or state actors, defining the practical benchmark for illegality, adapting it to the changing circumstances, and applying it to particular expressions. As a result, platforms effectively blend law enforcement and adjudication powers, and sometimes even lawmaking powers, and yet are not subjected to adequate constitutional checks: N. Elkin-Koren, M. Perel (2020), Separation of functions for AI, *Lewis & Clark Law Review*, 24(3), 861.

between natural and legal persons. The internal policies define the perimeter of the rights of the members of the community: from the protection of personal data, to the freedom of speech – where they also implement international law principles[19] – to the use and removal of inappropriate images, or copyrighted content,[20] to the content of contracts between users, whose fulfilment is checked by the platform,[21] to the systems with which the reputation of the members of the community is built (and destroyed). Thus, digital transnational companies have regulatory power, when they set and impose on their digital community rules and practices (policies) that such community must abide by and that only partially – and by now incidentally – coincide with the law of one or more states in which they operate.[22] This even occurs to the point that these

---

[19]   Facebook's Oversight Board Charter states that 'Freedom of expression is a fundamental human right', balanced with 'authenticity, safety, privacy, and dignity'. The Charter also instructs the Board to 'pay particular attention to the impact of removing content in light of human rights norms protecting free expression'.

[20]   YouTube Content ID is a good example. The system enables YouTube to automatically screen user-uploaded content and identify copyrighted content using a digital identifying code. It is also algorithmically set to determine which specific level of similarity between an uploaded video and an original copyrighted work would trigger the matching feature, which will then submit a signal to the right holder, allowing her to choose whether to remove, monetize, block, or disable the allegedly infringing material before it becomes publicly available. YouTube effectively exercises judicial power when it determines which content constitutes an infringement of an original copyrighted work. It also exercises executive power when it acts to remove, disable, or filter such content.

Amazon uses AI to proactively adjudicate apparently illegitimate uses of brands. Powered by Amazon's machine learning (ML), Project Zero continuously scans Amazon's online stores against key data points that brands provide (e.g., trademarks, logos, etc.), and proactively removes suspected counterfeits before they reach a customer.

[21]   The internal policies of social networks (Facebook is the most advanced) impose on those who register and become part of the community a series of constraints that the user undertakes to respect, regardless of whether they correspond or not to applicable and binding rules in the country from which the user accesses the platform. They apply, for example, to the rules on hate speech, the use of inappropriate sentences, and the use of protocols relating to inappropriate images ('community standards'). They also apply to the methods used to control effective compliance with the platform rules, or penalties in the case of recognized violations, ranging from admonition, warning, temporary suspension from the community, to final ban. Furthermore, they apply to the appeal systems against the penalties imposed, which allow the user to justify his position. In summary, a true system of production of rules, of application, of verification of their respect, of sanctions and a jurisdictional system that I would not define as primitive.

[22]   Facebook's Community Standards ban pornography, hate speech, graphic violence, torture of animals, and are significantly less permissive than US First Amendment Doctrine, and more similar to European Union standards. The opposite applies to Twitter's internal rules (see below, section 3 of this chapter).

companies often openly oppose state laws, refusing to implement national laws or remodelling them in the process of adopting them.[23] This engenders, on the one hand, the risk of competition between legal systems and, on the other, during the delay in enforcement, the inclusion in the process of digital transnational systems, which apply and execute national laws, sometimes compliantly, and sometimes only consistently with them. Consistency with multiple systems is often privileged over full compliance with a single system: the *lex mercatoria* applied.

Although platforms' policies may be inspired by the contents and procedures of regional or national sectoral regulations (of the European Union, the United States, China), the current radicalization of international economic relations does not allow for a synthesis (above, Chapter 1, section 2). Also (but not only) for this reason are the internal policies of digital transnational companies becoming increasingly important not only as transnational law – in the terms in which it is shared, at least among all those belonging to this category – but as a real legal order.

2.3   The Executive Power of Digital Platforms

Digital transnational companies exercise executive power when they intervene, often in real time and in any case with absolute efficacy (algorithmic, we should say, by now), to implement their policies and therefore make the behaviour of the members of the community compliant with the rules.

2.4   The Judicial Power of Digital Platforms

Digital platforms exercise judicial power when, following a violation remaining uncorrected, they punish the violator with proportional measures up to excluding him, temporarily or definitively, from the community; or when they intervene to settle, following an appeal (always within their legal system), a dispute between users of the community: suppliers, distributors, buyers, consumers or professionals, etc. (below, section 3). The tool currently used for this

---

[23]   We refer in Europe, inter alia, to the debate on the Copyright Directive (Directive (EU) 2019/790 of the European Parliament and of the Council of 17 April 2019 on copyright and related rights in the Digital Single Market and amending Directives 96/9/EC and 2001/29/EC) and to the decision of some digital platforms not to implement it fully. We also refer to Facebook's recent proposal to the European Commission on the protection of personal data (White Paper 'Charting the Way Forward: Online Content Regulation'), suggesting that there should be global, rather than national, policies on what is permissible, and that internet companies should not incur any liability for the contents loaded on their platforms, otherwise free speech would be limited.

purpose is the clause which derogates from national jurisdictions and entrusts the resolution of the dispute to the tools specifically created by the digital platform (i.e. eBay settles more than 60 million disputes yearly), supposedly arbitral but in any case, de facto jurisdictional, and in the near future, by the contract, which 'acts on its own accord', self-executes, prevents and resolves disputes, today via an oracle, tomorrow via an algorithm (above, Chapter 1, section 7).[24] As a matter of fact, from a blockchain perspective, in an evolved system, oracles will be replaced directly by the algorithm.[25]

Not to mention payment instruments, which are also autonomous – still subject, for the moment, to state or transnational regulatory law – up to the creation of a real (private) currency, a historical attribute of the sovereignty so far of the main legal system, that is, the state system (below, section 4).[26]

---

[24] Smart contracts registered in the blockchain are not only irrevocable but also capable of evolving automatically the contractual relationship governing all the negotiation (and therefore also pre-contractual) and application phases. Implementing common law models, such contracts foresee all possible developments and can prevent, before they even regulate, possible pathologies, eliminated together with the subjective and discretionary elements in the application of the contract (the software is by definition trustless). Therefore, being self-executing and self-enforcing, each smart contract represents separately a reproposition of that Medieval 'common law', the *ius mercatorum*, the one and only for all orders, because it is outside all of them and does not need them, being sufficient in itself, almost as if it were a 'private order'. It does not require rules outside those encoded in the software, nor dispute resolution tools, because the failure to fulfil obligations is simply impossible.

[25] See, among others, E. Marique (2020), Sanctions on digital platforms: balancing proportionality in a modern public square, *Computer Law and Public Security Review*, 36, article 105372; E. Marique, Y. Marique (2019), Sanctions on digital platforms – beyond the public/private divide, *Cambridge Journal of International Law*, 8(2), 258–281.

[26] Cryptocurrencies have long been an element of folklore in the system but have had the merit of exposing the development of distributed ledger technologies, of which they are an application, to public attention. Born in 2009 (the first and most famous is Bitcoin) from an original idea by an inventor (Satoshi Nakamoto is his pseudonym) they initially constituted an investment asset. They then evolved into various different types. The issue suddenly took on a different connotation when, in June 2019, Facebook announced the start of the procedures for the distribution of a virtual currency, called Libra. The potential pool of users (2.3 billion users are active on Facebook monthly) immediately posed the issue of the stability of a currency subject to uncontrolled volatility and therefore to the conditions that virtual currencies must respect. Telegram, in turn, has initiated a similar path. In a few weeks, many central banks (the Bank of England first, then the ECB too) put the creation of a public virtual currency on the agenda. The Chinese government, for its part, is almost ready to launch its virtual currency. For a payments system as a transnational order see: A. Janczuk-Gorywoda (2015), The new transnational payments law and global consumer trade: online platforms as providers of private legal orders, TILEC Discussion Paper, DP 2015-024.

2.5   Digital Platform Orders

These communities have all the elements of a legal system: they are 'concrete' orders,[27] equally legitimate as the others because they exist regardless of external recognition. They evolve, transforming themselves. They are transnational, because they operate within the states, of which they respect certain rules and principles, but also outside (in different state systems) and beyond the states (subjects of transnational law). This last aspect is perhaps the most controversial, since one of the relevant issues today is precisely to verify whether and to what extent digital transnational companies have gained legal international or transnational subjectivity. We shall deal with this topic in Chapter 4.

The digital transnational companies qualified as above are partly derivative and partly original entities,[28] which evolve over time, strengthening their character of originality, as they progressively become also more independent from the (state) system that originates them *pro parte* (insofar as they are incorporated there) and therefore from subordinate and imperfect they become progressively more perfect.[29] Their independence (via insubordination, if measured in relation to the state order that originates it) then tends to become absolute.

Originally merely functional, as being instrumental to specific and limited activities, digital transnational companies gradually become full companies by reference to the increase in the functions and activities carried out, or the

---

[27] C. Schmitt (1934), *On the Three Types of Juristic Thought*, Praeger.
[28] S. Romano (1918), *The Legal Order*, Routledge, 141:
In the first place, it is possible to have original institutions, which are those in which a legal order is not placed by other institutions and which is therefore, as regards its source, independent. Conversely, there are derivative institutions, whose order is established by another institution, which thus affirms, in this regard, its superiority over the first, which therefore remains subordinate to it. Between these two opposing cases, an intermediate third is given, when there are institutions whose order is partly original and partly derived.
[29] S. Romano, *The Legal Order*, above, note 28, at 143–144:
One can distinguish perfect institutions, which are always original and which can be simple or complex, from imperfect ones, that rely on other institutions with respect to which they are, not only presupposed, but coordinated or subordinate. They are often derived: but they can also be original, if they are simply coordinated or not entirely subordinate to the former.
and (p. 147), thus configures the relationship between states:
[A] third figure is given by the case that two or more orders are independent of each other, in their direct relations, but they depend together on a higher order: in a way which can be mutually relevant through the latter, as it coordinates them. International law, which stands above those of several states, offers very interesting examples of this.

services provided.[30] They are born in the market as market instruments, but they progressively become legal systems. The technological evolution illustrated above also transforms transnational companies on an ontological and not merely qualitative level, making them no longer partial but complete.[31] As independent systems, transnational companies are not irrelevant; on the other hand, for state legal systems, they are not taken as a fact but as a legal datum, as an 'other' system.

2.6   Digital Platform Orders and *Lex Mercatoria*

If, therefore, the possibility of admitting a transnational system constituted by the *lex mercatoria* is still uncertain (above, section 1), it seems – for the same reasons that raise doubts about the former – the existence of private transnational legal systems should instead be admitted, as they overcome all the limits and contradictions of the former. Because they are based not only on custom but also on agreements. Because they present unity in the primary (relationship) and secondary (organizational, in the Hartian sense[32]) norms of

---

[30]   It has been suggested that platforms, as regulatory providers, resemble nation states or have become the 'new governors': M. Cantero Gamito (2017), Regulation. com. Self regulation and contract governance in the platform economy: a research agenda, *European Journal of Legal Studies* 9(2), 53, 56; K. Klonick (2018), The new governors: the people, rules, and processes governing online speech, *Harvard Law Review*, 131, 1598.
Similarly, even if from a different point of view: G. Teubner, The corporate codes of multinationals, above, note 15, at 8 states that 'the corporate codes are neither prescribed by national legislation, nor adopted, nor integrated. More pertinent is the notion of conflict of laws: the autonomous legal orders of the multinationals collide with national and international laws. In this collision between autonomous legal orders, both undergo a deep process of change'.
[31]   S. Romano, *The Legal Order*, above, note 28, at 199 ff., identified in the company a system that was in part irrelevant to the state, as it was not taken into account by it, being 'not recognized as such by the [state order] which takes into consideration certain facts and some relationships that it contemplates and regulates but in a different way, attributing to them the only figure that is compatible with some of his basic principles'.
[32]   H. Hart, in *The Concept of Law* (1961, Oxford University Press), distinguishes between primary rules (rules of conduct) and secondary rules (empowering rules). Hart separates secondary rules into three types: the rules of recognition, the rules of change, and the rules of adjudication. The rule of recognition is a collection of standards and requisites that govern the validity of all rules. Rules of change confer and prohibit power of the creation, extinction and alteration of primary and secondary rules. Rules of adjudication empower individuals to make authoritative determinations of the question whether, on a particular occasion, a primary rule has been broken; they govern the election and procedure of the judiciary.

the community. Because the organizational rules (as regards regulatory, executive and jurisdictional power) are complete.

2.7   Autonomy or Independence of Digital Platform Orders

These legal systems would be autonomous if derived from another system, independent if based on a fundamental rule not set by another system, and therefore not constituting a link with the latter. The practice of digital transnational companies shows a progressive autonomy of these orders, which is starting to transform them into independent systems, since they regulate inter-individual relationships within the order, bearing in mind the constraints represented by the rules of other systems (state or international organizations) to which, however, they do not conform *tout court*. These are permeable orders (sometimes defined as 'porous' in the literature[33]). The question therefore becomes that of the relationship between the digital transnational system and the other systems and of the verification of the existence of adequate mechanisms of *renvoi* or – in the negative – of the applicability of the classic *renvoi* of state systems. The issues of public order, both internal (of private transnational systems but also of the state systems that interact with them) and international also arise in a peculiar way.

A characteristic that must be considered in the investigation is that these orders are 'private': they are accepted by the community that applies them but are imposed by the transnational company that constitutes them and modifies them at will. The question of legitimacy therefore certainly arises, but not that of the democratic nature of the order, which is denied by definition (above, Chapter 1, section 5).

3.   THE LEGISLATIVE, EXECUTIVE AND JUDICIARY POWERS OF DIGITAL PLATFORMS: CHECKS AND BALANCES

Digital platforms thus exercise legislative, executive and judicial powers and therefore constitute real private orders.

However, if the first two powers are easily identifiable and constitute a mere evolution of the internal procedure of multinationals, which presents many examples even far from the digital world, the presence, as well as the way in

---

[33]   L.C. Baker, The emerging normative structures of transnational law, above, note 10, at 31.

which judicial power is (privately) exercised, is innovative.[34] In fact, all digital platforms, closed or open, provide for internal dispute settlement mechanisms. Their existence is not only admitted by the states but also expressly requested by national regulation and, de facto, legitimized.[35]

Lastly, the provision in the Digital Services Act Proposal by the European Commission in December 2020 is meaningful in this sense, as it requires online platforms to work with independent, certified dispute settlement bodies with which users can lodge complaints when they believe their content has been wrongfully removed. Pursuant to Article 18 of the Proposal, users should go through the platforms' internal complaint procedures before being entitled to call upon an independent dispute settlement body.[36] It seems to me a sort of application of the international law principle of prior exhaustion of domestic remedies,[37] which strengthens the setting of a relationship between states and digital platforms in terms of the relationship between public and private legal orders.

The mechanisms adopted by the digital platforms for the resolution of disputes with and between users – the issue relating to disputes with employees

---

[34]   E. Haber (2016), Privatization of the judiciary, *Seattle University Law Review*, 40, 115–172; P. Ortolani (2016), Self-enforcing online dispute resolution: lessons from Bitcoin, *Oxford Journal of Legal Studies*, 36(3), 595.

[35]   The EU General Data Protection Regulation (GDPR) has recently taken the privatization of the judiciary a step further by adopting a right of erasure (right to be forgotten): a 'right of individuals to have their data no longer processed and deleted when they are no longer needed for legitimate purposes'. Prior to GDPR adoption, the European Court of Justice (ECJ) granted EU individuals a more limited right to be delisted under an interpretation of the Data Protection Directive. In both cases, for-profit, commercial entities – not the state – are positioned as the judiciary to decide on fundamental rights. See also: R. van Loo (2020), The new gatekeepers: private firms as public enforcers, *Virginia Law Review*, 106, 467.

[36]   Proposal for a Regulation of the European Parliament and of the Council on a Single Market For Digital Services (Digital Services Act) and amending Directive 2000/31/EC, COM/2020/825final, at Article 17 (Internal complaint-handling system), and 18 (Out-of-court dispute settlement).

[37]   S. Vezzani (2013), Prior exhaustion of internal remedies in cases involving the international responsibility of the European Union, *The Italian Yearbook of International Law*, 22(1), 59–89; A.O. Enabulele (2012), Sailing against the tide: exhaustion of domestic remedies and the ECOWAS Community Court of Justice, *Journal of African Law*, 56(2), 268–295. G. Thallinger (2008), The rule of exhaustion of local remedies in the context of the responsibility of international organisations, *Nordic Journal of International Law*, 77(4), 401–428; R.P. Mazzeschi (2000), Exhaustion of domestic remedies and state responsibility for violation of human rights, *The Italian Yearbook of International Law*, 1, 17–43; R.W. Rideout (1965), The implied requirement of the exhaustion of internal remedies, *Modern Law Review*, 28(3), 351–355.

is different, it follows more consolidated dynamics and is less relevant for our purposes – range from extremely detailed substantive and procedural rules, to less binding and more consolidated mechanisms. Surprisingly, the former do not always refer to (closed) social networks and the latter to open platforms, as would be expected.

Among the social networks, the one with the most advanced system is probably Facebook. In 2019, Facebook set up an Oversight Board for Content Decisions, a group of forty experts who review Facebook's most challenging decisions to allow or remove content from Facebook or Instagram. The Board decisions' legal grounds are the Oversight Board Charter, a constitution-like document[38] that lays down the structural relationship between Facebook, the Oversight Board and the Trust[39] that sits between them. The Charter principles are implemented by the Bylaws, which resolve many questions left open by the Charter.[40]

The Board has broad subject-matter jurisdiction[41] and, by exercising independent judgement, it has the power to reverse Facebook's decisions to

---

[38] Oversight Board Charter, Facebook, https://about.fb.com/wp-content/uploads/2019/09/oversight_board_charter.pdf (https://perma.cc/H53N-PHP4). The document provides for seven Articles: Members; Authority to Review; Procedures for Review; Implementation; Governance; Amendments and Bylaws; and Compliance with Law. The Charter also sets out rules on Board Composition; Selection and Removal of Members; Board Authority and Power; Appellate Procedure; and Structural Independence.

[39] The Charter states that 'the Board, the Trust and Facebook will work together to fulfill the Charter and the Board's purpose'. The Board is to 'review content and issue reasoned, public decisions within the bounds of this Charter ... [and] provide advisory opinions on Facebook's content policies'. The Trust is to fund the Board's budget and appoint and remove members. Facebook is to commit to the Board's independent oversight of content decisions and the implementation of those decisions, funding the Trust and appointing trustees.

[40] The Bylaws are split into four Articles detailing the relationship between Facebook, the Trust, the Oversight Board, and the people who will be able to appeal through the Board.

[41] The Charter does not mention what content would be eligible for review. Excluding content that was removed in compliance with local laws, and following an exhaustion of appeals through Facebook, 'a request for review can be submitted to the board by either the original poster of the content or a person who previously submitted the content to Facebook for review'. This statement implies that the Board has the authority to review not only content that is removed ('original poster of the content') but content that is kept up ('person who previously submitted' content for review). A Case Selection Committee, comprised of five Board members, reviews the cases, and a majority vote is necessary to move a case to panel review.

remove contents, as well as recommend changes to Community Standards.[42] The Charter also specifies that any prior decisions by the Board on a specific content will have 'highly persuasive' precedential value. The Board's decision – which must include a specific 'determination of content', as well as the reasoning and explanation for the decision – is sent to the entire Oversight Board for review, where it must receive a majority vote in order to be formally adopted. The decision is binding and Facebook will implement it promptly, within seven days of the release of the Board's decision, 'unless implementation of a resolution could violate the law'; domestic law, one should suppose, as the Board applies principles of international law (i.e. human rights-related principles) directly. Yet, the reference is still unclear, for these principles should prevail over domestic law. The independence of the Board – which will obviously be measured and evaluated over time[43] – guarantees a primitive

---

[42] Policy recommendations are advisory on Facebook, which must 'transparently communicate about actions taken and results'. See: K. Klonick (2020), The Facebook Oversight Board: creating an independent institution to adjudicate online free expression, *Yale Law Journal*, 8, 2419–2499, at 2464. E. Doeuk (2019), Facebook's 'Oversight Board': move fast with stable infrastructure and humility, *North Carolina Journal of Law & Technology*, 21(1), 3; M. Meroni (2019), Some reflections on the announced Facebook Oversight Board, EUI Centre for Pluralism and Media Freedom; H. Bloch-Wehba (2019), Global platform governance: private power in the shadow of the state, *SMU Law Review*, 72, 28, 33–39.

[43] Pursuant to the Charter outlining the Board's operations and structure, the Board will hear cases in which Facebook decided to leave up or remove content from Facebook or Instagram according to its Community Standards. The Board will select the cases it focuses on, and Facebook will be able to refer cases to the Board for consideration. Users may also be able to appeal to the Board, following on from Facebook's existing appeals process.

To avoid conflicts of interest, current or former Facebook employees and government officials won't be able to serve as Board members, among other disqualifications. Candidates for Board membership should embody certain principles, including showing commitment to the Board as an institution. Board Members should be (1) experienced at deliberating thoughtfully and collegially, as an open-minded contributor on a team; (2) skilled at making and explaining decisions based on a set of policies; and (3) familiar with matters relating to digital content and governance, including free expression, civic discourse, equality, safety, privacy, and technology. Qualifications will be disclosed to the public.

Within two weeks after closing each case, Board members will issue an explanation for their decision, and their decision will be final. They can also recommend changes to Community Standards for Facebook to review, and Facebook will report back to the Board publicly, explaining whether they will take up the recommendation.

For a detailed investigation on the Board's jurisdictional, intellectual and financial independence, see: K. Klonick, The Facebook Oversight Board, above, note 42, at 2481 ff.

but effective separation of powers.[44] Facebook is actually the frontier outpost of an orderly status of the social networks: the Oversight Board is a private, independent arbitration system, which guarantees to Facebook's community members a 'due process'.[45]

Conversely, Twitter, despite exercising an enforcement of content control that is certainly more incisive than that of Facebook,[46] does not provide for claims or appeal procedures. Neither does Google.[47]

---

[44]   According to Facebook's CEO Mark Zuckerberg 'The idea is to create a separation of powers, so that while Facebook is responsible for enforcing our policies, we aren't in the position to make so many decisions about speech on our own. This Board will be tasked with upholding the principle of free expression while ensuring we keep our community safe.' A different perspective is proposed by N. Elkin-Koren, M. Perel (2020), Separation of functions for AI: restraining speech regulation by online platforms, *Lewis and Clark Law Review*, 857–898.

The authors introduce a separation of functions approach to restraining the power of platforms while enhancing the accountability in AI-driven content moderation systems. Namely, they propose to facilitate independent tools embedding public policy. These tools would run on the platforms' data and would include their own optimization processes informed by public policy.

According to the authors, such separation between independent public tools and private data may enhance public scrutiny of private law enforcement of speech restrictions.

[45]   The Charter and the Bylaws guarantee to Facebook's members: (1) notice of what the rule is, (2) notice that they have allegedly violated the rule, (3) notice that a procedural system exists for review of the alleged violation, (4) notice of what that procedural system entails, and (5) notice of the ultimate decision reached. For a detailed investigation see K. Klonick, The Facebook Oversight Board, above, note 42, at 2479 ff.

[46]   Above, Chapter 1, note 154.

[47]   Google policy is to not 'get involved when merchants and customers disagree about facts, since there's no reliable way to discern who's right about a particular customer experience'. Google's judicial role is only relevant in the European Union due to the implementation of the GDPR's right to be forgotten, which requires search engines to decide whether each request to delist a web page satisfies the statutory conditions. Pursuant to the Regulation, the data subject may send the search engine an online removal request. The search engine is required to examine whether the data subject has the right and whether his right overrides their economic interest and the interest of the general public in having access to that information upon conducting a search relating to his name.

Sometimes, complaints by users are allowed, but without default procedures for the resolution of the dispute (Uber), or through a mere mediation procedure (Airbnb).[48] Technological tools also prevent disputes.[49]

As for the dispute resolution systems used by open platforms (marketplaces), they range from a mediation function that the platform assumes, such as the Amazon Payments Buyer Dispute Programme, if the purchase is not covered by the Amazon guarantee,[50] or the eBay dispute resolution mechanism,[51] to a form of *sui generis* arbitration, envisaged for example in Alibaba's contracts, which intervenes directly, using a third party, if necessary, who certifies the quality of the products, and provides a final award.[52]

---

[48] The Airbnb Resolution Centre is an online portal where users can request a formal resolution with their host or guest and request compensation for damage. The Airbnb mediation procedure provides for mediation by 'peace officers'; should parties be unable to reach an agreement, each party can ask Airbnb to make the final decision 72 hours after the initial request is opened. Airbnb states that it does not need to justify the reasons behind its suspensions.
Airbnb suspends accounts if a host rejects too many reservations, responds too slowly, or receives low ratings. A broader set of foundations for suspension includes complaints from guests about specific incidents. See: C. Petersen, V.G. Ulfbeck, O. Hansen (2018), Platforms as private governance systems – the example of Airbnb, *Nordic Journal of Commercial Law*, 1, 38.

[49] A predictive dispute-prevention strategy is based on predictive analytics and machine learning. For example, the Airbnb patent describes artificially intelligent technology that scans people's online life to 'determine a trustworthiness score or compatibility score of the person based on the behavior and personality trait metrics using a scoring system'. The tool can lower a score if the user has 'authored online content with negative language, or has interests that indicate negative personality or behavior trait'.

[50] By implementing its guarantee programme, Amazon provides refunds to buyers if an item does not arrive within three days of the expected delivery date, the buyer received the wrong item, or the buyer returned the item to the merchant without receiving a refund. If the item meets one of these criteria, Amazon deducts the funds from the seller's account. The seller receives an email detailing the buyer's grievance and must respond within three days. Based on a review of this information, Amazon decides whether to rule for the buyer or seller. If the platform decides to uphold the refund request, merchants can appeal within 30 days by providing further evidence. Although a high 'defective order rate' is a primary avenue for account suspension, a seller can file a complaint about another seller by clicking a 'Report abuse' link.

[51] The eBay Dispute Resolution Mechanism offers, through Square Trade as a dispute resolution provider, a free web-based forum which allows users to attempt to resolve their differences on their own or if necessary, through a professional mediator. See: L. Del Duca, C. Rule, K. Rimpfel (2014), eBay's de facto low value high volume resolution process: lessons and best practices for ODR systems designers, *Arbitration Law Review*, 204–219.

[52] Chapter 10: Quality Problems, Inconsistent Descriptions, and Infringement of Alibaba Transaction Dispute Rules, gives Alibaba the power to: determine that the

Its nature of the award is confirmed by Alibaba itself, since the termination mechanisms of the dispute resolution process provide for cases of *lis pendens* and tools to avoid a conflict of judgments.[53]

The mediation provided by Amazon and the decision (de facto an award), provided by Alibaba present, albeit to varying degrees, elements of impartiality with respect to the parties. This element is obviously considered adequate, when the platforms are mere marketplaces that provide brokerage services. The situation should be different for platforms that also sell their own goods (Amazon, in fact), since in this case the element of impartiality is lost (above, Chapter 1, section 3). However, it does not seem that the procedures applied by Amazon in these cases are different.

That the degree of detail of the dispute resolution procedure and the more or less binding nature of the final decision do not depend on the type of platform (closed or open) is a surprising and extremely interesting fact, since it highlights the (different) degree of awareness of digital platforms about the tools available to 'close' their legal systems or make them at least less 'porous' and therefore less sensitive to the regulatory measures of states.

4.   FROM PAYMENT SYSTEMS TO PRIVATE CURRENCIES: THE PATH FORWARD

Two other elements are relevant, in order to understand the developments of digital platforms towards the dimension of orders. The first is given by payment systems, the second by private currencies; the first is current, the second is about to become such.

---

products have quality problems or inconsistent descriptions (Article 51); determine the quality in accordance with the test results (Article 52); determine that the products do not infringe upon the rights of others (Article 53); designate a qualified third-party testing or appraisal agency to conduct testing and appraisal, and the results of the said testing or appraisal shall be treated as the basis for identification (Article 54); support returning of products and refund to the buyer or support a refund, with the seller to contact the buyer directly to handle the return of products (Article 55); support partial refunds (Article 56); determine the proportion in sharing the relevant expenses so incurred according to the degree of liability (Article 57).

[53]   Article 58, Chapter 11 (Termination) of Alibaba Transaction Dispute Rules, provides that Alibaba.com has the right to terminate the dispute resolution process when the arbitration institution that has jurisdiction over the dispute involved has rendered an award, or when either party notifies Alibaba.com that the dispute has been submitted to an arbitration institution of competent jurisdiction for arbitration or both parties have agreed to submit the dispute to another trade dispute settlement institution for settlement.

Both are part, in the European Union, of the regulatory strategy of the Commission which tries, via rules, to acquire a role as a global pivot by relying on the Brussels effect, on the effectiveness of the rules and on the global sharing of principles and protections proposed by the Union. I am referring to a comprehensive 'Digital Finance Package', which includes a 'Digital Finance Strategy', a 'Retail Payment Strategy', and legislative proposals for a 'DLT Pilot Regime' and for more 'digital resilience' in the financial sector (above, Chapter 1, section 2).[54]

Online payment systems are a means of facilitating access to platforms that sell products and certainly represent a relevant market, for antitrust purposes, but also as a specific (vertical) regulation silo. PayPal has built on this a very peculiar business model[55] that other platforms have followed (most recently, WhatsApp Pay, but also Telegram). The European Union intervened to regulate the sector by opening up to competition a market that the banks were not seizing in a sufficiently proactive way.[56] The intervention is aimed (also) at interrupting the chain that connects, on the one hand, the payment system with the credit institution from whose account the provision is made and, on the other hand, the payment with the digital platform that mediates the sale.

As for private currencies, they have undergone a fast evolution. From forms of investment (such as Bitcoin, Ethereum and other cryptocurrencies)[57] they are turning into real trading currencies, released from real coins, as per the original intentions. The intervention of central banks has, for the time being, transformed that evolution by directing private currencies towards autonomous stablecoins, anchored, however, to real single currencies or to a basket of currencies.[58]

---

[54]   Above, Chapter 1, notes 84–85.
[55]   A. Janczuk-Gorywoda (2016), Online platforms as providers of transnational payments law, *European Review of Private Law*, 24(2), 223–251; E. Pacifici (2015), Making PayPal pay: regulation and its application to alternative payment services, *Duke Law & Technology Review*, 13, 89–115.
[56]   Above, Chapter 1, note 85.
[57]   J. O. McGinnis-K. Roche (2019), Bitcoin: order without law in the digital age, *Indiana Law Journal*, 94, 1497.
[58]   A cryptocurrency is a digital currency made secure through an encryption process. The best known cryptocurrencies are based on the blockchain. A stablecoin, on the other hand, is a digital asset designed to simulate the value of fiat currencies such as the dollar or the euro, and allows users to transfer value around the world quickly and economically, while maintaining price stability. Facebook announced in the summer of 2019 the launch of a cryptocurrency, Libra. Faced with the reaction, in September 2019, of many central banks (US Federal Reserve, Bank of England and ECB, among others), the project was downsized to a stablecoin (Diem). On the other hand, central banks are working (ECB and US Federal Reserve, among others) for the launch of public digital currencies (e.g. digital dollar, digital euro).

In September 2020 the European Commission made a Proposal on 'Markets in Crypto-Assets Regulation' (MiCA).[59] The MiCA includes all types of crypto-assets that are not yet covered by EU financial law (especially MiFID II), and provides for specific rules on the initial capital reserves, the security of the IT infrastructure, the corporate governance structure, and the suitability of the management board, as well as rules against market manipulation and insider trading on crypto-asset trading platforms.

Payment systems and (public and private) virtual currencies are instruments that replace (the first), or integrate (the second) those offered in the state systems and follow, at present, the same rules.[60] The significant dimension of this evolution – for the very limited purposes of the investigation I am propos-

---

[59] The Proposal for the Regulation creates various regulation categories: Crypto-assets generally, as a 'catch-all' category (e.g., bitcoins, ether, litecoins, etc.); utility tokens (e.g., Filecoin token, Basic Attention Token, etc.); ART – asset-referenced token (e.g., Diem, BasketCoin, etc.); EMT – e-money token (e.g., USDC, Diem, euro, etc.). ART and EMT are stablecoins, depending on whether they are pegged to a single fiat currency (e.g., euro, US dollar, etc.) (EMT), or are linked to several fiat currencies, commodities such as gold, or the value of other crypto-assets (ART). For these two 'stablecoin' categories, there are also additional requirements if the token is considered 'significant' – for example, if a broad usage and a large issuance volume are expected. This addition was obviously made with the Diem project in mind.

[60] C. Buttigieg, S. Cuyle (2020), A comparative analysis of EU homegrown crypto-asset regulatory frameworks, *European Law Review*, 639–659; D.A. Zetzsche, R.P. Buckley, D.W. Arner (2020), *Regulating Libra*, Oxford Journal of Legal Studies, 1–33; D.A. Zetzsche, R.P. Buckley, D.W. Arner (2020), Decentralized finance, *Journal of Financial Regulation*, 6(2), 172–203; F. L'heureux, J. Lee (2020), A regulatory framework for cryptocurrency, *European Business Law Review*, 31(3), 423–446; R. Hockett (2019), Money's past is fintech's future: wildcat crypto, the digital dollar, and citizen central banking, 2 *Stanford Journal of Blockchain Law and Policy*, 2, 1; R. Hockett (2019), The democratic digital dollar: a peer-to-peer savings & payments platform for fully inclusive state, local, and national money & banking systems, Cornell Law School Research Paper No. 19-37; R. Hockett (2019), Payment polyphony and monetary hierarchy, Working Paper; H. Nabilou (2019), How to regulate Bitcoin? Decentralized regulation for a decentralized cryptocurrency, *International Journal of Law and Information Technology*, 27(3), 266–291; C. Rueckert (2019), Cryptocurrencies and fundamental rights, *Journal of Cybersecurity*, 5(1), 1–12; A.L. Seretakis (2019), Blockchain, securities markets, and central banking, in P. Hacker, I. Lianos, G. Dimitropoulos, S. Eich (eds), *Regulating Blockchain Techno-Social and Legal Challenges*, Oxford University Press, 213–228; H. Arslanian, F. Fischer (2019), The continuing evolution of cryptoassets, in H. Arslanian, F. Fischer (eds), *The Future of Finance: The Impact of FinTech, AI, and Crypto on Financial Services*, Palgrave Macmillan, 217–231; O. Hari, U. Pasquier (2018), Blockchain and distributed ledger technology (DLT): academic overview of the technical and legal framework and challenges for lawyers, *International Business Law Journal*, 5, 423–447; P. Yeoh (2017), Regulatory issues in blockchain technology, *Journal of Financial Regulation and Compliance*, 25(2), 196–208.

ing – is not a possible divergence of the rules in the future, but their function in terms of 'closure' of the ordering of the platforms, which is less and less dependent, even under this profile, on that of the states.

In a nutshell, the risk is that in regulating private virtual currencies, states and central banks do not take into account the fact that, beyond the specific function they perform, these currencies constitute an instrument for closing the private system of digital platforms, which thus becomes increasingly independent and impermeable.

Apparently, when the virtual currency meets the blockchain, the independence of the digital platform issuing this currency becomes complete (above, Chapter 1, section 7). This effect allows us to understand the reaction of central banks and the consequent transformation of the virtual currencies announced by Facebook and Telegram into stablecoins. The direction, however, is clear and the conclusion, at present, seems inevitable.

5.   DIGITAL PLATFORMS AS PRIVATE, SOVEREIGN TRANSNATIONAL ORDERS

This first part of the legal analysis leads to a result that was not taken for granted, but should not be considered surprising. Digital platforms, even if not classifiable in a stable way because they are highly dynamic, in pursuit of markets and of maximum efficiency, increasingly tend to transform themselves into independent bodies, into ecosystems (on an economic level) and therefore, on a legal level, into legal orders.

Private legal systems were studied by Santi Romano back in 1918. Digital platforms, however, have peculiar characteristics that distinguish them from other private systems, on a qualitative level. They are in fact increasingly autonomous from state systems, and tend to become independent from them. They apply internal law which – as explained by Facebook in the Charter – introduces elements and principles of international law in a system that is often more restrictive than the local law in which it operates. So it is, for example, with regard to free speech in the United States (above, Chapter 1, section 5). It is therefore a matter of qualifying the internal (domestic) law that digital platforms apply. We shall do this in Chapter 4, section 3.[61] The evolution of practice and case law will be more or less fast, due to the ability of digital platforms to replace state law with international interindividual law. Substitution is obviously relative, not absolute: digital platforms only regulate parts of

---

[61]   See below, Chapter 4, section 3. This is a typical international interindividual law.

community's activities; however, they are increasingly numerous and decisive aspects, not just related to economic purposes.

On the legal side, the progressive independence of the legal order leads – together with effectiveness – to sovereignty, which must be investigated and qualified, in relative terms and therefore in relation to other legal systems.

Faced with this evolution, the responses of state law are currently mostly regulatory (antitrust is also part of this scheme) and address digital platforms as companies. The paradigm shift is not adequately grasped, in my opinion, by states and regulators, and therefore deserves to be further investigated, in itself and in the effects it produces.

A point of the analysis developed in the first chapter appears clear, and I believe we must start from here: the internal and external plan of digital platforms (digital legal systems, it must be concluded, based on this second chapter), and therefore the rules of the digital community and the relationship between this and other communities, digital or state, must be distinguished. We have seen this with regard to competition law, regulation, the impact on democratic principles, the relevance of ethical principles (when they are really such and not something else). This result is not easily understandable if the survey is limited to the markets and the related regulation. On the other hand, it becomes much clearer if reported on a juridical, orderly level. This is the development that I propose in the next chapter.

3. Plurality of private transnational legal orders and relations with other legal systems

Now we have classified the digital transnational companies as legal systems, in this section we deal with the relationship between these and the other legal systems. In Chapter 4 we investigate the profile of the legal personality that can be recognized in companies that identify themselves with their digital transnational order.

The mainstream literature has so far considered multinational and transnational companies as without international legal subjectivity.[1] Due to the denial of the existence of a transnational system, part of the literature has also regarded these companies as having no transnational legal personality.[2]

We have seen in the previous paragraphs that digital transnational companies have acquired such characteristics that they do configure, each according to the elements that constitute them, real legal systems of transnational nature. If this is true, the question of recognizing international or transnational legal personality in digital transnational companies should come later. Conversely, the assessment of the relationship between international and transnational

---

[1] Below, Chapter 2, section 1.

[2] Among others, see: M. Noortmann, A. Reinisch, C. Ryngaert (eds) (2015), *Non-State Actors in International Law*, Hart Publishing; V. Chetail (2014), The legal personality of multinational corporations, state responsibility and due diligence: the way forward, in D. Alland, V. Chetail, O. de Frouville J. Viñuales (eds), *Unity and Diversity of International Law. Essays in Honour of Prof. Pierre-Marie Dupuy*, Martinus Nijhoff; C. Walter (2012), Subjects of international law, in R. Wolfrum (ed.), *The Max Planck Encyclopedia of Public International Law*, Vol. IX, Oxford University Press, para. 28; A. Bianchi (2011), The fight for inclusion: non-state actors and international law, in U. Fastenrath, R. Geiger, D.E. Khan, A. Paulus, S. von Schorlemer, C. Vedder (eds), *From Bilateralism to Community Interest: Essays in Honour of Judge Bruno Simma*, Oxford University Press, 40 *et seq.*; R. Miller (2008), Paradoxes of personality: transnational corporations, non-governmental organizations and human rights in international law, in R. Miller, R. Bratspies (eds), *Progress in International Law*, Brill, 381; P. Dumberry (2004), L'entreprise, sujet de droit international? Retour sur la question à la lumière des développements récents du droit international des investissements, *Revue Générale de droit International Public*, 108(1), 103 *et seq.*

systems constituted by each digital transnational company having the characteristics described above should come first.

1.   PRIVATE TRANSNATIONAL LEGAL ORDERS AND STATE ORDERS

If the legal order of digital platforms is the order of digital transnational companies ('communities' we should say), its relationship with state systems – meaning that of origin (of incorporation of the company) and those in which this legal order operates and to whose rules it is (should be) subject – is one of independence, partial but progressive. The dualistic approach helps clarify the terms of the relationship. The digital transnational systems are in fact totally independent as regards their internal order, while they are partially dependent on others (state systems and regional organizations) as regards the rights and duties that they can recognize with respect to them, just as, for example, the states recognize with respect to the international community.

1.1   The Progressive Emancipation of the Legal Orders of Digital Platforms

Since they are not static but highly dynamic, the legal systems of digital transnational companies quickly emancipate themselves from other legal systems, on which they depend less and less. This is the case for the substantive rules but also for the procedural ones, for the primary (relationship) and secondary (organization, in Hartian sense) rules as illustrated above.

As for substantive law, the platforms apply rules that are inspired by (and integrate) the principles of international law and then create a system consistent with their application. The example of free speech in the United States is emblematic: both Facebook and Twitter have applied more restrictive rules than those of the federal law of the United States, since free speech in their legal systems does not constitute – as is the case in the US Constitution – a right prevailing over others, but must be moderated according to these rules (on information, data protection, etc.).[3]

As for procedural law, Facebook is again the frontier outpost, since it has established a system similar, or in any case comparable, to that of a state jurisdiction.[4]

For these reasons, agreements between states and digital transnational companies begin to be numerous, to regulate not only the activity of the latter in

---

[3]   Above, Chapter 1, section 5.
[4]   Above, Chapter 2, section 3.

the territory of the former, but also the methods and limits in which the rules of state regulations must be enforced by the digital transnational companies.

Sometimes indeed, digital platforms operate as states' 'regulatory agents' and guarantee the implementation of national laws (i.e. fiscal rules, but also in respect of hate speech, the fight against terrorism, paedophilia, etc.[5]).

One must, however, distinguish between elements of platforms' internal functioning, which are identical notwithstanding where users are located – and thus are fully self-regulated – and their external effects, which diverge depending on the geographical location at stake and need a form of co-regulation.

To the point that today the co-regulation – which involves forms of collaboration between the digital platforms and the states in which they operate (above, Chapter 1, section 2) – can be considered the only adequate modality of relationship between the state orders and those of the digital platforms, with a voluntary acceptance, expressed or implicit, of the independence of digital legal orders.[6] States, international organizations and digital platforms' co-regulation replaces thus the consolidated production of transnational

---

[5]   Public regulators are increasingly relying on platforms in their regulatory activity, drawing on their superior operational capacities, data pools and direct access to platform users. Platforms are therefore increasingly taking over a role as regulatory intermediaries: cooperation between home-sharing platforms and regulators is not limited to enforcement of local time limits for vacation rentals but also concerns other regulatory goals, for example collection of local taxes. But relevant examples are also the protection of personal data, copyright, the rules on the liability of the platforms for violations, by users, of the rules on money laundering, on defamation, on cybercrime, paedophilia, etc. See: C. Busch (2019), Self-regulation and regulatory intermediation in the platform economy, in M. Cantero Gamito, H.W. Micklitz (eds) (2019), *The Role of the EU in Transnational Legal Ordering: Standards, Contracts and Codes*, Edward Elgar Publishing, where the author states that

a future regulatory framework for the platform economy should not only address platform operators as market intermediaries, but should also consider their role as actors participating in the regulatory chain, be it as a provider of private ordering services or as a regulatory intermediary implementing public ordering. In this sense a future EU policy for platform regulation should be focused on a co-operative regulatory approach combining elements of regulated self-regulation and regulatory intermediation.

[6]   M. Fink (2018), Digital co-regulation: designing an above-national legal framework for the platform economy, *European Law Review*, 47–68; D. Koukiadis (2015), *Reconstituting Internet Normativity: the Role of State, Private Actors, Global Online Community in the Production of Legal Norms*, Nomos; C. Marsden (2011), *Internet Co-regulation: European Law, Regulatory Governance and Legitimacy in Cyberspace*, Cambridge University Press; D. Harvey (2017), *Collisions in the Digital Paradigm: Law and Rule Making in the Internet Age*, Hart Publishing; R. Van Loo (2017), Rise of the digital regulator, *Duke Law Journal*, 66, 1317.

rules and standards (guidelines, codes of conduct) addressed to transnational corporations.

Sometimes the digital platforms' transnational rules become true sources of national law, thanks to the commitment by states to enforce them in state courts or through private enforcement mechanisms.[7] The transnational private legal orders of digital platforms operate thus with the endorsement and support of states.

Sometimes these rules override state laws. We have recently seen it with Covid-19 exposure notification applications; many states (including Germany, in Europe) have had to change the laws just enacted because they required software not compatible with the technical standards released by Google and Apple and automatically downloaded by all mobile devices.[8]

1.2   Platform Law

The notion of platform law, the autonomous order of digital platforms, has now been defined by scholars and accepted by many subjects of international law (international organizations, states, transnational corporations).[9] This

---

[7] H. Collins (1999), *Regulating Contracts*, Oxford University Press, at 46–57. R. Wai (2005), Transnational private law and private ordering in a contested global society, *Harvard International Law Journal*, 471 ff.. See also A. Janczuk-Gorywoda (2015), The new transnational payments law and global consumer trade: online platforms as providers of private legal orders, TILEC Discussion Paper, DP 2015-024, where the author states that: 'PayPal's represents a relatively uniform and autonomous transnational legal order', but 'state laws continue to infiltrate it with important substantive rules ... nevertheless, the influence goes both ways: transnational private legal orders and national legal systems interact with each other and mutually shape each other'.

[8] Initially (April 2020) the German government had authorized the use of a technology that required centralized data management. The law was then changed (May 2020) to make the system compatible with the platform spread by Google (Android) and Apple which provided for decentralized data management (at the smartphone level).

[9] See among others: O. Lobel (2016), The law of the platform, *Minnesota Law Review*, 87–166, at 93–94: the author considers the law of the platform not in terms of the law that platforms generate, but in terms of the regulatory environment within which platforms operate and how established features of the legal system map onto the economic shifts that platforms have introduced; F. Zoll (2016), The rise of the platform economy, *Journal of European Consumer and Market Law*, 5(1), 3–10; M.K. Land (2020), The problem of platform law: pluralistic legal ordering on social media (in P. Schiff Berman (ed.), *The Oxford Handbook of Global Legal Pluralism*, Oxford University Press), states that platform law is composed of four central elements: contract law (contractual provisions governing the respective rights and duties of users and company); substantive common law (norms: communications about expected norms,

shows that platforms are not only addressees of transnational (soft/hard) rules and standards – and therefore, are not only subject to public regulation – but actively participate (even through private co-regulation) in the transnational law formation. For these purposes, both the internal activity of the digital platforms and especially the external activity – the agreements that they stipulate between them and states, or international organizations – matter.

1.3 Recognition by States of the Private Jurisdiction of Digital Platforms

The digital platforms' private jurisdictional power is recognized by states and international organizations.

Facebook's Oversight Board's decisions are a good case: states may recognize them as precedential authority when courts adjudicate on platform speech issues.

The European regulation seems to follow this path, even if it is still at an early stage: the European Commission Proposal for a Digital Services Act requests digital platforms to provide internal complaint-handling systems (Article 17), giving out-of-court national dispute settlement bodies competence to review platforms' decisions on internal disputes (Article 18). This is a clear recognition of the private jurisdiction of digital platforms' internal dispute settlement bodies, and a direct implementation of the principle of prior exhaustion of domestic remedies.

Via regulation – as happened with the General Data Protection Regulation – European Courts can also request digital platforms to adjudicate and enforce

---

procedures and sanctions, content moderation and user account practices; decisional law (internal guidance and policies used to moderate content and govern user account suspension and termination); procedural common law (procedures for flagging, reviewing and removing content and sanctioning users); technical law (technical and system design choices).

As for a UN recognition of a 'platform law': D. Kaye (2018), Report of the Special Rapporteur on the Promotion and Protection of the Right to Freedom of Opinion and Expression (UN Doc. A/HRC/38/35, 6 April 2018), where he recommends that social media companies begin to collect and share with users their decisional law:

> The companies are implementing 'platform law', taking actions on content issues without significant disclosure about those actions. Ideally, companies should develop a kind of case law that would enable users, civil society and states to understand how the companies interpret and implement their standards. While such a 'case law' system would not involve the kind of reporting the public expects from courts and administrative bodies, a detailed repository of cases and examples would clarify the rules much as case reporting does. (p. 63)

claims related to certain rights,[10] also using digital platforms' internal dispute settlement mechanisms to enforce their jurisdiction extraterritorially.[11]

1.4   Coordination and Conflict-of-Law Rules

If the digital transnational orders tend to become autonomous from the state ones, the issue of their coordination and therefore of the (reciprocal) *renvoi* from one order to another arises: from the state to the digital transnational one, and vice versa. To this end, the analogic use of the *lex mercatoria* practice does not seem correct to me. In fact, starting from the assumption that the *lex mercatoria* lacks unity, being made up of distinct sets of rules for the various sectors ('vertical silos') or the various aspects of international trade, the transnational case law considers it relevant only as an alternative or complementary method to conflict. And therefore it may be relevant, based on the common will of the parties, or when explicitly referred to in an international convention, but it cannot be referred to by a conflict of law provision, since the latter is formulated in order to be addressed to state systems or international organizations.[12]

---

[10]   See Case C-131/12, *Google Spain SL v. Agencia Española de Protección de Datos*, 2014 ECR 317, ruling that Google must honour a claimant's request to 'delist' information from its search engines but acknowledging that the claimant's right must be balanced against concerns for access to information, and placing adjudication of that balancing test on a case-by-case basis in the hands of Google. See, among others: R.C. Post (2018), Data privacy and dignitary privacy: Google Spain, the right to be forgotten, and the construction of the public sphere, *Duke Law Journal*, 67(5), 981–1072; I. Saphiu (2015), Google Spain and Google, *European Public Law*, 21(4), 691–702; P. de Hert, V. Papakonstantinou (2015 Google Spain: Addressing critiques and misunderstandings one year later, *Maastricht Journal of European and Comparative Law*, 22(4), 624–638; O. Lynskey (2015), Control over personal data in a digital age: *Google Spain v. AEPD and Mario Costeja Gonzalez*, *Modern Law Review*, 78(3), 522–534; M. Peguera (2015), In the aftermath of Google Spain: how the 'right to be forgotten' is being shaped in Spain by courts and the Data Protection Authority, *International Journal of Law and Information Technology*, 23(4), 325–347.

[11]   See Case C-18/18, *Glawischnig-Piesczek v. Facebook Ir. Ltd*, Judgment, 2019 ECR 821. See: D.J.B. Svantesson (2020), Scope of jurisdiction online and the importance of messaging – lessons from Australia and the EU, *The Computer Law and Security Report*, 38, 105428 (at 5–7); Z. Morawska-Zakroczymska, D. Gęsicka (2019), Case Note to the Judgment of the Court of Justice of 3 October 2019 in Case *Eva Glawischnig-Piesczek v. Facebook Ireland*, C-18/18, 25 *Comparative Law Review*, 25, 345–356.

[12]   Consider, by way of example, Article 4.1 of the 1980 Rome Convention on the law applicable to contractual obligations under which, in the absence of choice by the contracting parties, 'the contract is governed by the law of the country with which it presents the closer connection'.

We can affirm, on the basis of what has been observed so far, that digital transnational systems present those characteristics of unity and completeness that according to many are missing in the *lex mercatoria*. Furthermore, these legal orders could well be considered – as transnational communities – on a par with those of international organizations (below, section 3). It is therefore possible that a digital transnational order may be referred to a conflict-of-law rule to identify the applicable law.

Of course, such *renvoi* will be more probable if the rule in question is common to more than one transnational digital order; hence the relevance of a codification of uniform law (below, Chapter 5, section 3). Again, between the two possible forms, it is more probable that the *renvoi* is not total, and therefore allows the referring legal system not to adopt the referred rule *tout court* but only some of its elements, making its application conditional on certain legal qualities or assessments that depend on the referring order.

As for the mutual hypothesis that a digital transnational system will refer to a state system in case of conflict, it is more than likely. Think of the *renvoi* to the rules of the country in which the member of a social network has his domicile or citizenship.

1.5   *Renvoi* and Public Order

If we admit the possibility of *renvoi*, in both the cases outlined, we must address the issue of the effectiveness of the public order limit, the application of which presupposes that the conflict-of-law rule has identified the applicable law in a different order than the referring one. Obviously I am referring here not to 'internal' public order, which is relevant in terms of administrative law (public safety) or private law (mandatory due to the private will of certain legislative provisions[13]), but to international public order, which is relevant in terms of transnational relations and is aimed at guaranteeing the internal coherence of the system and preserving the fundamental principles which it is inspired by.

Again, I believe the answer should be positive. We start from the first case, in which the public order limit is challenged in a state system. The practice of using the public order limit to restrict the application of the law of a referred state order incompatible with the fundamental principles of the referring order is fully valid even if it refers to cases where the referred order is a 'non-state'

---

[13]   We refer here also to the 'public order of protection', born in the French legal system as opposed to the 'public order of direction', that gives rise to various consequences in terms of discipline: relative and not absolute nullity. See: G. Farjat (1963), *L'Ordre public economique*, Bibliothèque de droit privé, 118 ff.

one. The interest in the protection of the referring order is in fact valid regardless of the state or non-state nature of the referred order, which is irrelevant for these purposes.

Less evident but equally possible is the application of an 'international' public order limit by a digital transnational order against a state order referred to by the conflict-of-law rule. Consider the case of a request by a government (not necessarily a dictatorial regime) to access personal data (health, sexual or political orientation) and the profiling of individuals who are part of a community or a social network. Consider also the request of a government to censor – or not to censor – the opinions expressed by a member of the community (and here the 'Trump saga' offers concrete and already debated examples: above, Chapter 1, section 5). If the issue is placed on the level of the relationship between legal systems, these requests, even if 'legitimate' on the basis of the law of the requesting country and *in abstracto* applicable on the basis of the conflict of law rules, could be barred by the public order limit of the digital transnational system. This is a restriction on which the contractual relationship between the digital platform and the individual user is also based (or should be).

2. PRIVATE TRANSNATIONAL ORDERS AND INTERNATIONAL LAW

We now come to the relationship between international law and digital transnational systems.

If we were to follow the monistic approach, this relationship cannot exist by definition, because the plurality of legal systems is denied *in nuce* – since state legal systems are only articulations of the international legal order – as well as the existence of non-state orders relevant to international law: if necessary, they will only be relevant for interindividual law.[14]

Even following certain dualistic approaches, a relationship between private transnational legal systems and the international legal system cannot exist, if this can apply only for states. Things change when we move on to the 'moder-

---

[14] For a recap of the different theories, see the writings of G. Arangio-Ruiz and in particular, among others: (2008), La persona internazionale dello Stato, *Digesto delle discipline pubblicistiche*, UTET; (1951), *Gli Enti Soggetti dell'Ordinamento Internazionale*, Giuffrè; (1972), *Diritto Internazionale e Personalità Giuridica*, Coop. Libraria; (2003), Dualism revisited: international law and interindividual law, *Rivista di diritto internazionale*, 909–999; (1975), L'etat dans le sens du droit des gens et la notion du droit international, offprint from *Österreichische Zeitschrift für Öffentliches Recht*, 3–63, 265–406.

ate dualism' theses, which admit an interrelation between a plurality of orders, potentially even non-state ones,[15] subject to a few considerations.

Firstly, digital private legal systems directly apply rules and principles of international law. In some cases, a reference is explicit. This is the case with the Facebook Charter, which applies international human rights principles, and which also prevails over the Constitution of the United States, as the Charter guarantees a reconciliation of rights in which free speech is not an absolute and therefore prevalent right – as it is in the US Constitution – but it is a relative right and applies consistently with other equal rights.

Secondly, as already mentioned, unlike the transnational order – when it is recognized as existing[16] – custom is not the only source of international law that digital transnational systems can access. The agreements between these and numerous states, aimed at regulating reciprocal relations, constitute a practice that highlights the awareness of the legally relevant reality (above, Chapter 2, section 2). It is no longer a matter of protection provided to companies indirectly through agreements between states (as in the case of the protection of foreign investors): the digital transnational company negotiates and signs agreements and protocols with the state. Protection is direct. It is a relationship of peers between legal systems. Therefore, and also because of what I said in the previous paragraph regarding the relationship between digital transnational systems and national systems, here we can admit not only the relevance of the transnational digital legal system, for international law, but also its (progressive) independence.[17]

---

[15] See among others: A. Cassese (1985), Modern constitutions and international law, *Le Recueil des Cours de l'Académie de Droit International de La Haye (RCADI)*, 192, 331 ff.; E. Cannizzaro, B. Bonafé (2014), Beyond the archetypes of modern legal thought: appraising old and new forms of interaction between legal orders, in M. Maduro, K. Tuori, S. Sankari (eds), *Transnational Law: Rethinking European Law and Legal Thinking*, 78 ff.

[16] The reconstruction of G. Arangio-Ruiz leads to the result of an international law understood as a law between 'powers', de facto entities, and not based on rules of relationship or organization of an international order. On the fact that the definition of 'international order' is inappropriate and not entirely harmless, see: La persona internazionale dello Stato, above, note 14, p. 67 and Dualism revisited, above, note 14, 997–998.

[17] If we consider that international legal subjectivity is today almost unanimously denied to multinational and transnational companies, we understand how this different approach determines a substantial change in terms of general theory and in relation to the subjects (below, Chapter 4). Also understood is the decisive relevance that is acquired by – and should be attributed to – uniform codification activity. However, it seems to me that this awareness is not particularly widespread today.

3.   PRIVATE TRANSNATIONAL ORDERS AND TRANSNATIONAL SYSTEMS

If we do not recognize the existence of a transnational legal system, because we do not attribute to the *lex mercatoria* those characteristics of unity and completeness that are necessary to guarantee its systematic nature and not only its mandatory nature, the issue of its relationship with digital transnational systems does not arise.

In the opposite case, we can assume a relationship between an 'open' and constantly evolving transnational order, such as the *lex mercatoria*, and the digital 'transnational' orders – 'closed' but also evolving towards a progressive emancipation from state systems – whenever arbitration courts settle a dispute by applying the rules or policies of the digital transnational corporation, or codifications and general principles are elaborated on it.

It is possible that digital transnational companies have an interest in harmonizing common rules and practices, also in order to oppose them more effectively to state systems when they are not entirely compliant with them, or that states or international organizations have an interest in subjecting the activities of digital transnational companies to generally applicable rules of conduct and minimum standards.

It emerges from these examples that the relationship between transnational legal systems and digital transnational orders is of independence, since the rules and codes of the former can be applied to the latter only in case of voluntary acceptance, which presupposes participation in their formation. This is the point of interconnection of the transnational order with the digital transnational systems and which the latter should, in my opinion, grasp and develop.

4.   RELATIONSHIP BETWEEN PRIVATE TRANSNATIONAL ORDERS

Digital transnational systems, being made up of transnational companies that present the characteristics listed above, are in principle completely independent from one another. However, it is easily predictable and highly probable that forms of interrelation between digital platforms will develop: to share behaviours (i.e. they ban and take down conspiracy theories and misleading false claims regarding the Covid-19 health crisis), and practices (i.e. the Santa Clara Principles on Transparency and Accountability in Content Moderation),[18]

---

[18]   https://santaclaraprinciple.org. The Santa Clara Principles on Transparency and Accountability in Content Moderation were drafted by a group of content-moderation academics and joined by the Electronic Frontier Foundation (EFF), the American

to codify standards (as Google and Apple did in the Covid-19 notification of exposure), to create uniform rules (such as Facebook's 'Community Standards'[19]), but also to 'query' data from another platform or to exchange data, which take on different values and meanings depending on the use they are intended for, with a level of detail and conditions that may change according to the kind of digital platform (open or closed), the needs (purpose), but also the constraints (regulatory, for data protection or competition).

Moreover, the evolution of the market leads to a consolidation of the platforms and therefore to an integration between the respective systems. There will therefore be more complex systems, in which some digital transnational legal systems will be superordinate to other, subordinate systems. The latter will have limited autonomy and will apply the norms and practices of the former, similarly to what already happens in international law, such in cases of annexation by a state of territories of another state. This has already happened, for example, with Facebook, which bought WhatsApp and Instagram, with Microsoft and LinkedIn, Amazon and Deliveroo, etc. (above, Chapter 1, section 3); all acquisitions that generated uniformity of rules and practices.

Furthermore, as mentioned above (Chapter 2, section 3) the more the practices of internal law of the platforms are consolidated and become best practices, the more they turn into standards. The Community Standards and Facebook's Charter Oversight Board can influence other digital systems. Reference between digital private legal systems, therefore, as regards their substantive and procedural domestic law, is more than possible, it is probable.

As for the external level, and therefore the relationship between digital private systems, in transnational law and increasingly, possibly, in the near future, in international law, the collaboration between platforms for the purposes of codification can certainly be of some help. We shall see this in Chapter 5, section 3.

Civil Liberties Union Foundation of Northern California, the Center for Democracy and Technology, and New America's Open Technology Institute. The Principles declared three 'initial steps' the companies must take in order to provide 'meaningful due process' on platforms. The third principle urged online speech platforms to create 'meaningful opportunity for timely appeal' for their users and in the long term to consider 'independent external review processes.'

[19] See above, Chapter 2, section 3. Digital platforms may replicate the process of creating an oversight board or design their own process to create their adjudicatory bodies, implementing the same rules and procedures.

4. Digital platforms as subjects of transnational and international law

In the supranational legal space in which they operate, digital platforms are private legal orders and, as such, enjoy legal personality.

The Internet Is Not 'the Place'

From the outset, it is necessary to clear the field of a misunderstanding relating to the 'place' in which the digital platforms operate. The literature has focused on the qualification of the internet as a 'non-place' or as a figurative territory (Lessig).[1] Digital platforms are thought to operate within this perimeter. Starting from this assumption, different legal theories on the activity of digital platforms have been set up at institutional and, sometimes, order level (the internet order and its governance).[2]

It seems to me that these theories have a common flaw, which consists of trying to reproduce, as regards the activity of digital platforms, the classic approach of international subjectivity, based on people, territory and govern-

---

[1]   L. Lessig (1999), *Code and Other Laws of Cyberspace*, Basic Books; L. Lessig (1996), The zones of cyberspace, *Stanford Law Review*, 48(5), 1403–1411. See also: I. Brown, C.T. Marsden (2013), *Regulating Code: Good Governance and Better Regulation in the Information Age*, MIT Press, 117–139; T. Schultz (2008), Carving up the internet: jurisdiction, legal orders, and the private/public international law interface, *European Journal of International Law*, 19(4), 799–839; U. Kohl (2004), The rule of law, jurisdiction and the internet, *International Journal of Law and Information Technology*, 12(3), 365–376.

[2]   D. Condorelli, J. Padilla (2020), Harnessing platform envelopment in the digital world, *Journal of Competition Law & Economics*, 16(2), 143–187; M.C. Buiten, A. de Streel, M. Peitz (2020), Rethinking liability rules for online hosting platforms, *International Journal of Law and Information Technology*, 28(2), 139–166; E.I. Obergfell, A. Thamer (2017), (Non-)regulation of online platforms and internet intermediaries – the facts: context and overview of the state of play, *Journal of Intellectual Property Law & Practice*, 12(5), 435–441; U. Kohl (2013), Google: the rise and rise of online intermediaries in the governance of the internet and beyond (Part 2), *International Journal of Law and Information Technology*, 21(2), 187–234; K.J. Boudreau, A. Hagiu (2009), Platforms rules: Multi-sided platforms as regulators, in A. Gawer (ed.), *Platforms, Markets and Innovation*, Edward Elgar Publishing.

ment. This is the reason why they search for a place (or 'non-place'), similar to a territory, underpinning an order (the internet order).

However, it is now a consolidated fact that subjectivity, on a transnational and international level, is based on the double assumption of independence and effectiveness.[3] Therefore, 'the Place' in which to measure it is not the internet: it is international relations. In the previous chapters we have seen that digital platforms enjoy independence and effectiveness. It is a question here of understanding whether these requirements are relevant on the level of transnational law alone, or also of international law.

Independence and Supranational Law

The evidence of the practice requires more in-depth studies and a consistent theoretical reconstruction. In this chapter I intend to verify the collocation of digital platforms in supranational law on the basis of the main theories on subjectivity. The aim is not to provide an autonomous vision or to profess any preference for a specific reconstruction, but to assess whether there is an approach more consistent with the evolution of the practice I have illustrated. The shift from the perspective of the system on which we focused in Chapter 3, to that of subjectivity, is justified by the need to make this verification between the practice and the main theoretical reconstructions and takes on a different connotation due to the approach followed (see Chapter 1).

International Personality

The definition of international personality is not univocal. The classical notion identifies it in the presence of three constituent elements: the capacity to conclude international agreements; the capacity to establish diplomatic relations; and the capacity to bring international claims (state-analogy conception).[4] The alternative conception, which relies on a single criterion: the capacity to be invested with rights and obligations by international law,[5] is no less rigorous,

---

[3]   J. Grzybowski (2017), To be or not to be: the ontological predicament of state creation in international law, *European Journal of International Law*, 28(2), 409–432; M.N. Shaw (2017), *International Law*, 8th edn, Cambridge University Press; E. Ringmar (1996), On the ontological status of the state, *European Journal of International Relations*, 2, 439–466.

[4]   For a general investigation see: R. Portmann (2010), *Legal Personality in International Law*, Cambridge University Press.

[5]   H. Lauterpacht (1970), The subjects of international law, in E. Lauterpacht (ed.), *International Law. Collected Papers of Hersch Lauterpacht, Volume 1: The General Works*, Cambridge University Press, 147.

compatible with the *ratio* expressed by the International Court of Justice in the *Reparation* case[6] and consistent with the evolution of contemporary international law.

The legal literature and the practice do not consider multinational and transnational companies as subjects of international law. Few authors admit a limited legal personality of transnational companies, in specific areas (i.e. investment law, human rights obligations).[7] For this reason it is necessary to

---

[6]   An entity is a subject of international law only if two cumulative conditions are fulfilled: it 'is capable of possessing international rights and duties, and that it has capacity to maintain its rights by bringing international claims' (ICJ, *Reparation for Injuries Suffered in the Service of the United Nations*, Advisory Opinion, ICJ Reports 1949, 174, at 179).

[7]   This is still the mainstream view today. See in particular: I. Brownlie (2003), *Principles of Public International Law*, 6th edn, Oxford University Press, 65; P. Malanczuk (1997), *Akehurst's Modern Introduction to International Law*, 7th edn, Routledge, 102; C. Domincé (1996), La personnalité juridique dans le système du droit des gens, in J. Makarczyk (ed.), *Theory of International Law at the Threshold of the 21st Century. Essays in honour of Krzysztof Skubiszewski*, Brill, 154 and 165; K.P. Sauvant, V. Aranda (1994), The international legal framework for transnational corporation, in A.A. Fatouros (ed.), *Transnational Corporations: The International Legal Framework*, Vol. 20, Routledge, 84; P. Merciai (1993), *Les Enterprises Multinationales en Droit International*, Bruylant, 198–201; F. Rigaux (1991), Transnational corporations, in M. Bedjaoui (ed.), *International Law: Achievements and Prospects*, Martinus Nijhoff, 129; L. Henkin (1989), International law: politics, values and functions, *Le Recueil des Cours de l'Académie de Droit International de La Haye* (*RCADI*), 216, 199; A. Cassese (1986), *International Law in a Divided World*, Clarendon Press, 103.

A limited personality derived from international law is admitted by P.M. Dupuy (2004), *Retour Sur la Théorie des Sujets du Droit International*, Studi di Diritto Internazionale in Onore di Gaetano Arangio-Ruiz, Editoriale Scientifica, 74 and 84; P.M. Dupuy (2002), L'unité de l'ordre juridique international: cours général de droit international public, *RCADI*, 297, 105–118, and more recently, by V. Chetail (2014), The legal personality of multinational corporations, state responsibility and due diligence: the way forward, in D. Alland, V. Chetail, O. de Frouville, J.E. Viñuales (eds), *Unity and Diversity of International Law. Essays in Honour of Prof. Pierre-Marie Dupuy*, Martinus Nijhoff, 105–130; P. Dumberry (2004), L'entreprise, sujet de droit international? Retour sur la question à la lumière des développements récents du droit international des investissements, *Revue générale de droit international public*, 108, 104–121; C. Leben (2008), L'activité des entreprises dans une economie mondialisée et le droit international public, in N. Boschiero, R. Luzzatto (eds), *I rapporti economici internazionali e l'evoluzione del loro regime giuridico – soggetti, valori e strumenti*, Editoriale Scientifica, 59–86. Driven to admit a limited international legal personality, few authors identify transnational and multinational companies as addressees of human rights obligations (see, among others, S. Ratner (2001), Corporations and human rights: a theory of legal responsibility, *Yale Law Journal*, 111, 488; D. Kinley, J. Tadaki (2004), From talk to walk: the emergence of human rights responsibilities for corporations at international law, *Virginia Journal of International Law*, 44, 944–946;

investigate if and to what extent the outcome can be different when it comes to a certain category of transnational companies, the digital platforms, which are de facto private legal systems (see Chapter 2).

1.   ATYPICAL DECENTRALIZATION, BASED ON MONISTIC THEORIES

If we try to simplify, by bringing together the different assumptions that reconstruct in monistic terms the relationship between international and national systems, we must start from the assumption of the decentralization of a single original universal legal order (that of the empire), which regulated the relations between the communities organized within the *civitas maxima* and has been articulated over the centuries into the various state legal systems, organs of the international legal community (*provinciae* of *civitas maxima*) and which now tends to take new forms of concentration (centralization) via international organizations.[8]

This approach is at the origin of the primacy of international law over state law – at the international relations level – a consequence of the twofold

---

A. Clapham (2006), *Human Rights Obligations of Non-State Actors*, Oxford University Press, 79), and recently, more broadly, on the subject of corporate social responsibility (among others: L.C. Baker (2005–2006), Multinational corporations, transnational law: the United Nations' norms on the responsibilities of transnational corporations as a harbinger of corporate social responsibility in international law, *Columbia Human Rights Law Review*, 37, 287).

A wider legal personality is recognized by J. Dunoff, S. Ratner, D. Wippman (2006), *International Law Norms, Actors, Process: A Problem-Oriented Approach*, Aspen Publishers, according to which corporations have long been major international law actors and have exerted considerable influence in the making of rules governing trade, investment, antitrust, intellectual property, and telecommunications; are indirect claimants in the World Trade Organization (WTO) dispute settlement system and direct claimants in investor–state arbitration; have long participated in 'governmental' teams before international organizations forums; have had direct voting rights in the International Labour Organization; have played standard-setting roles in other organizations such as the International Telecommunications Union; have been the de facto subjects of a large number of treaties dealing with everything from labour law to environmental protection; have been the direct subject of Security Council decisions, including its sanctions regimes; and, of course, have been the subject of or participated in substantial 'soft law' regulatory efforts, such as codes of conduct (at 216–234).

⁸   G. Arangio-Ruiz, (2003), Dualism revisited: international law and interindividual law, *Rivista di diritto internazionale*, 909–999, at 925 quotes K. Marek translating Hans Kelsen: 'Mais cela est l'image parfaite de l'unité du droit international et de l'ordre juridique interne: le droit international – qui a besoin des ordres juridiques internes pour s'accomplir – comme ordre universel se trouvant au-dessus des ordres juridiques étatiques particulieres, les délimite et les réunit dans un tout supérieur.'

assumption that, on the one hand, international and national law cannot coexist as independent legal systems and, on the other, that national laws are derived from international law, taking their legal status from it, on the basis of the principle of effectiveness.[9] The consequences that are relevant for our purposes include: the identification between the legal system and the state;[10] the notion of international law as the law of relations between national legal systems; the autonomy, not the independence of state systems from international law; the interindividual nature of non-international law.

These last two aspects become decisive, for our purposes, since they allow us – or, strictly speaking, oblige us – to admit the international legal personality of natural and legal persons, differentiating their rights and obligations in domestic and international law only to a different degree of operation. In fact, states exercise a more or less wide degree of autonomy in choosing ways and tools to impose such rights and obligations on individuals and companies, which in any case originate from international law, which itself organizes and defines all the interindividual institutions into which humanity is divided.

2.   PROOF OF THE PLURALISM OF THE ORDERS, IN DUALIST THEORIES

Dualist theories are based on the assumption of the independence of state systems from international law, the prevalence of which, not contested at the international relations level, is not recognized at the domestic law level, as it is subject to the express or implied action from time to time of the lawmaker, of the administration or of the national judicial bodies. International law therefore has no direct effect: even the instruments that allow automatic adjustment to international law are in fact instruments of internal law.[11]

---

[9]   It is according to this principle [of effectiveness] that international law empowers the 'Fathers of the Constitution' to function as the first legislators of a state. The historically first constitution is valid because the coercive order erected on its basis is efficacious as a whole. Thus, the international legal order, by means of the principle of effectiveness, determines not only the sphere of validity, but also the reason of validity of the national legal orders ... the basic norm of the international legal order [being thus] the ultimate reason of validity of the national orders, too. (H. Kelsen (1946), *General Theory of Law and State*, Harvard University Press, 367–368.)

[10]   H. Kelsen, in his *General Theory of Law and State*, identifies the state with its legal order, that is, with the legal structure of human society.

[11]   No rule of general international law requires states to adjust their legal system to international law. A different thing – as clarified by G. Arangio-Ruiz, in Dualism revisited, above, note 8, at 924 – is 'the so-called "direct effect" of international norms, as more or less infrequently agreed upon by states at the international level. In any such

Therefore, the national legal systems are independent (not autonomous) from the international legal system (hence the mutual 'exclusivity'[12]) and must consequently relate to one another (being both original) by means of reciprocal, formal (total) or material *renvoi*.[13]

The distinction continues between the personality of the state according to domestic law and to international law.[14] While remaining one and the same state (with an internal and an external 'face'), identity concerns the de facto entity, while the legal persons are two, since personality is relative and has legal relevance only if in relation to an order (national and international).[15] A corollary of the dualist approach is the recognition of an international

---

case, the direct effect derives from the domestic law of the states involved, not from the affected international norms themselves.' Therefore, it is evident that 'the operation of international rules within the national system remains – whether through the constituent, the legislator, the executive or the judges – a municipal law operation carried out by national organs under municipal law rules or principles' (at 930).

[12] G. Morelli (1967), *Nozioni di Diritto Internazionale*, CEDAM, 74–75, states that once we have identified the order taken as a given and from where we start, ... be it the international order or one of the various state systems, this order will not only be legal by postulate, but will also be the only order taken into consideration. All the other legal systems, precisely because they rest on fundamental norms whose juridical nature is not taken as data (and the choice of a fundamental norm necessarily excludes the assumption of any other fundamental norm), do not have the character of juridicality. The chosen order therefore appears to be necessarily exclusive. (My translation from Italian.)

[13] T. Perassi (1942), *Lezioni di Diritto Internazionale*, Foro Italiano, 26–30; A. Bernardini (1989), *Norme Internazionali e Diritto Interno, Formazione e Adattamento*, Pescara; A. Bernardini (1966), *Produzione di Norme Giuridiche Mediante Rinvio*, Giuffrè. By means of total *renvoi*, the legal order referred to determines the entire content of the rule that imposes the referring order: the latter sets identical rules, as regards content, to the rules of the order referred to, although formally distinct from them. By non-total *renvoi*, however, the order determines only some elements of the aforementioned rule, which is not taken into account in the referring order, since its application presupposes legal qualities or legal assessments that depend on the referring order.

[14] Hence the consistency with the practice whereby: (a) a state can be bound by a treaty concluded not in conformity with the domestic rules on treaty making and (b) a state could be liable for a breach of international law as a consequence of the conduct of individuals who are not state agents according to its national law.

[15] See also T. Perassi, *Lezioni di Diritto Internazionale*, above, note 13, at 45–46: [F]or a state, the personality of international law is a qualification that is given to it by the international legal order and does not exist prior to this. For similar considerations, the proposition, which conceives the international personality of a state as necessarily connected with its personality under domestic law, is to be discarded. Such an interpretation from time to time could be sustainable insofar as the two personalities were considered as two simple directions of a single personality, dependent on a single legal order: it is not sustainable if the interna-

personality, different from that of the states, extended to other independent or quasi-independent subjects.[16]

Based on the dualist approach, an international personality of natural and legal persons, who can operate only in a national legal space, is not admissible, because such space, and no others, is interindividual. In the absence of a universal interindividual public law, international norms do not produce constitutive effects for populations in terms of interindividual rights and obligations connected to the legitimacy or illegitimacy of an act.

Although there are many dualist theories and each one highlights a specific profile, on a juridical level – the sociological level being separate – dualism is studied in relation to the relationship between state law and international law, admitting a pluralism only because of the number of state legal systems.

3. THE DUALISM BETWEEN INTERNATIONAL (INTERSTATE) AND INTERINDIVIDUAL LAW OF ARANGIO-RUIZ

The dualistic approach of Arangio-Ruiz, original in many respects, is relevant for our purposes in that, by contesting the main contradictions of the dualist theories,[17] it distinguishes the legal entity of the state in domestic law from

---

tional and internal order of each state are considered, as should be done, as two different and distinct systems. (My translation from Italian.)
From here Arangio-Ruiz then moves further and challenges
the common claim that the entities subject to the international order are legal entities, because there is no legal entity that is not characterized by its own legal system and there is no legal entity that does not form an integral part of the legal system in which the legal entity exists as such. (1951, *Gli Enti Soggetti dell'Ordinamento Internazionale*, Giuffrè, 565, my translation from Italian.)

[16]   The monistic approach implies that the international legal order 'qualifies' the entities it deals with, such as 'states', 'insurgents', 'belligerents', 'governments in exile', distinguishing states from other entities and then, among the former, attributing international legal capacity. The dualist approach does not presuppose instead the legitimacy by international law of the subjects, such as being endowed with effectiveness and independence (understood not as 'over-ordination' but as 'non-subordination').

[17]   G. Arangio Ruiz in Dualism revisited, above, note 8, at 944 ff., disputes the qualification of the state in international law as a juridical person, since this is *in nuce* incompatible with the dualistic approach, which presupposes the independence of state orders from the international order precisely because they do not derive from it. Qualifying states as 'legal persons' on the international law level necessarily implies recognizing that they are subject to a superior legal order which attributes them such personality.

the state as a de facto entity in international law.[18] The state in internal, inter-individual law is identified with the legal system (Kelsen[19]) rather than with

---

[18]   G. Arangio-Ruiz, in Dualism revisited, above, note 8, at 950, states:
Unlike legal persons and other subdivisions of national law, coming into being as juridical structures through private or public legal acts, and unlike the State of national law itself, the establishment of which coincides with the formation of the community's legal system, States as international persons come into being *de facto*, continue to exist *de facto* and are eventually modified or dissolved *de facto* from the standpoint of international law.
In fact, Arangio-Ruiz continues (at 954),
[T]he setting up of legal persons in national law – and of the State itself under national law – is a juridical *event* (or *effect*) with regard to *both* the setting up of the entity and its elevation to legal personality. The setting up of a State in the sense of international law, is a juridically relevant *fact*, the only juridical *event* (or *effect*) attached thereto by international law being the attribution (to the factual entity) of legal personality, namely, international rights and obligations, or the capacity thereof ... It is in that sense that I maintain that the setting up of States and governments is, from the standpoint of international law, a factual, not a legal event.
Even more precisely (at 963), the author states that
the State in the sense of international law is neither Kelsen's (national) legal order nor S. Romano's (interindividual) juridical 'institution'. It is the factual entity that, under some 'control' from the national community's legal order and other (internal or external) sociological and historical factors – *but no comparable 'control' of international law at interindividual level* – handles the community's external relations. It is indeed that entity – not the national society, the community or its legal order – that is the member of the constituency of positive international law.
[19]   In this he agrees with Kelsen (Dualism revisited, above, note 8, at 948): 'The legal person of the State is – Kelsen *docet* – the legal order itself, or the portion of the legal order governing the State's structure, functions and status under the community's law.' The author believes 'the Kelsenian equation between law and state – the latter distinct from society or identified with this only when society is understood as a "social order" or "juridical community" (or State in a broad sense)' (G. Arangio-Ruiz (2008), La persona internazionale dello Stato, *Digesto delle discipline pubblicistiche*, UTET, at 26, my translation from Italian). In *Gli Enti*, above, note 15, at 556, Arangio-Ruiz affirms:
The entities in question are de facto units, entities (legally) simple. They present themselves, however, to the international legal order, in their historical–social unity and not as entities shaped by law. Instead of 'creations' of the international order (that need to exist) they are the products of historical–social causality and of all the factors composing them. The current claim that international law 'presupposes' the state means just that. It is therefore wrong to refer to states as legal entities or moral entities under international law. (My translation from Italian.)
The approach of Arangio-Ruiz, profoundly dualistic even if in an original way, differs from Kelsen's monistic approach, which also shares the assumption of the equivalence

the institution (Santi Romano[20]); in international law, on the other hand, it constitutes a de facto entity, a 'given' entity, which Arangio-Ruiz qualifies as a 'power'.[21] The international person of the state is characterized by independence, a factual condition, not attributed or delegated by international law.[22]

---

state–law, but not the statement, which the author considers unproven, that law is necessarily interindividual.

[20]   State organization rules are formed after the formation of the legal community. In this, Arangio-Ruiz agrees with S. Romano, when he affirms (Dualism revisited, above, note 8, at 947):

> The organization of the State takes shape within a legal community, not within a lawless aggregation of humans. Rather than just a *posterius* of State law, community law procedes in a relevant part the State's organization. The formation of any new secondary rules (in Hartian sense) are at most concomitant with the organization. While not sharing S. Romano's notion that the society's factual organization is a part of the law, I believe that this authoritative author is essentially right where he highlights that concomitance.

Similarly, in La persona internazionale dello Stato, above, note 19, he affirms that (at 26–27)

> Since the institution is the legal organization and not the organized entity, it identifies itself with the state rather than with society. The correction of S. Romano's assumption of the equivalence law–society (and therefore law–fact) lies, in our opinion, in the replacement of the extra-juridical concept of society – as the environment of production and action of the system, environment which, however, never identifies with the system itself – the juridical concept of state ... which is the reduction of S. Romano's thesis to Kelsen's, challenged by S. Romano precisely because he (rightly, we believe) rejects the idea that there is no law where there is no norm. (My translation from Italian.)

[21]   In Dualism revisited, above, note 8, at 955 n. 73, the author affirms:

> It was contended (as I continue to contend) that, contrary to the general view (of dualists as well as monists) that international law assumes, or works out, the same concept of state (or statehood) that is assumed or worked out by, under, or for the purposes of national law, international law assumes the state (and statehood) as *in fact made by history (the effective action of national law and international law rules themselves included)*. It follows that there is, in my view, a concept of the state as a ('given') person of international law, namely a *Staat im Sinne des Völkerrechts*, separate and distinct from the national law concept of the state (or statehood). The latter – namely, the state in the sense of national law – is simply either, as per Kelsen, an interindividual legal order or, as per S. Romano, an (interindividual) institution. The former – namely, the state in the sense of international law – is a factual entity and *only* in that sense a '*puissance*' taken by international law as a '*given*' entity.

[22]   In *Gli Enti*, above, note 15, at 561, Arangio-Ruiz states that

> states as such – that is, states as legal organizations of individuals – are, so to speak, 'unknown' to international law, which takes them into account only in their material quality as members of international society and recipients of the rules that regulate their relationships with other members of society: as de facto entities. (My translation from Italian.).

For Arangio-Ruiz, international law is interstate law, which is opposed to interindividual, typically (but not only) state law. The classification is broader (because it includes entities other than states) and more flexible (because it provides intermediate forms and developments that derive from the evolution of practice) compared to the classic dualistic classification between international and state law.

Starting from the dualistic approach – which recognizes the separation between the international and national systems and their respective independence – from which, however, it differs profoundly in terms of the qualification of the state in international law (not a juristic person but a de facto entity), the Arangio-Ruiz thesis allows the recognition of entities of international law other than the state of citizenship or incorporation, which exercises its independence in relation to both primary and secondary norms (organizational, and therefore in the exercise of legislative, executive and jurisdictional powers).[23]

4. THE CORRECT SUBJECTIVE QUALIFICATION OF DIGITAL PLATFORMS

We may, however, gain further insight following Arangio-Ruiz's approach, which qualifies the juridical person as the 'artificial centre of attribution of rights and obligations set up for the pursuit of the relevant private or public interest'.[24] The difference with respect to the conventional notion of juridical person as a 'given collective entity, different from human beings' is significant, since it gives value to a real datum: unlike the natural person, whose birth or death constitutes a mere fact, the juridical person is constituted, operates, undergoes changes, and is extinguished through legal acts and in forms that are classified within a specific legal system. The phenomenon is resolved entirely in the world of law and the issue arises therefore not in terms of effectiveness but of legitimacy. It is therefore a matter of qualifying a possible legal person-

---

[23] G. Arangio-Ruiz, in Dualism revisited, above, note 8, at 961 states: 'Data such as the "missing" international legitimation of States at *interindividual* level, the "missing" international-*interindividual* structuring of States, the "missing" *direct* international personality of individuals clarify and confirm each other.'

[24] G. Arangio-Ruiz, in Dualism revisited, above, note 8, at 946, opposes this definition to the

> dominant concept of legal persons – private and public, including the State of municipal law – as 'collective' entities or entities 'other than human beings', namely, to the notion of legal persons as given entities consisting either of a group of members or of beneficiaries, or of an organization, or of assets or of a finality, or some combination or other of two or more such elements, bound together somehow by the law.

ality of the digital platforms on the basis of an order that recognizes them as legal entities.

4.1   Digital Platforms as 'Powers'

Digital platforms are neither born nor developed within the international legal system. The digital platform cannot therefore be an international legal person; but, strictly speaking, not even the state is (in the sense of international law). The digital platform is, however, like the state, a de facto entity under international law, which is relevant insofar as it operates in that legal space as a 'power'. But this is a factual situation, which must be verified in its historical evolution. If the digital platform does not operate (or does not yet operate) in international law as a 'power' comparable to the state, it still operates in international interindividual law, which is opposed to international interstate law. The interindividual law obviously includes the set of primary and secondary rules (in Hartian sense) on which the legal ordering (and therefore the internal organization) of the digital platform is based.

For the purpose of verifying the de facto operation of the digital platform as 'power', the requirements historically deemed necessary for the attribution of legal personality to the state (people, territory, government) are not relevant, and not only because they are not decisive even in contemporary international law (they rather show effectiveness and independence), but because it is ontologically impossible to speak of international legal personality, these bodies being relevant for international law only 'in fact'. They are not the 'organs', but only the 'private individuals' of the international legal system. It applies to the state and, even more so, to other entities operating in the supranational legal area. This conclusion is important for our purposes, among other things, because it also enhances the privatistic concept of international law, which best represents intersubjective relationships between private individuals (primary norms), and refers public law in the strict sense, in international law, to secondary (organizational) rules.

4.2   The International Interindividual Law of International Organizations

Further insight on the action of digital platforms in the international legal space is given by the analysis – corresponding, *mutatis mutandis*, to the one developed by Arangio-Ruiz for international organizations, which – following its approach – presents, in my opinion, numerous analogies with digital platforms and therefore provides useful ideas. International organizations – simplifying in order to highlight their common features – have legal functions and instruments, primary and secondary norms (according to Hart's classification) similar to those of states. They have a very high degree of autonomy from the states that are members of them, to the point of being 'almost independent' of them. In any case, international organizations are systems which relate to both the systems of the states and the international ones.[25]

Based on this classification, Arangio-Ruiz qualifies the internal law of international organizations as a form of 'international interindividual law', distinct from the 'national interindividual law' of states. Among the forms of international interindividual law there are also the rules of private law that do not fall into international law or national law, including the *lex mercatoria* and other forms of transnational law.[26]

4.3   The International Interindividual Law of Digital Platforms

It seems to me that digital platforms can be considered, on the basis of this classification, among the forms of international interindividual law described by Arangio-Ruiz. They are not subject only to state regulations, with respect to which they operate with a degree of progressive autonomy and have primary and secondary, organizational, complete rules (above, Chapter 2). The interindividual character of these systems is not in question, nor is their supranational dimension (above, Chapter 3).

The possible transition from international individual law (which concerns the 'internal face', the legal personality of a digital transnational company

---

[25]   G. Arangio-Ruiz, in Dualism revisited, above, note 8, at 991–992:
     Be it as it may of its analogies with, and differences from, national legal orders, the internal systems of international bodies interact – as well as national law – with both international law on the one hand, and national legal systems on the other hand. (They also interact, incidentally, *inter sese*: an area that is even less explored.)

[26]   G. Arangio-Ruiz, in Dualism revisited, above, note 8, at 992–993:
     One must distinguish, precisely, international law from any *species* of interindividual law. The latter *genus* would include both the several national systems, on the one hand, and the several internal systems of international bodies, on the other hand, the latter systems to be acknowledged, in order to mark their international character, as unassembled bits and pieces of '*international interindividual*' law (as opposed to *national* interindividual law). It will be noted incidentally that the *genus* of international interindividual law seems also to encompass those sets of formations of (mostly unwritten) rules of private law that can be ascribed neither to international law proper nor to the private law (and conflict of laws rules or principles) of national legal systems. I refer particularly to '*droit privé des peuples*' and *lex mercatoria*. To the same class it might be possible to ascribe the rules applying to the transactions between States and private parties, namely the rules rightly or wrongly classified by some scholars, together, at times, with the law of international organs, as 'transnational law' ...

in the system with which it identifies itself) to international state law – and therefore to an equal relationship with other state systems: the 'external face' – allowed in abstract terms by the flexibility of this classification will obviously depend on factual circumstances and therefore on the evolution of the relationships between the orders of digital platforms and those of the states.

Now, certainly digital platforms enjoy or not an international personality (partial or full, functional, direct – insofar as deriving from primary norms – or indirect – insofar as deriving from obligations of states towards their actions) to the extent that this is recognized to transnational companies. Yet, the nature of the private legal order of digital platforms (on which the international interindividual law is based) radically changes the terms of the matter and produces direct effects on the level of the international personality. In fact, as legal systems that tend to be complete (and therefore are in the path that leads from autonomy to independence), digital platforms are de facto powers and potentially direct recipients of international norms.

4.4   A Compatible Approach: The Global Law

This approach seems to me fully compatible – if not also consistent – with the evolution of the part of contemporary research that admits the existence of a global law. By global law we mean, at different times, a 'systematization of anarchy',[27] or the 'management of a loosely entangled universe of autonomous governance frameworks operating dynamically across borders and grounded in functional differentiation among governance communities',[28] in which the main role is assigned, from time to time, to the state,[29] to the norm,[30] to the legal system,[31] and this also assumes, *in nuce*, a 'unified world order'.[32]

---

[27]   E. Dandford Martin (1933), Systematized anarchy, *Harpers*, February.

[28]   Among others: P. Allott (1990), *Eunomia: New Order for a New World*, Oxford University Press; M. Shapiro (1993), The globalization of the law, *Indiana Journal of Global Legal Studies*, 1(1), 37 ff.; K. Suter (2003), *Global Order and Global Disorder: Globalization and the Nation-State*, Praeger.

[29]   M. Delmas-Marthy (2003), *Global Law; A Triple Challenge*, Transnational Publishers.

[30]   P. LeGoff (2007), Global law: a legal phenomenon emerging from the process of globalization, *Indiana Journal of Global Legal Studies*, 14, 119 ff.

[31]   G. Ziccardi Capaldo (2018), *The Pillars of Global Law*, Routledge; A.M. Slaughter (2005), *A New World Order*, Princeton University Press; G. Della Cananea (2016), *Due Process of Law Beyond the State*, Oxford University Press.

[32]   S. Cassese (2010), Is there a global administrative law?, in A. von Bogdandy et al. (eds), *The Exercise of Public Authority by International Institutional Law*, Springer, 761–776; S. Cassese (2018), *A World Government?*, Global Law Press.

Global law is also, more conventionally, defined as 'the law of non-state governance systems', understood as governance communities that operate in a legal environment separate and independent from the state ones, as they do not derive from them.[33] Transnational companies that exercise powers similar to those of states are also included among the governance communities.[34] This reconstruction of the global law, which is based only on custom, presupposes a pluralism of legal systems and imposes coordination rules between them,[35] highlighting the private law nature of primary international rules.[36] In addition, it requires a non-state management of the evolution of the phenomenon and a consequent rethinking of the legitimacy requirements of the community and the order with which it identifies itself.[37]

---

[33] L.C. Baker (2012), The structural characteristics of global law for the 21st century: fracture, fluidity, permeability, and policentricity, *Tilburg Law Review*, 177–199, states (at 181):

> Unlike domestic legal orders, global law covers a wide number of distinct governance communities existing simultaneously and organized beyond the rule imposing power of states. ... global law communities may be understood as functionally differentiated societies organized for mutual benefit for specific objectives. They can include groups, institutions and networks.

[34] L.C. Baker, The structural characteristics of global law for the 21st century, above, note 33, at 183 points out:

> [T]hese entities can mimic the state in organization form; principal among them is the emerging class of self-governing multinational corporations that in many ways has begun to exercise governance authority within its own supply or value chains that resemble the legislative authority of states. But they can also assume other forms – they can manifest themselves as product or process certification organizations, as standard setting organs, as assessment entities, or as a *volk*-like group evolving customs and shared practices (e.g. cyber-communities).

Similarly, G. Teubner (2004), Societal constitutionalism: alternatives to state-centered constitutional theory, in C. Joerges, I.-J. Sand, G.Teubner (eds), *Transnational Governance and Constitutionalism: International Studies in the Theory of Private Law*, Hart Publishing.

[35] L.C. Baker, The structural characteristics of global law for the 21st century, above, note 33, states that

> polycentricity is the foundation of global law. ... Non-state actors provide a better view of the polycentric character of global law. Corporations may be subject to the laws of the states in which they operate and are chartered, they may be subject to the laws of the states in which their subsidiaries are chartered and operate, they may be subject to international law in conflict zones, and to international soft law standards administered through states, the U.N. system, and private entities, to the rules of listing entities, and to its own internal governance systems.

[36] They help to create a 'new form of transnational private law': G.P. Calliess, P. Zumbansen (2019), *Rough Consensus and Running Code: A Theory of Transnational Private Law*, Hart Publishing, 109.

[37] L.C. Baker (The structural characteristics of global law for the 21st century, above, note 33, at 185) points out that

Digital platforms' custom (internal, external, transnational), as well as agreements between digital platforms and with states, show a progressive, constant and almost consolidated transnational legal personality of many digital companies, as 'powers' (above, Chapters 2 and 3).

The digital platforms, as non-state governance communities, therefore operate in international interindividual law as defined by Arangio-Ruiz, as well as in international interstate law insofar as practice demonstrates their effective autonomy and progressive independence (also) from state systems. The independence of the private ordering of digital platforms, demonstrated in Chapter 3, constitutes proof, on a theoretical level, of their legal personality. I am confident of further confirmation from evolving practice.

However, the practice of digital platforms highlights a specific evolution of global law, which shows cooperation between digital platforms, states and international organizations. In this perspective, global law does not appear so much an alternative law to transnational law (with which, on the contrary, it identifies itself widely) and international law. It does not highlight a rift or a contrast between the practices of multinationals and states: they operate in the same environment.

The global law of digital platforms therefore constitutes an application of international interindividual (internal) law and international interstate (external) law. In these terms, which coincide with the conclusions of Arangio-Ruiz (evidently, with reference to other protagonists of international law) the existence of a global law of digital platforms can be admitted and indeed is fully confirmed by the practice (below, Chapter 5, section 4).

---

global law is about the law of system legitimacy in a heterodox world of governance organizations. It posits consent, not as a historical fact ... managed through the formal mechanics of voting, to a more dynamic and functional action-consent, in which the mechanics of and linkages between democracy, legitimacy and law/governance will have to be re-thought within contextually distinct governance spaces. ... The government of governance groups can be as democratic as the internet or as hierarchical as the multi-national corporation. That government must be able to manifest the group will, to make rules derived from and subject to the foundational rules (the constitution) of the group. The group must be able to discipline its members, enforce its rules and determine membership. The foundational premise rests on acceptance of the existence – independent of the control or authority of any one state or of the community of states – of a system of non-national, above-national or multi-national principles and rules applicable, in accordance with its own terms and logic, to public and private actors, natural and juridical persons.

5. Digital platforms and global law

So far, I have investigated digital transnational companies in terms of legal systems (Chapter 3) and legal entities (Chapter 4). But the 'substrate' of these legal entities, which identify with their transnational system, is made up of companies operating on the markets. To date, this seems to be the only aspect investigated in literature and governed by state orders.[1] From what I have said so far, however, it is clear that the attempt to subdue these companies, in their capacity as operators, to the constraints of the systems in which they operate, is bound to be ineffective, if not harmful.

It is ineffective from a threefold profile: because regulation and competition are inadequate to regulate relations between legal systems, for this is what digital platforms, as transnational digital companies are; because the tools that regulation and competition can use, however modernized they may be, prove substantially useless in the digital economy;[2] and because digital platforms have long enjoyed regulatory exemptions aimed at allowing the development of new markets. It would therefore be hard to insert them in an *ex post* regulatory matrix.[3]

---

[1] Above, Chapter 1, notes 1–4.

[2] Mainstream doctrine identifies the levers that legislators and regulators can use to intervene in the markets in regulation and competition. *Ex ante* the regulatory intervention, to correct the asymmetries (and therefore the failures) of the market, *ex post* the one to protect competition, to correct business behaviour.

The reality of the markets appears more complex than the theoretical models and the simplifications they produce. Regulation does not make up for a market failure: it regulates the dynamics that follow liberalization. The regulation does not intervene *ex ante*, since the information asymmetry holds back legislators and regulators with respect to potentially inconsistent market guidelines. Competition intervenes *ex post* but tends to regulate, not the market but specific companies, creating constraints with variable geometry, by definition asystematic, which regulators and legislators hardly ever put into the system.

[3] Transnational companies, mainly established in the United States, Russia or China and operating in many countries and almost all geographic areas, which have as their core business – although not always as a direct objective – the data management of the community they gradually build, have been able to grow and consolidate outside the rules of the markets, in the absence of a specific regulatory silo and in the presence, in Europe, of targeted exemptions, sandboxes *ante litteram*. In Europe, the e-Commerce Directive (2000/31/EC) provides for a substantial exemption of liability of ISPs (internet service providers) with respect to user activity on websites. The only

Yet, regulatory policy is not only ineffective: it is also harmful, because it leads us to believe that the phenomenon of digital transformation can be managed by state regulations with a mere modification of the rules, thus delaying an action that could instead be effective and adequate if otherwise oriented, if what we have seen in the previous chapters is true.

The instruments of regulation and competition are therefore valid for companies but ineffective for regulating the evolution of the systems in which they are being transformed, based on the assumptions and upon the occurrence of the conditions listed above. Of course, a matrix is needed, but of a different nature and character than the current one.

1. THE GLOBAL RESPONSE TO DIGITAL PLATFORMS: INADEQUACY OF THE REGULATORY MATRIX

The regulatory 'matrix', intended as silos of vertical (sectoral) and horizontal (general) rules that intersect is ontologically inadequate to regulate digital transnational platforms.[4] It is not so much a matter of measuring the incompleteness of the reforms or the contrasts between the silos, or the speed of evolution: that of digital markets being exponential, that of the regulatory one being, at best, linear (when efficient), a fact that gives rise to alternative

---

constraint is the obligation to execute a court order in the event of violations ('notice and take down'). This exemption of responsibility has allowed and perhaps contributed to developing a closed digital environment similar, as regards the activities carried out, services provided and products sold, to the physical world, but without the rules applicable to the latter. From the initial perspective, the exemption from regulation should have operated for a limited period. However, nothing is as definitive as the transitory, and when the time came, the operators had now become too large to be regulated by a national order or, as for the European Union, a regional one.

[4]   See: F. Bassan (2019), *Potere dell'algoritmo e regolazione dei mercati. La sovranità perduta sui servizi*, Rubbettino. Over the past thirty years, the European Union has created, developed and increasingly refined what I have on several occasions called 'vertical regulatory silos': parallel sector disciplines and therefore by definition non-converging, autonomous to the point of justifying sectoral codifications (electronic communications, energy, banks, insurance companies, financial markets, etc.). The progressive removal of these vertical rules from the unity of a code (civil, in the continental Union) has led the European legislator to create a balance, strengthening general, intersectoral rules to which the 'silos' will be anchored. Competition law immediately appeared the most suitable. Two other new regulatory bodies were quickly added, which responded to some of the main needs of a welfare system that the European Parliament increasingly required and invoked: the protection of the individual both as a consumer and as himself, for data protection. Again, codes: 'horizontal silos' with the claim of mutual independence and partial autonomy from the continental civil code, which they were, however, forced to confront.

solutions, including that of the 'regulatory circle'.[5] It is the regulatory matrix that is structurally incompatible with digital evolution.[6]

It follows that vertical and horizontal silos find limited implementation (or often none) in a digital environment. Furthermore, the progressive divergence of vertical silos has created intermediate gaps that digital platforms have been eager to sneak into. The void tends to be filled up, it is a law of physics and there is nothing shocking about it.

Today scholars follow the tracks of the markets and are therefore specialized in silos, vertical or horizontal. Therefore, research in competition law has focused first on the market of data, which for economists is economic goods (exchangeable and with a quantifiable value) and for jurists is fundamental rights (available or not).[7] Then, when it became clear that data does not constitute a market, because per se it is not dynamic but static when 'disconnected' from users, scholars turned to the topic perceived (because so represented) as decisive: the algorithm, which makes data alive, because it gives them meaning. And therefore the levels and methods of transparency of the algo-

---

[5]   Above, Chapter 1, section 2, note 45.

[6]   Competition law, consumer protection, and personal data protection apply to all sectors but 'intersect' each vertical silo at a specific point from which different applications originate due to the resilience of the markets, the degree of liberalization, and the powers attributed to the supervisory and regulatory authority.

That the vertical silos were parallel soon proved to be an illusion, when the markets began to converge. Electronic communications with postal services. Electricity with gas, water and waste industries. Banks with insurance companies (with mixed products) and with financial markets for investments, alternative products for a banking activity that is no longer profitable and therefore unsustainable for cyclical (negative rates) and structural (compliance charges) reasons.

That the vertical silos were not independent from horizontal silos then became immediately evident, on a theoretical level because the horizontal silos constituted the anchorage of the vertical silos to the unity of the European Union order, and in practice because that was how the national courts and the European Court of justice understood them, in resolving conflicts of powers and attributions; of course, each in its own way.

[7]   See among others, as for the economic approach: E. Curry (2016), The big data value chain: definitions, concepts, and theoretical approaches, in J. Cavanillas, E. Curry, W. Wahlster (eds), *New Horizons for a Data Driven Economy*, Springer; J. Tirole (2017), *Economics for the Common Good*, Princeton University Press; Y. Demchenko, W. Los, C. de Laat (2018), Data as economic goods: definitions, properties, challenges, enabling technologies for future data markets, *ITU Journal: ICT Discoveries*, Special Issue No. 2. On the other side, according to Recital 1 of EU General Data Protection Regulation (2016/679):

[T]he protection of natural persons in relation to the processing of personal data is a fundamental right. Article 8(1) of the Charter of Fundamental Rights of the European Union (the 'Charter') and Article 16(1) of the Treaty on the Functioning of the European Union (TFEU) provide that everyone has the right to the protection of personal data concerning him or her.

rithm have become the objectives of protection[8] (above, Chapter 1, section 6). This too, however, is a typically deceptive target. The transparency of the algorithm is just another hole that is dug only to be filled in later.[9]

The research into the protection of personal data appears more modern but only if seen in view of the regulation of the markets (above, Chapter 1, section 4). The 'silo' of consent, through which everyone directs and limits the use of his data, but the right to oblivion and privacy by design or by default as well, are only apparently adequate tools in the current regulation. If viewed from the perspective of relations between legal systems, however, they run the risk of being ineffective (because ontologically inapplicable to the blockchain, where data by definition is public and cannot be deleted) or even harmful, when data protection is used by digital transnational companies to deny data sharing and therefore, in fact, to 'close' their own order.[10]

The standstill created by the interest of the lawmakers and of the market in maintaining the status quo – even admitting the implicit goal of market consolidation – may be an explanation, but only a partial one.[11] The missing part is the error of vision and perspective: while chasing market dynamics, lawmakers and regulators have focused on the activity and have lost the dimension of the subjects, the digital transnational companies, and their quick and almost completed transformation into legal systems (above, Chapter 3).

---

[8]   See: R. Brauneis, E. P. Goodman (2018), Algorithmic transparency for the smart city, *Yale Journal of Law & Technology*, 1(20), 103; J.A. Kroll, J. Huey et al. (2017), Accountable algorithms, *University of Pennsylvania Law Review*, 165(3), 633–705; A. Datta, S. Sen, Y. Zick (2016), Algorithmic transparency via quantitative input influence: theory and experiments with learning systems, Conference Paper, in IEEE Symposium on Security and Privacy, 598–617.

[9]   Above, Chapter 1, note 76. Digital platforms change the algorithms used dozens of times a day. Digital platforms allow companies to query the data they have: it is one of the services they offer to the market, but they are the ones who make the queries, not the clients, who pay to have the results of the analysis, whose seriousness and objectivity are guaranteed by the market. And in any case, there are already – and many more will be developed – agreements between digital platforms to share the data needed when the data available are not enough.

[10]   We refer, among others, to the Facebook's proposal to the European Commission on the protection of personal data (White Paper, Charting the Way Forward: Online Content Regulation), February 2020.

[11]   I am referring to the ongoing debate within the European Union on the need to change regulations and competition to allow the market to achieve the necessary strength to ensure that European companies can compete on international markets, where size has now become one of the decisive elements.

2. A NEW MATRIX AND ITS TOOLS: FROM REGULATION TO NEGOTIATION

2.1 Companies and Orders

If the assumptions investigated in the previous sections are true, the matrix must change: from an illustration of the relationship between the rules within the state system, it becomes part of the theory of the relationships between legal systems, including private transnational ones, connected even when more or less independent. Independent as regards the internal rules of each digital transnational system, in the relationship between users in the community (in international interindividual law, according to the approach of Arangio-Ruiz but also of the global law if correctly interpreted) and in the relationship between platform and users (presently tied to standards, tomorrow to principles and uniform codification). Connected, when not coordinated (increasingly) with state regulations as regards external activity, and relevant 'de facto'.[12]

If this is the trend, the effects on the markets appear obvious. Each transnational digital system is a market in itself, in proportion to the degree of closure of the platform, it being irrelevant whether it follows the behaviour of the platform or constitutes an indirect effect of its structure (network effects).

And in fact, using the classic tools of competition (cross-flexibility of supply and demand) it is clear that, on the demand side, leaving a social network is in fact costly, partly due to the number of 'friends' or followers, which it is impossible to rebuild in another system. The economic theory has measured these exit costs.[13] On the offer side, then, the referral algorithms with which each platform enhances the data made available by each member of the community give each user the exact picture of the reality they share (which is different from objective reality). This is so true that Amazon can now implement anticipatory shipping, based on the algorithmic certainty that the products delivered, even if not requested, will not be returned because they are deemed necessary by the recipient.[14]

It is therefore clear that each closed digital platform, due to the economies of scale and purpose, the indirect network effects, the possibility of collecting – in the absence of competitors – a large amount of data on both sides of the

---

[12] Above, Chapter 4, section 4.
[13] Above, Chapter 1, note 131.
[14] Amazon has obtained a patent for what it calls 'anticipatory shipping' – a system of delivering products to customers before they place an order. Amazon says it may box and ship products it expects customers in a specific area will want – based on previous orders and other factors. According to the patent, the packages could wait at the shippers' hubs or on trucks until an order arrives.

market, the barriers to access (for competitors) and exit (for users), constitutes a market in itself (and therefore, according to traditional schemes, competition in the market must be replaced with competition for the market). It is also the access point to that market (gatekeeping action). And it also sets the rules of behaviour in that market (legislator, regulator, arbitrator).

All this is evident if we start from the theoretical analysis of the relationship between orders that we developed in Chapters 2–4, but it is confirmed by the bottom-up analysis that starts from the markets (above, Chapter 1, sections 2 and 3). The evolution towards the blockchain further radicalizes the conclusions on both sides, since it requires the closure of the system and of the market, respectively, to guarantee its operation (above, Chapter 1, section 7).

2.2   Divergent Starting Points, Shared Results

If the two branches of research, which start from divergent, when not actually opposite, points (theory and practice, general and particular, legal systems and markets) lead to a common, shared result, the tools that, based on the same conclusions, they allow use of are very different.

As private transnational systems, digital platforms exercise regulatory, executive and jurisdictional functions (internal profile) over their own community. As for the external profile, these systems relate to others, national, transnational (when admitted) and international and are increasingly less often the addressees – more or less passive – of the rules set by other systems, which will be applied if and when implemented by the digital transnational order. Which happens more easily if the rules are negotiated, not imposed. In this perspective, the mechanism of the *renvoi* between legal systems is also noteworthy, which, as we have seen, is not only possible but partly already adopted in practice.

As operators in the market, on the other hand, digital platforms are subject to an increasingly lesser extent – inversely proportional, however, to the progressive independence of the systems with which they identify themselves – to the regulation and competition rules of host states. With reference to the former, it is up to the platforms themselves to push the evolution towards negotiated solutions compatible with the development of the markets, which the regulators (not to mention the legislators) are not able to foresee. The mechanisms of the regulatory circle are useful for this purpose.[15]

---

[15]   Above, Chapter 1, section 2.6.

2.3 ... And a Point in Common

A point in common in the two-sided analysis (legal systems and markets) is the need for the evolution of that private transnational law that allows for the harmonization of methodologies, contents and perspectives otherwise compromised by the current geopolitical evolution, in which barriers and lists are decisive signals. This is therefore one of the possible directions to follow: the progressive development of a uniform law (private, as it regulates relations between the subjects) which, if not the solution to all the conflicts listed here, certainly represents a way of overcoming the contrasts between states, between states, international organizations and companies, between digital transnational companies, and between legal systems. This is (also) because the international and transnational practice highlights the need to coordinate – in a constant and more consistent way than it does now – the uniform codification of private law with a much more developed (public) transnational regulation, which on the one hand requires companies to comply with standards, technical rules, principles, and guidelines that extend over a wide span between soft and hard law, and on the other hand delegates their application to companies. Transnational private and public law should therefore, if not converge, at least be consistent.

3. NEW CENTRALITY OF UNIFORM LAW INSTRUMENTS

We have tried to demonstrate that the object of the analysis cannot be – as it appears in the current debate – the regulation of digital platforms, through an evolution of vertical regulatory silos and a modernization of horizontal silos (competition, data protection, consumer law).[16]

On a theoretical level, digital transnational companies are less and less subject to the rules of the country in which they operate, to the extent that they become private transnational legal systems that connect in a more or less 'porous' and osmotic way with state systems, with that of the European Union, with the transnational system (if recognized), and with international law.

On the practical level of the markets, the rules have proved ineffective, both because the markets have evolved in order to circumvent checks and balances, and because the rules apply to companies, but do not regulate the relationships

---

[16] Communications from the Commission to the European Parliament, the Council, the European Economic and Social Committee and the Committee of the Regions: A European Strategy for Data (COM(2020)66) and Shaping Europe's digital future (COM 2020)67), both 19 February 2020.

between legal systems. Based on these assumptions, we have proposed a different matrix, which contemplates both the profiles of (digital transnational) subjectivity and (trans-sectoral) activity.

3.1   Negotiation of Public/Private Rules

If state public law is ineffective, or if its effectiveness is limited to implementation left to self-regulation, the negotiation of the rules between orders can be useful: between digital transnational orders and state orders, above all. This can take place at public law level, as regards digital platforms' external activity, to integrate the regulation of the markets with the best practices via the regulatory circle. But it can also take place, above all and more effectively, at private law level, which best meets the subjective and objective needs of the current developments. Subjective, because digital transnational systems identify themselves with digital platforms and therefore with corporations. Objective, because the object of the evolving law is the relationship between the subjects of transnational law or, in broader terms, of international interindividual law. Yet, we have already seen how the private formulation of international law better represents intersubjective relationships between private individuals (primary norms).

3.2   The Codification of Uniform Private Law

Therefore, the codification of uniform private law must regain importance, as it might systematize negotiations that otherwise, if bilateral, would be ineffective, even more than inefficient. States must participate in this codification, and, of course, transnational digital platforms, as separate legal systems, should too. The harmonization of the contractual rules that regulate the coexistence in the platforms between the members of the community and between them and the platform would also allow for a less dramatic use of the typical regulatory tools. These are generally aimed at preventing behaviours detrimental to the interests of users, which would be mitigated by a uniform codification, which would also offer adequate protection tools and sanctions, in any case certainly better than those offered by public regulation.[17]

---

[17]   Public regulation in many markets (vertical silos) also significantly affects the relations between private individuals. But the effectiveness of this intervention is less realistic when this relationship cannot be regulated, for example because of territorial constraints, as happens with Big Data markets (see the GDPR discipline in Europe). For this reason it appears necessary, and urgent, to recover the communicating vessel of the codification of private law.

The need for a fast evolution towards a harmonized set of rules is required due to the speed of the technological revolution. This applies to smart contracts, where a significant number of clauses is determined on the basis of discretionary assessments, presently unquestionably imposed by the platform (e.g. the methods and restrictions for the access to data by the parties; the oracles; the knots of the blockchain; third parties; the identification of oracles; the selection of databases which oracles can access in order to solve conflicts; the definition of the algorithms that replace the decisions of the oracles; the payment options relating to both the usable currency and the instruments available; the technologies and methods available for use to the parties; etc.). It also applies to the primary relationship rules of digital platforms (from contracts between users to contracts between the platform and members of the community, which impose rules and behaviours and can govern a matter – for example, data sharing terms and methods – otherwise hard to reach by public regulation) and to secondary, organizational rules (from the enforcement of the policies adopted by the platform to assessments of such enforcement).

In a nutshell, the myth of the completeness of public regulation, generated by the liberalization of the markets, should lead to the awareness of the need for a uniform private law codification consistent with it, which in my opinion is not yet sufficiently developed. But we have seen how public regulation and private codification are communicating vessels; that the latter can make up for the shortcomings of the former; and that in the era of transnational digital corporations the codification of private law is more consistent with their gradual transformation from companies into subjects of transnational law and, in the end, into private transnational orders.

Obviously, the topic of digital platforms and their relationships with state orders and with international law can not be held to be unravelled with this conclusion. I hope, however, that this first step will facilitate the start of a debate on a level no longer limited to the regulation of markets.

4. THE GLOBAL LAW OF DIGITAL PLATFORMS: A NEW PARADIGM

According to the conclusions we have drawn, the law of digital platforms must be brought to international interindividual law (platforms' law, according to the UN)[18] and, to an extent that is not yet clear but increasingly evident, to international interstate law. The first concerns the internal face of the platforms, the second their external face. The first also includes transnational law, insofar as it is applicable to platforms (above, Chapter 2, section 2).

---

[18] Above, Chapter 3, note 9.

We also concluded, based on practice, that the approach according to which the private perspective of international law best represents the intersubjective relationships between private individuals (primary norms) and refers public law, in international law, to secondary (organizational) rules (above, Chapter 4, section 4), is correct.

We also found: that public and private regulation are communicating vessels; that public regulation operates only in the spaces that the private one leaves free, implementing, among others, the principles of subsidiarity and proportionality; that the structure through which public regulation can regulate is mainly that of co-regulation (above, Chapter 1, section 2).

We then assessed: that digital platforms are private systems, autonomous from state systems and, in the near future, independent from them; how the relations between these private systems and the state systems, as well as transnational law and international law, should be qualified; that the internal law of platforms (platform law) belongs to international interindividual law, while their external law can increasingly be drawn to international interstate law; that platforms are subjects of transnational law and increasingly also of international law.

Based on these conclusions, the evolutionary path towards a global law of digital platforms is manifold, and develops through the following points.

The first consists in the codification of the contractual relationships between digital platforms and their communities, as well as the relationships between the users of the community itself. I am referring here to the internal law of platforms, and therefore to international interindividual law, based on the three increasingly separate powers, through which the platforms govern their communities (above, Chapter 2, section 3). On the one hand, codification can be of uniform private law – within UNIDROIT or UNCITRAL – and can therefore concern contracts. On the other hand, it can develop through the adoption of general accepted practices and principles (GAPP), drawn up jointly by the platforms, possibly also within the framework of international organizations (i.e., OECD).

The two solutions, not necessarily alternative to each other, have as their object a private regulation, possibly agreed and certified by international organizations. These international forums (UNIDROIT, UNCITRAL, OECD, etc.) would allow, among other things, the prevention of possible actions by national or EU regulatory or competition authorities, which could otherwise qualify similar negotiations between companies as agreements potentially incompatible with the internal market due to their effect of preventing, restricting or distorting competition.

The second path of development of the global law of digital platforms consists of the production of agreements between the platforms and between them and states or international organizations, both as regards international interindividual law and also interstate law. We refer to the cases, now numerous, in which the platforms operate as agents of the states (above, Chapter 2, section 1), to those in which they impose on the states their technology-embedded law (i.e. the Google–Apple agreement on the notification of exposure to Covid-19 – above, Chapter 1, sections 2 and 4), and to those in which platforms and states negotiate on the regulation of the operation of the platforms themselves (i.e., tax law).

The third development path concerns the participation of digital platforms in the definition, by states – as regards their own systems – and by supranational (EU) and international organizations (ITU, OECD, etc.) – as regards transnational and international law – of rules, standards and application protocols. I refer to both the technical side (5G, Cloud, etc.), and the fundamental principles and rights, in the definition of a welfare that cannot be addressed by mere ethical rules. This evolution implies and assumes the transposition on a transnational, but also international level, of the principles and methodologies of co-regulation, in the meaning I have proposed in this research, and with reference to both the codification and the application of general principles, which no longer coincide with the outdated regulatory silos, but with specific applications.

The three evolutionary lines outlined here impose a definition of the global law of digital platforms (above, Chapter 4, section 4) and suggest its perimeter and contents: it cannot identify itself with a new global governance, which would capture only one of the evolutionary profiles listed above (the third). Yet, it cannot either be reduced to the law of non-state governance systems, which would apply only to interstate/interindividual law, the internal law of platforms (platform law). The practice reveals a much more complex and intricate interweaving between digital platforms, user communities, states, supranational and international organizations. The result is a joint operation of national laws, transnational and international law, primarily private, secondarily public (as regards organizational rules), and also subsidiary (as regards regulation).

A definition of the global law of digital platforms consistent with the conclusions I have drawn coincides with Arangio-Ruiz's theoretical approach (Chapter 4, section 4). In fact, he classifies and separates – for international organizations, but we have seen that the pattern is also applicable to digital platforms – the internal side (international/interindividual) and the external side (international/interstate). The latter applies to the relations between platforms, as well as between platforms and states and supranational and international organizations.

The global law of digital platforms is therefore the international interindividual law constituted by the exercise of the three powers in the legal order of the platforms on the one hand, and the international interstate law constituted by the relations between the legal order of the platforms and those of states and supranational and international organizations, on the other.

This approach, and the resulting definition, are even more relevant in the perspective of the evolution of digital platforms. They will grow and will incorporate into their systems further and more significant relationships of the social life of their community: from payment systems to digital currencies, from centralized to decentralized cloud, to distributed systems and technologies (DLT), to the Internet of Things (IoT), with products and services connected to the network and interconnected with one another.

Actually, as we have now seen, this evolution produces an overlap between ecosystems (on the economic level: digital platforms, AI, blockchain) and of orders (on the legal level). It is therefore desirable that this evolution takes place in a legal environment (transnational and international) that is ready to endure and support such a complexity of multilevel and inter-order relationships.

Index

Printed and bound by CPI Group (UK) Ltd, Croydon, CR0 4YY

27/10/2024

14580410-0004